Readings in

Curriculum Development for the Gifted

David M. Jackson

Special Learning Corporation

TM

Readings in

Curriculum Development for the Gifted

David M. Jackson
Former Executive Director,
National/State Leadership Training Institute
on the Gifted and Talented
Reston, Virginia

Special Learning Corporation

42 Boston Post Rd. Guilford, Connecticut 06437

Special Learning Corporation

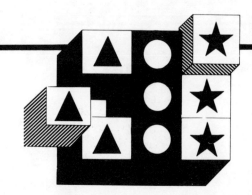

Publisher's Message:

The Special Education Series is the first comprehensive series designed for special education courses of study. It is also the first series to offer such a wide variety of high quality books. In addition, the series will be expanded and up-dated each year. No other publications in the area of special education can equal this. We stress high quality content, a superb advisory and consulting group, and special features that help in understanding the course of study. In addition we believe we must also publish in very small enrollment areas in order to establish the credibility and strength of our series. We realize the enrollments in courses of study such as Autism, Visually Handicapped Education, or Diagnosis and Placement are not large. Nevertheless, we believe there is a need for course books in these areas and books that are kept up-to-date on an annual basis! Special Learning Corporation's goal is to publish the highest quality materials for the college and university courses of study. With your comments and support we will continue to do so.

John P. Quirk

First Edition

1 2 3 4 5

0-89568-188-9

SPECIAL EDUCATION SERIES

* ● Abnormal Psychology: The Problems of Disordered Emotional and Behavioral Development
● Administration of Special Education
● Autism
* ● Behavior Modification
Biological Bases of Learning Disabilities
Brain Impairments
● Career and Vocational Education for the Handicapped
● Child Abuse
* ● Child Psychology
● Classroom Teacher and the Special Child
* ● Counseling Parents of Exceptional Children
Creative Arts
● Curriculum Development for the Gifted
Curriculum and Materials
* ● Deaf Education
Developmental Disabilities
* ● Developmental Psychology: The Problems of Disordered Mental Development
* ● Diagnosis and Placement
● Down's Syndrome
● Dyslexia
* ● Early Childhood Education
● Educable Mentally Handicapped
* ● Emotional and Behavioral Disorders
Exceptional Parents
● Foundations of Gifted Education
* ● Gifted Education
* ● Human Growth and Development of the Exceptional Individual

● Hyperactivity
* ● Individualized Education Programs
● Instructional Media and Special Education
● Language and Writing Disorders
● Law and the Exceptional Child: Due Process
* ● Learning Disabilities
● Learning Theory
* ● Mainstreaming
* ● Mental Retardation
● Motor Disorders
Multiple Handicapped Education
Occupational Therapy
● Perception and Memory Disorders
* ● Physically Handicapped Education
* ● Pre-School Education for the Handicapped
* ● Psychology of Exceptional Children
● Reading Disorders
Reading Skill Development
Research and Development
* ● Severely and Profoundly Handicapped
Social Learning
* ● Special Education
● Special Olympics
* ● Speech and Hearing
Testing and Diagnosis
● Three Models of Learning Disabilities
● Trainable Mentally Handicapped
● Visually Handicapped Education
● Vocational Training for the Mentally Retarded

● Published Titles   *Major Course Areas

TOPIC MATRIX

Readings in Curriculum Development for the Gifted provides the college student in special education, and the classroom teacher with a comprehensive overview of the subject. The book is designed to follow a basic course of study, and suggest techniques that may assist the classroom teacher.

COURSE OUTLINE:

Curriculum Development for the Gifted and Talented	Readings in Curriculum Development for the Gifted	Related Special Learning Corporation Readers

I. Introduction to the Education of the Gifted
  A. Student evaluation
  B. Curriculum planning
II. Screening and Identification Procedures
III. Instructional Approaches/Fostering Creativity
IV. Basic Support for Curriculum
	I. Curriculum Planning and Evaluation
	II. Screening and Identifying for Gifted Program Membership
	III. Program Examples
	IV. Basic Support for Curriculum: Teacher Preparation and Community Involvement
		I. Readings in Gifted and Talented Education
		II. Readings in Foundations of Gifted Education
		III. Readings in Special Education
		IV. Readings in Administration of Special Education

CONTENTS

PREFACE

Why not talk with some gifted-talented-creative young people before beginning your study of this volume? You might ask the young people how they feel about the pace of instruction in their school, and about the extent to which they usually feel challenged by the problems offered as part of their instruction in school.

Such conversations are likely to provide a realistic basis for examining existing curricula for the gifted, and for thinking critically about the philosophical and theoretical foundations of a gifted program which differs significantly from the program offered to all, or almost all, children and youth.

Readings in Curriculum Development for the Gifted is a collection of articles gathering the latest information on new programs, new testing methods, and possible expanded definitions of "gifted and talented" for the future. It is the purpose of the reader to give specific techniques for working with the gifted student as well as ideas for starting and supporting a gifted program in your school.

CURRICULUM PLANNING AND EVALUATION

In the past few years we have developed some eminently practical ways to select students for membership in gifted programs so that their community's racial and ethnic composition is mirrored in the special program population. Further, particularly in the field of mathematics, we have found ways to relate educational strategies and teaching methods to learners' characteristics.

The following section offers instruction on methods used to rate specific student behaviors. Besides covering the state of the art, the articles also discuss, as in the case of "Gifted IEP's: Impact of Expectations and Perspectives" the problems in developing present educational levels,

annual goals, and short term objectives are presented. While the section concentrates on the role of the teacher in the identification process, it is important to realize the role of the parent as well as the multidisciplinary team.

Finally, researchers are experimenting with measurements of social intelligence, coping skills, congnitive style, learning potential, audiovisual perceptional and electrical responses of the brain. As our understanding of intelligence increases, so will the sophistication of our tests. We may be preparing for "individualized testing" sometime in the near future. With that who can say where the definition of "gifted and talented" will lead?

Gifted Education.... are you ready for the challenge

by Guy G. Gorden and Carolyn Regan

Dr. Gorden, former Assistant Superintendent for the Kingsville (TX) Independent School District, and was instrumental in developing the CHALLENGE program. Mrs. Regan is the CHALLENGE program coordinator in that district. The high school CHALLENGE has been selected by the Texas Education Agency as its only Senior Level Demonstration School in Individualized Instruction for 1978-1980.

The preaching-practicing gap in gifted education is immense and probably growing. School districts across the nation are jumping on the "gifted" bandwagon. Even so, many authorities in gifted education believe that most programs for the gifted talk a good game but come across with few wins.

The lack of success of gifted programming may be related to several factors; financing, inadequate curriculum and methodological approaches, prejudice against elitism, and probably most important - lack of commitment.

When our school district decided to attempt to serve the needs of our gifted children, we made a commitment to overcome the above obstacles. To do so, we first sought commitment to the program by a variety of publics. A twenty-five member steering committee was formed to develop a program plan to submit to the Board of Education. School personnel, community members, and students were members of this planning group.

The steering committee concentrated on addressing four general areas in the written plan:

1. philosophy and program goals with goal indicators;
2. written plan for local gifted education;
3. publicity: design and implementation; and,
4. budgetary considerations.

The steering committee considered the following program features essential in the written plan:

- There should be a socially and psychologically defensible definition of the gifted.

- The program should provide for appropriate entry and placement of pupils into the school and grade level.

- It should be characterized by fluidity of individualized scheduling and work.

- It should reflect a sustained sensitivity to the interrelatedness of the content to be learned and of the processes to be cultivated and nurtured.

- The advance planning should provide for continuity - both as regards the educational life of each pupil and as regards the maintenance and further development of the program. [1]

The written plan, submitted to the Board of Education by the steering committee, encompassed K-12 gifted education and was unanimously adopted by the Board. Seven thousand dollars in planning monies were allocated for the developmental phase and CHALLENGE, Gifted Education in the Kingsville Independent School District was born.

THE WORKING MODEL

CHALLENGE is interfaced very closely with the "Enrichment Triad Model"[2] conceived by Joseph Renzulli. Of primary importance to us was that the gifted learner has two dimensions that must be addressed. These are (1) the student's specific content interests and (2) his or her preferred style(s) of learning. [3] Also, learning experiences for the gifted must be "qualitatively differentiated". These differentiated learning experiences should be based upon the *interests* of the student and should be the cornerstone of all enrichment activities.

The Enrichment Triad Model involves three types of enrichment activities. The first two types, General Exploratory Activities and Group Training Activities, are considered by Renzulli to be appropriate for all learners; however they are also important in the overall enrichment of gifted students.

Type III Enrichment, Individual and Small Group Investigations of Real Problems, is the major focus of this model. Renzulli suggests that approximately one-half of the time that gifted students spend in enrichment activities should be devoted to these types of experiences.

PROGRAM WITHIN THE DISTRICT

With a sparse span of high school programs to survey as models, our school district designed a gifted program to meet the assessed needs. The program, CHALLENGE, harmonizes with the existing scheduling, offering diversified opportunities in differentiated education to gifted and talented students.

Elementary students were identified only in the academic area and are involved in a program of horizontal enrichment in academics and in creativity. This is an in-classroom teaching situation with the classroom teachers using community resources, independent study, and classroom learning centers.

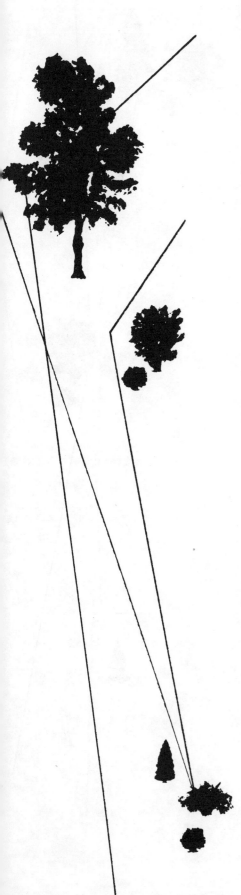

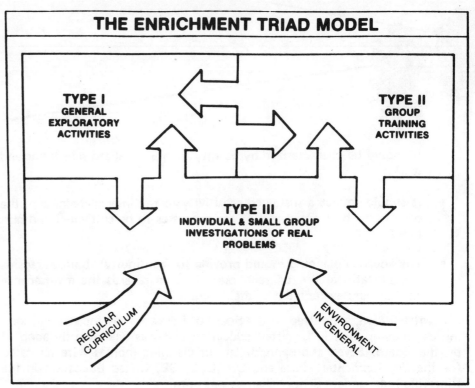

THE ENRICHMENT TRIAD MODEL

TYPE I GENERAL EXPLORATORY ACTIVITIES

TYPE II GROUP TRAINING ACTIVITIES

TYPE III INDIVIDUAL & SMALL GROUP INVESTIGATIONS OF REAL PROBLEMS

REGULAR CURRICULUM

ENVIRONMENT IN GENERAL

The problem of identification is one of using the best available measures in order to arrive at an assessment of pupil potential which is as accurate as possible. Screening should be thought of as a preliminary step toward identification, in which multiple measures including group intelligence and achievement tests, teacher judgment, teacher check lists, and other measures are used. The final assessment of potential should be made with a measure which permits the pupil to perform at his true level and not with one which imposes ceiling limitations. This insures a proper basis for adequate curriculum planning.[4]

Academic screening began April 1977, when teacher recommendations were made on students in grades 9 through 11 at that time on the high school campus. The system's two middle schools nominated students in grade 8. Parent nominations were solicited through the media with forms being available on the three secondary campuses.

Screening for CHALLENGE included:

- Standardized Achievement Test Composite of 90th percentile

- Grade point average of 8.0 on a 9 point scale.

- High scores in PSAT, ACT and SAT in verbal and/or math

- attention to strong discrepancies between the Standardized Achievement Test and other test scores, and/or teacher recommendation, and/or grade point average.

All nominees were screened on their respective campuses by its Campus Screening Committee. These committees were composed of the campus administrator, a counselor and two teachers. Upon completion of student identification, numbers of students in each subject area were determined. The curriculum format structure was begun.

CHALLENGE CONTENT COURSES

Sufficient numbers of students were recommended for English I, English II, English III, World History, American Government and Biology I to create homogeneous sections for the identified CHALLENGE students.

Content courses are basic academic courses emphasizing enrichment through content-oriented learning experiences and individual investigation of real problems. Advanced learning techniques are used in providing students with skills and abilities that better enable them to deal with problem solving. Professional people in the community conduct seminars or serve as speakers. Retired persons with specialized knowledge in a vocation or hobby serve as mentors. Texas A & I University facilities such as Conner Museum, Jernigan Library, Agriculture Farm and the Foreign Speakers Bureau are a valuable class resource. Many individual professors have donated time and expertise to the CHALLENGE Program. Other facilities serving as resources are Kingsville Naval Air Station and museums in nearby Corpus Christi.

Regular content teachers are used who have expressed a desire to work with CHALLENGE students. The teachers possess a broad knowledge base including superior knowledge in one field, with understanding of related fields and their application in analyzing and arriving at solutions to problems.

Content class advantages are

- Class enrollments are from 16 to 18 students

- Students interact freely and enjoy relating to their peers

- True individualization is possible

- No special staffing is needed

CHALLENGE REGULAR CLASSES

Individual needs of identified CHALLENGE students are met in existing classes where there were not enough students for a class to be scheduled. Heterogeneous accelerated or regular classes are in subjects ranging from British Literature to music.

Teachers of these classes were provided with lists of identified CHALLENGE students so they could provide enrichment activities in addition to regular class work. A CHALLENGE resource teacher coordinates and assists regular class teachers in off campus contacts for resources and in supplying needs for enrichment projects.

CHALLENGE ELECTIVE

All identified students are offered the Elective course. This type of course offering would be described by Gallagher as placing greater emphasis on changes in *content,* with particular stress on a high level of abstract understanding of various content fields. Major curriculum reform and modification efforts in the sciences, history, anthropology, and other content areas have aided this development.[5]

In addition, much attention has been paid to the advancement of new techniques and procedures that encourage independent thinking, problem-solving and problem-seeking behavior. This modification has been based

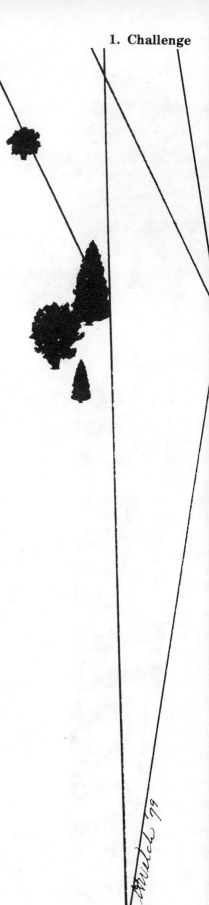

1. PLANNING

on the notion that a rapidly changing culture makes facts obsolete before they can be used by the growing child, so that the only productive educational strategy is to help the child modify, adapt, and learn how to discover new facts for himself.[6]

The CHALLENGE teacher is a facilitating individual who has an understanding of the curriculum content and the nature of the classroom discussion process and interaction as well as insight into the growth potential of the individual student.

The Elective course has a limited number of students and is offered two periods a day. This allows the Elective teacher adequate time for preparation and for making community contacts for field trips and speakers.

Activities for the Elective have been diversified in study. The two class sections have engaged in these areas.

- Preparation for college entrance exams - - PSAT, SAT, ACT

- Individualized projects according to interests

- Development of decision making skills and problem solving

- Career exploration

- Leadership development

- Exploration of subject matter interests not offered in regular high school curriculum

- Introduction to computer technology and use of statistical data

- CEE Advanced Placement Program course - - English

- How to use various resources, e.g., university library

- Field trips - - group or individual

- Use of community resource people in the classroom

- Cross age teaching - - to elementary and middle school CHALLENGE students in areas of physics, language arts, music and art

- Job interview skills

Torrance, like Gallagher and Renzulli, believes that the most important thing that gifted high school students can do is to become an expert in something - - in some skill, job, or area of knowledge. This is something that will challenge "all out" performance - - acquisition of knowledge from all sources, practice, experimentation, invention, testing, and improved strategies. Such efforts should not wait for high school graduation, college, or graduation from college, or graduate school.[8]

The CHALLENGE Elective has gone beyond the textbooks, revealing hidden talents, strengthening self-concept and awakening unused potential.

MECHANICS OF A WORKING MODEL

The Campus Screening Committee over-sees the progress of all CHALLENGE students. Criteria for maintaining grades and program requirements were designed and used when students or parents needed consultation.

CHALLENGE, in pilot stages, has operated on a small local budget. Two additional employees were added, a coordinator for the district's gifted and talented educational program and the high school resource teacher.

Clerical help, professional literature, staff development, distinctive materials, audio visual equipment and the use of a school district van for transportation seem to have been top priority program budgetary items.

The CHALLENGE Council monitors the program. The Council is made-up of two community representatives, teachers, students, principals, administrators and the coordinator. A schedule of program activities and projects is made available to Council members as their observations and participation with students are valuable to program evaluation.

Integral components of the total CHALLENGE program are inservice with staff, community involvement and awareness, and program evaluation. Evaluation has been continuous and focuses on the objectives which either were met or not met.

Results of a recent Student Questionnaire completed by 110 content students after four months of program participation were compiled. The students stated that CHALLENGE classes were more difficult than their regular classes. They stated that they had learned more in this type of class and that the classes were more interesting.

Perhaps the most important point that can be made however, is related to gifted education in general and that is that each school district must plan and implement gifted programs on the basis of its local needs. The emphasis, however, must be on programs that are qualitatively different from regular programming.

The day of gifted education in our public schools is long past due. The only question remaining is - - are you ready for the CHALLENGE?

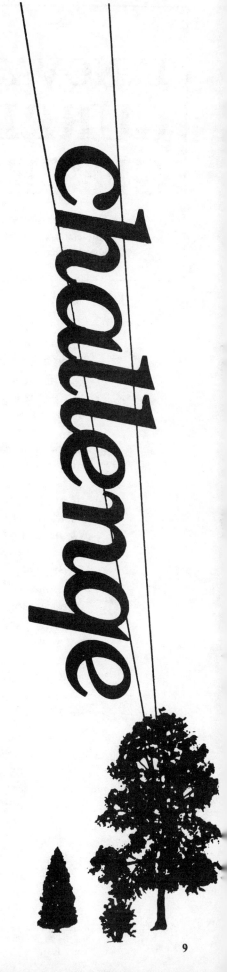

[1] T. Ernest Newland. *The Gifted in Socioeducational Perspective.* Englewood Cliffs, New Jersey: Prentice-Hall, Inc., 1976.

[2] Joseph S. Renzulli. *The Enrichment Triad Model: A Guide for Developing Defensible Programs for the Gifted and Talented.* Wethersfield, Conn.: Creative Learning Press, 1976.

[3] An instrument that is currently available to assist teachers in the identification of learning style preferences is called the "Learning Styles Inventory." For futher information about this instrument write to Linda H. Smith, University of Connecticut, BOX U-64, Storrs, Connecticut 06268.

[4] Ruth A. Martinson and Leon M. Lessinger. "Problems in the Identification of Intellectually Gifted Pupils." In Walter B. Barbe and Joseph S. Renzulli (Ed.), *Psychology and Education of the Gifted.* New York: Irvington Publishers, Inc., 1975.

[5] James J. Gallagher. *Teaching the Gifted Child.* Boston: Allyn and Bacon, Inc., 1975.

[6] Ibid., p. 88.

[7] Elizabeth Monroe Drews. "Beyond Curriculum." In John Curtis Gowan and E. Paul Torrance (Ed.), *Educating the Ablest.* Illinois: F. E. Peacock Publishers, Inc., 1971.

[8] E. Paul Torrance. "How Gifted High School Students Can Continue Growing Intellectually." In John Curtis Gowan and E. Paul Torrance (Ed.).

INNOVATIONS IN EDUCATION: CURRICULA FOR THE GIFTED AND TALENTED

Delmo Della-Dora, Professor and Chairperson, Department of Teacher Education, California State University/Hayward and President, (national) Association for Supervision and Curriculum Development

In preparing this paper it occurred to me that I have experienced most of the major approaches used for the gifted and talented, either as a student or an educator, since their formal inception in the United States.

Detroit was one of the first school systems to use "x, y, z" groupings in the 1930's when I was in elementary school and intermediate school. We were all aware of being grouped by ability and took it to be just the "natural" way of doing business. I also attended Cass Technical High School in Detroit, majoring in chemistry and metallurgy. This program consisted of three years of chemistry (general, qualitative analysis, quantitative analysis, and organic), three years of English and math plus two years of social studies and one year of biology, of physics, of metallurgy, of Latin, and of foundry. A group of us then went on to the first attempt at an advanced placement program at Wayne State University in 1943.

Professionally, I've participated in the Wayne County Study of Programs for the Gifted in 1957-61 and served as a teacher, administrator or consultant in some 40-50 school districts in the Wayne County (Michigan) area which were developing, operating and/or evaluating programs for the gifted.

My personal experiences in the 1931-43 period, my professional experiences for about 10 of my 29 years in the profession, and my visit to some 10 states this year in my service as President of ASCD lead me to make these eleven generalizations. If your concern is to have effective and innovative approaches to planning curricula for the gifted and talented, these may be helpful to consider in your planning.

1. *Strategies for curricular planning should be characterized as providing for honest involvement of all those to be affected.* What I have observed most often in my travel to 10 states this fall is that "strategies" are often designed *to do something to*, rather than *with* others. That is, "Let's plan processes which can be used to manipulate others into doing what we want them to do."

    Honest involvement means bringing in teachers, students, and parents along with administrators and supervisors in the first stages of planning, laying all the cards on the table and continuing to involve those interested and affected throughout the life of the programs.

From *New Directions for Gifted Education*, A Report on Bicentennial Midyear Leadership Training Institute at Kansas City, January 26-27, 1976. Sponsored by the National/State Leadership Training Institute on the Gifted and the Talented, March 1976.

2. *The innovations which are most successful and which persist for the longest period of time are ones in which all the participants had a voice.* Participants, in effect, feel that they "own a piece of the action", that it is *their* program and that, therefore, they have a commitment to make it succeed. We have had some evidence of this in research since the 1930's beginning with the Lewin, Lippitt, White classic study of the efficacy of democratic decision-making processes used in teaching. Similar pioneer studies in industry such as that undertaken at the Hawthorne Plan of General Electric indicated then (and subsequent studies continue to show) that when people are consulted and otherwise involved in decisions that affect them, they are likely to be *both* happier *and* more productive.

3. *Many of the plans for gifted and talented today are designed to repeat the same mistakes made in the 1930's and in the post-Sputnik era. We appear, in many states, compelled to use new or additional funds for the gifted to "do the wrong things even harder" than before.* To reverse an old cliche, "let's *not* just do something, let's just stand still"—until we examine what has been done previously and, most importantly, determine *why* so many programs for the gifted and talented have failed, up to and including the present. The most serious mistakes usually begin in the identification process because of lack of agreement about what giftedness means. In this connection, I believe nothing productive or innovative for the gifted and talented will be developed by people who have not informed themselves about the findings of J. P. Guilford on the nature of intelligence, who do not know what research indicates about the results of the most commonly used forms of ability grouping, and who are not aware of the major work done by Getzels and Jackson concerning the nature and nurture of creative students as opposed to the nature and nurture of students with high IQ's.

4. *The people who control the allocation of funds for programs for the gifted and talented must themselves be at least open-minded and, hopefully, even creative or the programs that result will be unimaginative and unsuccessful.* The people who are actually going to operate the programs should also be characterized as being open-minded and creative *and* have an opportunity to use that open-mindedness and creativity in planning and operating good programs. It is easy to establish procedures for checking on programs if the guidelines are prescriptive and descriptive *but innovation and creativity are products of innovative and creative people who can be trusted.* You cannot simultaneously make it easy for the legislature or state department or some other supervening agency personnel to check to see if funds are allocated as prescribed using rigid guidelines, *and also* have programs which gather and use formative data as part of a productive and dynamic process of teaching and learning.

5. *Innovative programs must be designed to promote the values which are basic to the survival and improvement of a democratic society.* Among those values are ones inherent in our Constitution and our Bill of Rights, namely, that each person should have the opportunity to learn up to his or her potential, that the learning is done in such a way that it does not interfere with the rights of any other person and finally, that attention is given the skills, knowledge, and com-

mitment needed to improve the democratic quality of life in this country. We have had some programs for the gifted which fostered a sense of superiority among gifted students and/or a sense of superiority on the part of the teachers involved and/or, a sense of superiority on the part of their parents. It is harmful to gifted students, their teachers, and their parents to assume that they are somehow *superior as human beings* because they are more able in certain aspects of learning just as it is harmful to all others to believe they are somehow *inferior as human beings* because they are not officially certified as "gifted" or "talented".

Another dimension of learning to live in a democratic society is highlighted by the research which shows that authoritarianism and democratic attitudes are related to the continuum which has tolerance for ambiguity and tentativeness at one end and need for closure and for definiteness at the other end. Programs which promote ability to tolerate ambiguity and tentativeness can result in less authoritarian citizens.

6. Up until now most programs for the gifted have focused on qualities common to white, middle-class, conforming students and less so, or not at all, on qualities found among the children of the poor, among students from racial and ethnic minority backgrounds, and also among the more creative or non-conforming white middle-class children.

    Therefore, our definitions of giftedness, our means of assessing, and our program planning must be comprehensive enough to include gifted children who are also poor, who are from racial and ethnic minority backgrounds, and whose values or lifestyles may differ from that found to be most acceptable in traditional school programs.

7. *Research and experience show that there are kinds of giftedness and many kinds of talents. It follows, therefore, that there must be a variety of curricula and a variety of instructional approaches in each school if we are to develop the potential of gifted and talented.* The most common means of identification used for gifted and the most commonly utilized programs for the gifted have been found to produce no improvement in learning generally and, in some cases, the ones who are called gifted even seem to do less well in "classes for the gifted". The most common means of identification are either intelligence tests and/or achievement tests—sometimes accompanied by either teacher recommendation, psychologist/counselor recommendation, or both. The cut-off scores are usually at the upper two percent of the population based on the criteria used. These students are then often grouped together for part of the day or all day and study more advanced material or go at a faster rate through regular academic content.

    Our experience in the Detroit area, and the work of others, indicates that these means of identification tend to pick up "convergent" thinkers (to use Guilford's terms) who are, in most cases, already learning as well as they can in regular classrooms. We even had reports from counselors in the more affluent suburbs that these types of approach seemed to produce more anxiety and pressure among students who were already either achievers or over-achievers.

One effect was more business for local psychotherapists from these overstriving children of overstriving parents.

8. *Innovative programs must take into account the available evidence which shows that thinking, feeling, physical reactions and behaviors are all affected when any part of one of these areas is affected. We can refer to terms like "cognitive", "affective" and "motoric" and "overt behaviors" when we wish to deal with one aspect of a whole human being, but must recognize that this doesn't alter the fact the human beings react as whole beings to all experiences.* The terms "cognitive" and "affective", in particular, are often posed on an either/or basis in some discussions of programs for the gifted. We do not have the choice which such a description implies. Affect and cognition are interwoven and interact with each other regularly. For example, in matters of racial prejudice, religious bias, and social class bias we know that *knowledge of the facts*, by itself, does not reduce prejudice in any of these areas. The *feelings* that gifted students have (as well as the non-gifted) cause them to perceive selectively and to learn selectively based primarily on their previous feelings or attitudes.

   Thus, in establishing program goals, the innovative approaches which are most likely to succeed are ones designed to elicit and account for the *feelings* and *behaviors* which accompany new knowledge, new experience, and new skills and which will attempt to help students integrate all three of these dimensions of their being in learning.

9. *Innovative programs should have as their central theme the development of self-direction and responsibility for self among learners.* This includes the ability to *establish* learning goals, to identify and use available resources, to formulate and test hypotheses for arriving at goals, to know how to evaluate one's own progress, and to alter goals and/or define new goals as warranted. In some circles, teachers who learn how to diagnose and prescribe *for* students are highly praised. In other places, teachers who individualize instruction *for* students are prized and viewed as noble and skillful people. However, these kinds of people, noble as their motives are and conscientious as their effort may be, are cheating themselves and students in important respects.

   The students are missing the opportunity to learn *to be responsible for themselves* and the teachers are wearing themselves out, treating themselves inhumanely, trying to do something for others which is best done for oneself. If half that teacher time and energy were devoted to helping students learn a variety of methods for *self*-diagnosis and *alternative self-prescriptions* for learning, the students would learn more and teachers would have more time and energy to be whole human beings themselves. Teaching students how to help each other learn is also a useful and effective approach.

10. *Worthwhile innovations can come into being and be maintained only if resources are provided for regular, ongoing supportive, and complementary services; chief among them being money for planning, research, development, and inservice education.* This should equal from six percent to fifteen percent of the budget allocated for operating funds, as is true in business and industry.

11. *Finally, innovative programs should encompass all the major goals of education in a democratic society, not just those which can be measured easily and cheaply.* In most of the 10 states I have visited this year, comments often heard were along these lines: "Yes, all goals are important, but let's be practical. There's no good way to measure problem-solving skills or racial prejudice, etc. We have to stick to the tests on the market." And so, goals and programs for the gifted become what the inexpensive, easily-administered tests can measure. The consequences of such action are to narrow the *real* goals of education and to limit types of programs to one small slice of narrowly defined educational objectives—which may have *nothing* to do with whether the gifted student is achieving anything of relevance for now or for the future. However crudely done, we can assess *any* goal area of consequence in some manner which is useful for teaching and learning. If it hasn't been done before, it's past time to begin. We cannot stop in our search for ways to assess any goal until, and unless, we decide the goal itself is not worthwhile.

It has often been said that if we fail to study our history we are doomed to repeat it. The time and energy of good educators and the money available for education today are both in short supply. Let's not squander our limited resources following paths which have led to nothing worthwhile or to negative results in the past. We can do a better job of teaching the gifted and talented. We know something about what *does* work and what *does not* work. Let's build on some 40-75 years of experience and research in creating innovative and effective curricula.

REFERENCES

Combs, A. (ed.) *Perceiving, Behaving and Becoming: A New Focus for Education.* Washington, D.C.: Association for Supervision and Curriculum Development, 1962.

Della-Dora, D. and House, J. (eds.) *Education for an Open Society.* Washington, D. C.: Association for Supervision and Curriculum Devemopment, 1974.

Getzels, J. and Jackson, P. W. *Creativity and Intelligence: Explorations with Gifted Students.* New York: Wiley, 1962.

Goldberg, M., et al *The Effects of Ability Grouping.* New York: Teachers College Press, 1966.

Guilford, J. P. *The Nature of Human Intelligence.* New York: McGraw-Hill, 1967.

McCelland, D. *The Achieving Society.* New York: Van Nostrand, 1961.

Milton, T. "Authoritarianism, Intolerance and Ambiguity, and Rigidity, Under Ego and Risk-Involved Conditions". *Journal of Abnormal Psychology* 55:1957, pp. 29-33.

Roethlisberger, F. J. and Dickson, W. *Management and the Worker.* Cambridge: Harvard University Press, 1939. ("Hawthorne effect" study reported.)

White, R. and Lippitt, R. *Autocracy and Democracy.* New York: Harper & Row, 1960.

DEVELOPING MULTIPLE TALENTS IN EXCEPTIONAL CHILDREN

C. JUNE MAKER

Articles and presentations directed toward teachers of exceptional children often include the exhortation "Develop the child's strengths as well as ameliorate his weaknesses!" Teachers are told to look for the peaks as well as the valleys in individual profiles. What often happens, however, is that the valleys are so low and the weaknesses so noticeable that we find ourselves spending so much time on remediation that there is very little time left for developing the potential gifts and talents. Methods courses concentrate on remedial techniques, articles discuss new strategies for "skill development," and textbooks emphasize methods for diagnosing and ameliorating weaknesses.

A real commitment to a talent oriented approach requires more than one teacher's belief in the necessity of developing the child's strengths. Often the child's talents may be in areas not usually considered "academic." In fact, these talents may interfere with the planned curriculum, or may even be seen as a nuisance because they are unusual or unconventional. The child's participation in such activities may be relegated to the realm of free time or after school and weekend activities. Chesler (1974) gave the following two examples of learning disabled children with special talents:

Emphasis on the development of talents can accomplish several desirable goals. First, a child can develop talents into career interests or satisfying hobbies. Second, self concepts can be greatly improved through the child's own perception of his or her activities as well as through peer perception of his or her activities. Third, deficit areas can often be improved by working through areas of strength.

Though most of us would not question the first two results, many would probably be skeptical about the third. There is, however, evidence from research that emphasis on the development of certain kinds of strengths can improve weak areas. For example, Carlson (1974) reported the use of a multiple baseline-successive treatments model in which she used a child's creative strengths in fluency and elaboration to increase academic achievement and evaluative efforts. She reported substantial improvements in the child's goal directed behaviors, her ability to assess her own progress, and several areas of academic achievement. Torrance (1977) also reported the use of strengths in fluency and flexibility to develop originality. Most of the children in Torrance's report also improved in math, spelling, and reading achievement scores.

Calvin Taylor's (1963) "multiple talent" approach has received a great deal of attention in general education, as well as in education of the gifted. Taylor, a researcher in the field of creativity, stated that schools have traditionally dealt with and encouraged only one type of talent—academic—and that by limiting our efforts in talent development to this one area, we give only 50% of our students a chance to be "average or above." As we increase our emphasis on areas such as creativity, communication, planning, forecasting, decision making, drama, and performing or visual arts, Taylor stated that as many as 90% may have a chance to be above average in *some talent area.* Taylor is *not* saying that 90% of all children are gifted, but that they may be above average in some talent area if we emphasize enough talent areas. Whether

1. PLANNING

he is correct about the percentage is not particularly important. What is important is that we all know from experience with children that most do have at least one strong area. The multiple talent approach has been used successfully in many classrooms, and has been the subject of quite extensive programs of research in curriculum development and implementation. Reports of this work can be found elsewhere (Taylor, 1962, 1963, 1964a, 1964b).

Other approaches to the development of multiple talents or strengths have been developed by Torrance (1962, 1974) and Meeker (1967, 1969). Torrance suggested using a checklist of "creative positives" to identify creative talents of disadvantaged and handicapped children, and using these talents as vehicles for the development of academic abilities. Meeker took an approach based on Guilford's (1967) Structure of Intellect model of human intelligence. She developed an elaborate system for assessing very specific intellectual strengths and deficits, and provided guidelines for systematically working through strong areas to develop weak ones.

The following section presents several teaching ideas based on Calvin Taylor's multiple talent approach and lists a number of publications to which the teacher can refer for many more teaching techniques.

ACTIVITIES FOR DEVELOPING MULTIPLE TALENTS

Map Activities

The activities in this section suggest ideas for developing multiple talents through using a state map. The map of Illinois was used in this example, but you can use any state map and simply change the names and places. The same types of activities could be designed for use with telephone directories, catalogues, newspapers, and other items from around the house.

The activities are designed for students without teacher direction except for Activity 3 under Dramatic Talent. They can also be used for whole class participation. Many of the activities can be used in developing more than one talent, so do not be overly concerned about the placement of each activity.

DECISION MAKING

1. Your father's new job requires him to travel to Quincy, Jacksonville, and Springfield because the company's three offices are located in those cities. You bought your new home in Macomb only 2 years ago. Decide (a) whether your family should move, (b) if they move, which town they should live in, and (c) what kind of car Father should have.

2. Explain your reasons for making each of the decisions.

3. Decide where you would live if you could live anywhere in Illinois.

4. List all the routes you could take to get from DeKalb to Paxton. Decide which is the best route to take and explain why you made this decision.

5. Your family is considering moving from Vandalia to Fairfield. List all the arguments you can think of for and against moving.

FORECASTING

1. Predict what a map of Illinois will look like in the year 2000.

2. Predict what would happen if all the interstate highways were suddenly destroyed.

3. Predict what the map would look like if Chicago were at the southern tip of the state.

4. Explain how a map of Illinois was different 20 years ago.

5. Explain how this map would be different if there were no large cities in the state.

6. List all the things a map maker had to know before making the map of Illinois.

PLANNING

1. You have a week's vacation and would like to go on a camping trip. Plan a trip to a place in Illinois. You may want to consider some of the following:

   a. How many miles you are traveling.
   b. How much time to spend at each place.
   c. How much food to take.
   d. What kind of equipment to take.

2. Plan a trip from Harrisburg to Chicago. Tell what routes you would take. Can you make the trip in 6 hours? If not, how long will it take?

3. You have a cousin who lives in Sandwich, a friend who lives in Watseka, and grandparents who live in Waterloo. You have 2 weeks vacation from school and want to visit all of them. Plan your vacation. Some things you may want to consider are:

   a. Time to spend with each.
   b. How to get there.
   c. Which routes to take.
   d. Places to stop on the way.
   e. What to take.
   f. What to do with your pets while you are gone.

4. Make a list of all the things an engineer would have to consider before building a new interstate highway across Illinois.

5. List all the reasons you can think of that would make Peoria a bigger city than Mt. Vernon.

COMMUNICATION

1. Using a map, explain to someone how to get from Rockford to Joliet.
2. Without using a map, tell someone how to get from Rockford to Joliet.
3. Explain to a deaf person how to get from Rockford to Joliet.
4. List as many words as you can that describe a map.
5. Make a map for a blind person.

CREATIVITY

1. Design some symbols that could be used to make maps better. You might want to make symbols for such things as:

   a. Road construction.
   b. Service stations that are open all night.
   c. Telephone booths.
   d. Motels.
   e. Toy stores.

2. List all the ways this map could be used.
3. List all the ways that a map of Illinois is like a water tower.
4. List all the ways that a map of Illinois is different from a map of Kentucky.
5. List all the things that could happen if all the bridges over rivers were torn away.

DRAMATIC TALENT

1. Pretend you are a map of Illinois. Tell the class about the state as if you were a map.
2. Make up a play about the five characters listed. They are trying to eliminate all the maps in the world.

   a. A city.
   b. An interstate highway.
   c. A river.
   d. A small town.
   e. A state park.

3. Teachers make a map out of the classroom and let different students act out different parts of the map. Some can be symbols of such things as interstate highways, airports, rivers, county markers, secondary roads, colleges or universities, etc., while others are numbers, letters, or paper. You may want to just select a small area rather than the entire state for this activity.

4. Make up a skit using the following three items as props:

   a. A map of Illinois.
   b. A piece of toast.
   c. A record.

ARTISTIC TALENT

1. Make a picture using only map symbols.
2. List all the ways that you could make this map more beautiful.
3. Make a map collage.
4. Make a map without drawing any lines.
5. Enlarge one section of this map.

MUSICAL TALENT

1. Find or make up a rhythm for each of the map symbols. How is the rhythm of an interstate highway different from the rhythm of a two lane paved road? How is it different from an unpaved road? How is the rhythm of a county line different from the rhythm of a river?
2. Make up a sound for each of the map symbols. How is the sound of a city different from the sound of a small town like Bogota? How is the sound of a state park different from the sound of an airport?
3. Make up a Map Song using the sounds and rhythms you have created.
4. Choose a musical instrument and make up a song about Springfield.
5. Find a song that best expresses your feelings about maps.

ACADEMIC ABILITY

1. Find where you live on the map. Make an X with your pencil. Find a place that is 20 miles from your town.
2. Compute the distance from Springfield to where you live. If your car gets 15 miles for each gallon of gas, how many gallons would it take to get to Springfield?
3. Find a town that is north of where you live. Circle it with your pencil.
4. Find a town that is south of where you live. Draw a line under it.

1. PLANNING

5. Put a check beside the river that is closest to your home.

6. Find the shortest route from Pleasant Hill to Tuscola.

Book Reports

Just by modifying the traditional format of book reports, a teacher can encourage the development of multiple talents. An added bonus could be more interest in reading!

The following activities can be used in a variety of ways: They can be listed as options on a learning contract, written on task cards and kept in a "book report" learning center, used as group activities, or kept as a file of teacher ideas to suggest book reporting formats to individual children.

DECISION MAKING

1. Write five things that would make your book better.

2. Make a list of the interesting words you found in the story and tell why you think they are interesting.

3. Write 10 words that tell about the story, and then decide which one of the words tells the most about your book.

4. Give your opinion of the book and the reasons for your opinion.

5. Try to convince someone who has a different opinion about your book that *you* are right.

6. Write descriptions of your favorite characters in the book.

FORECASTING

1. Predict what someone who reads the book 20 years from now will say about it.

2. Predict what some historical person would have said about the book if he or she had read it.

3. Find and list cause and effect relationships in the story.

4. Predict what a character in another book would say about your book.

5. Predict what you would say about this book when you are 25 years old (50, 99, etc.).

6. Write what might happen in the next chapter of your book.

PLANNING

1. Plan a play based on your book. (It does not have to be given—just planned.)

2. List all the things you would need to do before presenting a play based on the book.

3. Plan a bulletin board display for your book.

4. Plan a party to introduce your book to your friends.

5. List all the problems that a character in your book had that were caused by someone else in the story.

COMMUNICATION

1. Make a puppet of a character from your book.

2. Write an imaginary part that could go in your book.

3. Make up a new character for your book.

4. Write a different ending for your book.

5. Write a story based on your book.

DRAMATIC TALENT

1. Write or tell how the book is the same or different from your life.

2. Present a play based on your book.

3. Give a book report to the class as you think one of the characters from the book would present it.

4. Read your book (or a part of it) to some younger children.

5. Give a report to the class the way *your book* would give it.

ARTISTIC TALENT

1. Draw a series of pictures to retell the sequence of your book.

2. Make an original cover for your book.

3. Use crayon, chalk, paint, etc., to illustrate your favorite part of your book.

4. Make a bulletin board display for your book.

5. Make a comic strip of your book.

6. Make a poster to "advertise " your book.

7. Make a diorama.

8. Make a mural.

MUSICAL TALENT

1. Write a song or play about your book.

2. Find a song that expresses what you think or feel about the story.

3. Discover or make up a rhythm or sound for each character in your book.

4. Make up a musical sentence about your book (only using sound and rhythm).

5. If the characters in your book could only sing to each other, name some of the songs they would sing.

ACADEMIC ABILITY

1. Look up something about the author.

2. Write a report on the area in which your book takes place.

3. Write to the author of your book.

4. Write a report on the period of time in which your book takes place.

5. Write a report on anything in the book that interested you.

CREATING A LEARNING CENTER

Teachers can create a permanent "multitalent" learning center in any classroom, where children can choose from a variety of activities that would develop several talents. The ideas presented can serve as a beginning for such a center by simply being written on task cards and placed in a center with plenty of maps. If you are really interested in beginning a multitalent center, you could write these on 3 inch by 5 inch index cards and place them in separate recipe file boxes (a separate file box for each talent area). You can add other tasks for use with telephone directories, catalogues, newspapers, and other items.

RESOURCES

The ideas presented are only suggestions to get you started. A creative teacher can develop hundreds of activities in every talent area. The following resources contain ideas for developing multiple talents and cognitive strengths.

Igniting Creative Potential: A Report of Project Implode, 1971.
Bella Vista Elementary School
2131 East 7000 South
Salt Lake City, Utah 84121

This is an idea book with teaching activities in several talent areas for kindergarten through 12th grade. The project was based on Taylor's multiple talent approach.

Using the Creative Strengths of a Learning Disabled Child to Increase Evaluative Effort and Academic Achievement, 1974. Dissertation by Nancy Carlson, Department of Elementary and Special Education, Michigan State University.

This is a good resource of diagnostic batteries, teaching procedures, and evaluation instruments found to be useful in working with learning disabled children. The instruments and procedures could also be used for children with other handicapping conditions.

Clues to Creative Teaching, *The Instructor,* 1963-1964, p. 5.

This is a series of 10 monthly articles written by Calvin Taylor. Titles include "Bridges from Creativity Research to Teaching," "Learning and Reading Creativity," "Listening Creatively," "Developing Creative Thinking," and several others.

SOI Abilities Workbooks
SOI Institute
214 Main Street
El Segundo, California 90245

Based on Guilford's SOI model, Meeker has developed five workbooks — *Cognitive, Memory, Evaluation, Convergent Production,* and *Divergent Production.* Specific teaching activities cover all content areas and grade levels.

These are not the only resources, but will provide a beginning for developing many talents in our exceptional children.

REFERENCES

Carlson, N. A. *Using the creative strengths of a learning disabled child to increase evaluative effort and academic achievement.* Unpublished doctoral dissertation, Michigan State University, 1974.

Chesler, B. M. Who wants to wash the dishes? *Exceptional Parent,* 1974, *43,* 47-51.

Guilford, J. P. *The nature of human intelligence.* New York: McGraw-Hill, 1967.

Meeker, M.N. Creative experiences for the educationally and neurologically handicapped who are gifted. *The Gifted Child Quarterly,* 1967, Autumn, 160-164.

Meeker, M.N. *The structure of intellect: Its interpretation and uses.* Columbus OH: Charles E. Merrill, 1969.

Taylor, C.W. Be talent developers as well as knowledge dispensers. *Today's Education,* 1968, December, 67-68.

Taylor, C.W. *Creativity: Progress and potential.* New York: McGraw-Hill, 1964.(a)

Taylor, C.W. Multiple talent approach. *The Instructor,* 1963, *27,* 142, 144-146.

Taylor, C.W. *Widening horizons in creativity.* New York: Wiley & Sons, 1964. (b)

Torrance, E.P. *Perspectives on the status of the gifted: Current perspectives.* Presentation to the 1977 Summer Institute on the Education of the Gifted/Talented, Teachers College, Columbia University, New York City, June 20, 1977.

Torrance, E.P. Differences are not deficits. *Teachers College Records,* 1974, *75,* 471-487.

Torrance, E.P. *Guiding creative talent.* Englewood Cliffs NJ: Prentice-Hall, 1962.

A MULTI-LEVEL APPROACH TO THE IDENTIFICATION OF KINDERGARTEN GIFTED PUPILS

Charles W. Humes, Jr.
and
Del G. Eberhardt

Dr. Charles W. Humes, Jr. is Director of Pupil Personnel Services. Mr. De. G. Eberhardt is Coordinator of Research and Evaluation in the Greenwich Public Schools, Greenwich, Connecticut.

As the pendulum swings in its cyclical moves toward the side of the gifted, there is evidenced a regenerated interest in identification and programming for these exceptional children. The current interest and enthusiasm for the gifted has pushed the area of emphasis beyond the typical narrow band of service rendered in the intermediate grades. (Most programs seem to being and end in grades 4, 5, and 6—much to the dismay of parents.) One of the new foci is that of early school identification, i.e., kindergarten level. Conceptually, this receives little opposition, because if is agreed that early identification will facilitate suitable educational planning. Such early planning serves two purposes; 1) it recognizes the plasticity of cognitive structures at early ages and 2) it decreases the likelihood that children of advanced learning potential will find school boring. One of the more difficult problems, however, is the design of effective ways of identification when so little is known about them. Another dimension is that of identifying characteristics, i.e., do these children manifest the same behavior as seen in older gifted children but on a modified scale? Unfortunately, the answer is not clear because the prior environment is so important. Depending on the locale and sociocultural factors, the kindergarten childen may have been in nursery school, may have been exposed to Sesame Street, or may have had preschool diagnostic testing. Clearly, there is no standard environment that precedes entrance to school.

Over the years the identification of the young gifted has paralleled efforts made with the general school population. The use of teacher noninations and testing are the most common approaches as shown in some typical studies (DeHaan, 1957; Isaacs, 1968) and extend to the young gifted as well. However, there have been some interesting efforts to determine the value of paraental nominations. Cornishe (1968) attempted it in the elementary grades with Jacobs (1971) and Ciha at al (1974) assessing it prior

"A Multi-Level Approach to the Identification of Kindergarten Gifted Pupils," Charles W. Humes, Jr., and Del. G. Eberhardt, *North Carolina Association for Gifted and Talented Quarterly Journal*, Vol. 3, No. 1, Winter 1977.

to entrance into kindergarten. The later studies suggest that parental input has maximum value before the child enters school.

The study was designed and implemented in an effort to synthesize what has been practiced or reported. It utilized, in combination, some of the more popular assessment techniques that can have discriminating value in identifying high-level academically gifted pupils in a total system-wide kindergarten population. The approaches included parent nominations, teacher nominations, group testing, rating scales, and individual tests. While this study uses some of the same techniques that are familiar and commonly used, it purports to differ from previous studies in that the above mentioned approaches were utilized in a systematic, sequential manner. The study was designed to show the value of a multi-level approach in identification but also to suggest the relative value of some of the different techniques employed.

METHOD

The subjects in this study were 630 kindergarten students in a medium-sized (10,500) suburban, upper-income school district. Racial composition was predominately white. There was a total of 12 elementary schools represented.

During the kindergarten registration period in the spring of the year, all parents were asked to complete a **Parent Questionnaire**, which was designed to provide parent nominations. This produced 455 completed questionnaires. In September of the same year all kindergarten teachers (N=14) were asked to observe the parent-nominated pupils as well as other subjects. In November teachers submitted their own list of nominees, including those who registered late. In December the **Stanford Early School Achievement Test (SESAT),** Level 1 was administered to 171 pupils. In January, teachers were asked to complete a **Teacher Rating Scale** for those pupils who were above the cut-off points on the SESAT. Rating scales were completed on 73 pupils. The final step involved individual intelligence tests (**Revised Stanford-Binet Intelligence Scale, Form L-M**) administered to 61 pupils by regularly employed school pscyhologists.

ASSESSMENT TECHNIQUES

Accepting the literature findings that parent nominations with pre-school children are as effective as teacher nominations, the **Parent Questionnaire** was devised utilizing input from teachers,[1] administrators and psychologists. No specific reference was made to gifted pupils for the purpose of the questionnaire.

Dear Parent: We are interested in finding out more about children before they enter kindergarten. We know that learning styles differ and that some children have special needs. In order to assist us in this exploratory project, you may elect to complete the questionnaire below. Your responses may assist the principal and teacher in planning a more meaningful kindergarten program for your child.

Name of Child _____School_____

1. Does your child learn much more rapidly
   than others his own age?   Yes___No___

2. Does your child have a long attention
   span excluding TV viewing?   Yes___No___
3. Does your child display a strong desire
   to attempt tasks on his onw?   Yes___No___
4. Does your child show a great curiosity
   about his surroundings?   Yes___No___
5. Does your child show an unusually well
   developed memory?   Yes___No___
6. Is your child interested in a wide variety
   of activities?   Yes___No___
7. Does he (she) often display an unusually
   deep interest in a topic?   Yes___No___
8. Does your child tend to direct the activities of his (her) agemates?   Yes___No___
9. Does your child show any unusual
   musical or artistic talent?   Yes___No___
10. Does your child read?   Yes___No___
11. The approximate age that your child walked independently:
    before 9 mos.___, 9 mos.-15 mos.___, 16 mos.-22 mos.___, 23
    mos.-28 mos.___, after 28 mos.___.
12. At approximately what age did your child speak in sentences:
    before 12 mons.___, 12 mos.-17 mos.___, 18 mos.-23
    mons.___, after 24 mos.___.
13. Do you expect your child to have any
    difficulty in kindergarten?   Yes___No___

Only the first ten items were scored. The final 3 items were for informational purposes only. Prior field testing suggested that a high cut-off point should be maintained, therefore, 8 **yes** responses were necessary to qualify on the questionnaire. The **SESAT** (4 subtests) was chosen over a group intelligence test for the following reasons: 1) teachers are move comfortable with achievement rather than ability tests; 2) results of achievements test can lead more directly to programming; and 3) results of achievement tests are viewed by teachers and parents as less "fixed" and hence less likely to result in labeling. A preliminary analysis of the data indicated that the total score should be at the 96th percentile with no individual subtest under the 80th percentile.

The **Teacher Rating Scale** was a 20 item adaptation of the Renzulli and Hartman scale (1971). On this measure it was established that the cut-off point should be a total score of 45. The **Stanford-Binet** was selected because it is an instrument that has a greater potential for high scores than other well-known intelligence measures. The minimum score for final identification was set at I.Q. 135.

RESULTS

The end group of pupils who survived the various assessments numbered 41 or 6.5% of the total (N=630) kindergarten population which was within the accepted percentage range for the academically gifted.

Initial parent nominations totaled 115 or 24.4% with a range among the schools extending from 18-45%. The teachers nominated 91 or 14.4% of the total kindergarten population. The group receiving the SESAT amounted to 171 of which 92 were parent nominations and 79 were teacher nominations. (The total of prior parent nominations were not SESAT tested due to a variety of factors, e.g., leaving the district, absent on day of test, etc.) At this point the combined nominations discriminated 27.46% of the total kindergarten population.

TABLE 1

Pupils Nominated as Gifted by the Various Procedures and Later Identified

Predicator	Total Nominated	Correctly Identified	Percentage of Accuracy
Parents	94[1]	22	23.4
Teachers	91[1]	20	22.0
SESAT	171[2]	41	24.0
Rating Scale	73[2]	41	56.2
Stanford-Binet	63[2]	41	65.0

[1]Number of pupils receiving other instruments
[2]Number of pupils taking test

DISCUSSION

The objective of designing a model for the multi-level identification of kindergarten academically gifted pupils was apparently realized. The final figure of 6.5% was reasonable considering the above average intellectual composition of the school district. Although some bright level pupils may have been erroneously screened out, it is safe to say that all of the finalists do represent bona-fide gifted pupils at the high end of the continum.

The fact that 455 out of a total population of 630 only had the benefit of parent nominations presents a contamination factor. It could be argued that some of the remaining 175 pupils might have been nominated by parents even though they were passed over by teachers. Interestingly, only one parent refused to complete the questionnaire.

Despite professional concern that parents would overnominate it did not occur to the degree expected. Parents nominated 24.4% of the total population which certainly was not excessive and confirmed that parents can be utilized as gross screeners at the preschool level. (Ciha, Harris, Hoffman and Potter, 1974). Paradoxically, there were more nominations in lower socioeconomic status (SES) schools than those in higher SES schools with a range extending from 18% to 39%. One may hypothesize that parents in lower SES schools are less discriminating and perhaps more threatened by institutional questionnaires. As indicated elsewhere in the study the teachers tended to be more conservative and nominated 14.4% of the children.

The issue of parent effectiveness in nominations versus teacher effectiveness was examined. The data suggested that parents of kindergarten children are as effective as teachers in the preliminary identification of academically gifted pupils. The final identified group (N=41) showed that parents had been correct in 23.4% of the cases while teachers had been accurate in 22.0% of cases and this difference is not significant. This finding has been substantiated by other studies and despite the evidence there is continuing resistance by professionals to the Idea that parents can be both effective and helpful in such early identification. This is even more meaningful when one considers that there is evidence (Jacobs, 1972) that megative measured attitudes toward the gifted/talented may be present in kindergarten and first grade teachers. However, there was insufficient overlap so that neither parent not teacher nominations could be used exclusively. When there is high quality present in the teaching staff, as was the case in this district, the teacher nominations tend to be more realistic and accurate.

The final teacher ratings of the parent nominees and teacher nominees were markedly similar. The final group showed 21 favorable ratings for parent nominations and 20 positive ratings for teacher nominations. Thus we see further substantiation for the fact that parents are as effective as teachers in assessing those behavioral characteristics that appear to be present in young children who are described as gifted.

Early development of reading skills is sometimes listed as an outstanding characteristic of young gifted children. In this study it was found that 14 or 34% of the parent nominees who become finalists were described as being able to read prior to entering kindergarten. It seems safe to hypothesize that in a middle to high socio-cultural setting that one simple way to tentatively identify such children would be to check out reading skills.

CONCLUSION

These data indicate that it is possible to identify kindergarten children in a systematic, sequential manner using a variety of assessment techniques. However, even with such a comprehensive program there are some cautions to be observed.

The rigor of this approach is evident but it is still possible that some potential candidates were overlooked. Critical is the full participation of all parents and pupils. This represents a real problem with young children because of childhood illness, parent unresponsiveness, etc. Every effort should be made to get the fullest possible participation even though it means follow-up and retesting. If one were to eliminate some of the steps, and certainly this might be necessary due to time and financial conditions, it would tend to increase the risk of duplication and omission.

The parent vs teacher effectiveness argument should not be emphasized to a fault. Common sense dictates that both groups have something to offer in the initial identification of the early childhood gifted. What is needed is a recognition that both groups are definitely complementary. The parent will nominate some children that are overlooked by the teacher and vice versa. Perhaps the onus rests with the teacher although excessive parental protestations will not help matters.

Each school district must review its own demographic makeup before deciding on techniques to be used and cut-off points on instruments. In a high socioeconomic district one might be inclined to use more stringent criteria for programming purposes, for at times giftedness is both relative and absolute. Certainly in racial or ethnic situations one would want to establish criteria in keeping with a normal curve of distribution for the group. For example, the early development of reading skills might not be prevalent in culturally different or disadvantaged situations.

Another area of concern, not dealing directly with identification, is that of differentiated programming. While it is satisfying to identify the gifted it is crucial to do something once they are identified. Inability, or reluctance to program for the gifted will result in a lack of credibility of the process from both parents and teachers. Both will regard the effort as a mere academic exercise with the result that in future attempts at identification there will be but token acceptance and participation. It is not enough to defer meaningful programming until the pupils reach the intermediate grades.

In summary, it makes sense to identify and program for gifted pupils as early as possible. To wait may increase the risk of "turn offs" and wasted potential. On the other hand, all such efforts should be tailored to local conditions and populations using a multi-level approach.

[1]The authors are particularly indebted to Miss Lois Hebert and Miss Mary Livezey both of whom are teachers in the Greenwich Public Schools.

REFERENCES

Cornishe, R. L. "Parents', teachers', and pupils' perception of the gifted child's ability." *Gifted Child Quarterly*, 1968, *12*, 14-17.

Ciha, T. E., Harris. R., Hoffman, C. and Rotter, M. W. "Parents as identifiers of giftedness, ignored but accurate." *Gifted Child Quarterly*, 1974, *18*, 18.

De Haan, R. F. "Identifying gifted children." *School Review*, 1957. *65*. 41-48.

Issacs, A. F. "The search for talent beings within." *Gifted Child Quarterly*, 1965, *9*, 89-96.

Jacobs, J. C. "Effectiveness of teacher and parent identification of gifted children as a function of school level." *Psychology in the Schools*, 1971, *8*, 140-42.

Jacobs, J. C. "Teacher attitude toward gifted children." *Gifted Child Quarterly*, 1972, *16*, 23-26.

Renzulli, J. S. and Hartman, R. K. "Scale for rating behavioral characteristics of superior students." *Exceptional Children*, 1971, *38*, 243-47.

THE BALDWIN IDENTIFICATION MATRIX

Alexinia Y. Baldwin

☐ Assuming that a school district accepts the rationale for an expanded definition of the gifted, this district faces the dilemma of pulling together a workable, sider the traits included in the HEW definition of giftedness as constants (Marland, 1971). These constants are general academic ability, creative ability, psychomotor ability, and psychosocial ability. The next step would be to select an array of techniques for establishing exceptional strengths in the particular area.

The vertical axis (see Figure 1) of the matrix includes the selection of assessment techniques. The horizontal axis includes a scale of 1 to 5 that represents a ranking of scores for each child who is average or above in any or all of the areas listed in the definition. Upon completion of the matrix, the researcher totals the points made on all variables with 5 being the highest possible score that can be received on any one variable. The sum of the points received by each child on the horizontal axis equals the total score for the individual. The highest possible score equals the number of items on the vertical axis times five.

According to the plan for a community, children can be selected from the gross screening for particular program emphases, i.e., mathematics, science, general abilities, creative development. The profile can also be used to establish an equitable cutoff point for acceptance into districtwide programs of some type.

The BIM has been designed and used successfully in the Minnesota school districts to combine all of the assessment techniques into a profile that allows a child equal access to a specially designed program for children who exhibit exceptional ability in a wide range of areas. Some of the advantages of a BIM format include:

1. It allows a school district to use available information for assessment of a child's capabilities.
2. It produces a total score that gives the child from a different culture an opportunity to compete for recognition in a specialized program. This advantage also applies to the child whose talents or giftedness lies in areas that have traditionally been excluded from recognition.
3. It allows the district to assess the strengths as well as the weaknesses of those children who are exceptionally gifted in the traditional areas of assessment.
4. It gives the district an opportunity to tailor the program to the abilities exhibited on the profile sheet (a threshold program that helps children to develop the areas of weaknesses before entering the arena of high competition in this area).
5. It provides a starting point for curriculum development and an organizational structure for meeting the needs of the identified children.
6. It surfaces the underachiever.

Reprinted from *Educational Planning for the Gifted,* by Alexinia Y. Baldwin, by permission of The Council for Exceptional Children. Copyright 1978 by The Council for Exceptional Children,1920 Association Drive, Reston, Virginia 22091.

In conclusion, the BIM format is suggested as a way to more equitably assign students to gifted programs. It does not suggest or recommend that standardized instruments such as IQ tests and achievement tests be ignored. Rather, it

Student _Joseph Matrix_ School _Loman Elementary_
Age _9_ Grade _3_ Sex _M_ Date _5-6-78_ School District _Eastern_

Assessment Items	Scores					
	5	4	3	2	1	B-NA
1. Standardized Intelligence Test	140+ ( )	130-139 ( )	120-129 (✓)	110-119 ( )	100-109 ( )	
2. Achievement Test Composite Score	95%ile ( )	90-94%ile ( )	85-89%ile (✓)	80-84%ile ( )	75-79%ile ( )	
3. Achievement Test—Reading Score	Stan 9 (✓)	Stan 8 ( )	Stan 7 ( )	Stan 6 ( )	Stan 5 ( )	
4. Achievement Test—Math Score	95%ile ( )	90-94%ile ( )	85-89%ile (✓)	80-84%ile ( )	75-79%ile ( )	
5. Learning Scale Score	32 (✓)	28-31 ( )	24-27 ( )	20-23 ( )	16-19 ( )	
6. Motivational Scale Score	36 (✓)	32-35 ( )	28-31 ( )	24-27 ( )	16-23 ( )	
7. Creativity Scale Score	40 (✓)	36-35 ( )	32-35 ( )	28-31 ( )	20-27 ( )	
8. Leadership Scale Score	40 ( )	36-39 (✓)	32-35 ( )	28-31 ( )	20-27 ( )	
9. Various Teacher Recommendations	Superior ( )	Very Good (✓)	Good ( )	Average ( )	Below Average ( )	
10. Psychomotor Ability	( )	(✓)	( )	( )	( )	
11. Peer Nominations	( )	(✓)	( )	( )	( )	
12.	( )	( )	( )	( )	( )	
Column Tally of Checks	4	4	3	0	0	
Weight	x5	x4	x3	x2	x1	
Add Across	20	16	9	0	0	
Total Score	45					

Figure 1. Baldwin Identification Matrix—Sample Form

practical, nondiscriminatory format that will help the participants interpret the child's qualification for a specially designed program. In using this approach, the first step for the user of the Baldwin Identification Matrix (BIM) is to consuggests that additional instruments, which expand the data base and establish the acceptance of a broad range of abilities, be added.

REFERENCES

Marland, S. P. Jr. _Education of the gifted and talented_, Vol. 1. Report to the Congress of the United States by the US Commissioner of Education, 1971.

Scientists Research Ways To Assess Intellectual Growth

The figure above is a familiar one usually connected with tradition but having universal significance. What does it convey to your own imagination? Develop one idea or meaning it suggests to you and indicate how the figure conveys that impression. You need not feel bound by traditional interpretations.

The values gained from a four-year general college education, although generally revered and even exalted, have always been difficult to pinpoint. Colleges frequently espouse the virtues of increased logical and analytical thinking, better communications ability, and other intangible signs of intellectual growth. "But the task of developing a casual relationship between these achievements and general education—non-major-field—courses has seemed awesome even for the most experienced research scientists," says Mary Churchill, editor of *ETS Developments*, a publication of the Educational Testing Service.

Now, however, the need for research of this nature has grown, especially since colleges are being held accountable for the difficulty some graduates have in finding jobs, writes Churchill.

But as institutions prepare to confront the problem, faculty and administrators have found themselves with too little information and hardly any agreement as to how to proceed.

Accordingly, a set of measures is being developed by a group of research scientists and educators in California under the direction of Jonathan R. Warren, research scientist at Educational Testing Service (ETS), Berkeley, that will assess student performance in areas often considered general education objectives. "Rather than measuring specific course knowledge or grasp of a body of knowledge in a major field, the tests are being designed to reflect intellectual growth," said Warren. After being fully developed, the measures will examine the effects of different curricular approaches on students' achievement in four kinds of academic competence: communication ability, analytical skills, synthesizing ability, and cultural awareness.

"We make no presumption that these four areas exhaust the possibilities for assessing ideas and values that can be measured in general education," said Warren. "But I believe we have made a good beginning."

"There is broad interest in this project coming from many colleges and universities across the country," Warren added. "They are particularly concerned with strengthening the general courses that broaden students' learning." Ultimately, he said, a set of measures may be developed from which colleges can select questions that best suit their own objectives. These measures will be ready for experimental use in 1979.

Each of the four areas of academic competence has been carefully defined by the test development committee (made up of many faculty members in California colleges and universities), and sample sets of questions and descriptions of categories of responses have been developed.

Analytic Thinking

Students who are the best analytic thinkers are defined as those "quick to identify the essential components of ideas, events, problems, and processes. They distinguish the important from the unimportant, fact from conjecture, and make other distinctions imaginatively but usefully. They quickly pick out deficiencies or inconsistencies in statements or positions. They are realistically skeptical or critical, but not destructively so." Those in the middle group would be more methodical than perceptive, less imaginative, and might miss some subtleties. Students low in analytic skill have difficulty, according to the research definition, in getting beneath the surface of a problem, idea or situation.

Aspects of analytic thinking are measured by: (1) the ability to draw defensible inferences and (2) the ability to identify the central issue in a statement or argument.

Synthesizing Skill

Students exhibiting a high degree of synthesizing skill are adept at organizing apparently unrelated ideas into a common frame of reference, thereby constructing a general framework that can be applied to new situations. They find unifying themes in diffuse bodies of information. One question probes the student's ability to identify metaphorical meaning in the Taoist symbol of the yin and yang.

From the *Bulletin of the National/State Leadership Training Institute on the Gifted and the Talented*, Vol. 5, No. 11, November 1978. Barbara Johnson, Editor.

Other questions in the series measure student's ability to integrate material from a lengthly list of detailed information.

Awareness

Students high in awareness or sensitivity see the broad ramifications and implications of ideas, events, and issues. They are aware of the cultural roots of value systems other than their own and appreciate the historical development of human culture and the relationship of present values to those of the past. Students low in awareness, as defined by the research committee, lack both breadth and depth of perspective.

One question probes the student's political awareness and social understanding by asking for the implications of a quote for someone commissioned to make a film documentary on the lives of the elderly poor in an inner-city area.

"One half the world knows not how the other half lives."

—George Herbert

Communication

In this fourth area of academic competence, questions were developed that measure communication in some major fields, including history, poetry, and mathematics. Specific course knowledge, however, is not required. One question gives the students some jargon-filled information concerning life on the planet Pluto, and then asks them to construct a concise paragraph that conveys the information in everyday language.

Students high in communication ability are defined as those able to express themselves clearly and precisely, without unnecessary words, stating their ideas vividly but smoothly, economically, even elegantly.

Initially, the test developers were confronted with the problem of scoring open-ended questions that, Warren believes, serves to evaluate some general education goals more effectively than multiple-choice questions. However, two ETS Princeton researchers developed a procedure for scoring free responses to open-ended questions intended to measure creativity. This procedure, initiated in 1975, was adopted for the academic competencies scoring. In fact, the open-ended questions were developed with that scoring in mind.

"While the procedure is not foolproof, experience in pretesting has shown that a set of workable questions and scoring procedures can be produced," said Warren.

The following was taken from Dr. Joseph's Renzulli's A Guidebook for Evaluating Programs for the Gifted and Talented (a Working Draft).

Non-Test Measures of Student Growth and Performance

Table 5

Means, Standard Deviations, and Levels of Significance for Sociometric Status of Project Gifted Students, East Providence

Groups	Regular Class		Gifted Students		Difference	t	Level of Significance
	mean	s.d.	mean	s.d.			
Fourth Grade							
Sit Near	5.17	4.67	7.30	6.34	2.13	1.23	n.s.
Play With	5.27	4.35	7.90	6.23	2.63	1.61	n.s.
Work With	4.85	4.51	9.90	6.14	5.05	1.59	.05
Total	15.31	12.68	25.10	17.57	9.79	2.07	.05
Fifth Grade							
Sit Near	5.27	4.09	6.64	5.14	1.37	1.10	n.s.
Play With	5.19	3.93	6.79	5.06	1.60	1.33	n.s.
Work With	5.30	5.62	6.50	5.32	1.20	0.74	n.s.
Total	15.76	12.56	19.93	14.69	4.17	1.11	n.s.
Sixth Grade							
Sit Near	5.54	3.91	5.38	4.65	-.16	0.13	n.s.
Play With	5.20	3.78	4.23	4.66	-.97	0.85	n.s.
Work With	4.56	3.23	7.85	6.36	3.29	2.98	.05
Total	15.34	9.78	17.54	14.60	2.20	0.71	n.s.

From: Renzulli, J. S., *An Evaluation of Project Gifted*. Storrs: University of Connecticut, 1973.

b.   *Non-Test Meaures of Student Growth and Performance.* Rating scales, checklists, logs, and anecdotal recording systems are the types of non-test

From *A Guidebook for Evaluating Programs for the Gifted and Talented, a Working Draft*, by Joseph S. Renzulli, sponsored by the National/State Leadership Training Institute on the Gifted and Talented, and a Grant from the U.S. Office of Education, Department of Health, Education and Welfare.

instruments that are most frequently used to evaluate student growth and performance. Several examples of instruments that have been used for these purposes are included in Appendix B. While most ratings of student performance are designed to be completed by teachers, we note in Appendix B some examples of parent and student scales that focus on a combination of abilities, motivation, and general adjustment to participation in programs for the gifted and talented. At this point we must raise a question about the *appropriateness* of sources of data. While it is certainly valid to ask parents about their childrens' enthusiasm, attitudes toward various aspects of a special program, and activities that the parents can observe at home, we must be cautious when asking parents to rate student performance. Parents may simply not have the opportunity or knowledge to assess school performance adequately because they are somewhat removed from the center of the learning situation. When this is the case, their responses on performance rating scales may really be reflections of their youngsters' attitudes; and thus, so far as *performance* is concerned, we have used the wrong source of data. A good rule to follow in matching instruments with sources of data is simply never ask a person to second guess or answer out of ignorance. If respondents have not had numerous opportunities to observe the behaviors under investigation *directly,* then chances are they are not appropriate sources of data.

Constructing instruments that can be used to assess growth and/or performance presents certain problems for the evaluator. Very often the items included in these instruments are too vague to pinpoint the specific areas where growth has occurred. For example, a statement that asks the teacher to rate "The ability to use research skills," does not tell us exactly which skills the student has mastered. An approach that focuses on relatively specific behaviors within the general area of research skills will help us to overcome the problem of vagueness. For example, we might ask the teacher to rate a youngster on the following behaviors:

1. The student used the following sections of reference books to locate information: (Scale)

    a. Table of Contents   _ _ _ _ _
    b. Index   _ _ _ _ _
    c. Appendix   _ _ _ _ _
    d. Bibliography   _ _ _ _ _
    e. Preface   _ _ _ _ _

2. The student uses the following references appropriately in locating desired information:

    a. World Almanac   _ _ _ _ _
    b. Readers' Guide to Periodical Literature   _ _ _ _ _
    c. Dictionary of American Biography   _ _ _ _ _
    d. Etc.   _ _ _ _ _

3. When presented with information in the following forms, the student can interpret it and translate it into his own language:

    a. Graphs   _ _ _ _ _
    b. Tables   _ _ _ _ _
    c. Topographical Maps   _ _ _ _ _
    d. Diagrams   _ _ _ _ _
    e. Flow Charts   _ _ _ _ _
    f. Etc.   _ _ _ _ _

1. PLANNING

4. The student has demonstrated the following
   skills in analyzing and presenting data:
   - a. Calculation of Means   ------
   - b. Calculation of standard deviations   ------
   - c. Preparation of tables   ------
   - d. Preparation of graphs   ------
   - e. Preparation of trend analysis statements   ------

It is important to keep in mind that rating scales or checklists of this type must be developed in accordance with the specific content of particular instructional goals. The evaluator should carefully review the curricular information that he obtained through Front-End Analysis, decide what type of instrument he will use, and then translate the information into an appropriate evaluation instrument. At this point the evaluator may want to work with teachers and curriculum coordinators to make certain that the instruments reflect accurate translations of the intended learning outcomes. It is also important to remember that a combination of instruments can be used to evaluate a particular component. For example, if a fairly valid test is available to assess some of the research skills discussed above, the evaluator may want to use this test in conjunction with a homemade rating scale that will cover skills not included on the test.

One of the areas that sometimes emerges as a Key Feature in the area of student growth has to do with self-concept development or other areas of psychological adjustment. Generally, a great deal of psychometric know-how is necessary for instrument construction in this area and therefore it is recommended that evaluators consider already available instruments if they want to assess changes in self-concept. A book entitled *Self-Concept Measurement: An Annotated Bibliography* (Coller, 1971) is included in the Instrument Sourcebook section of the bibliography. We have, however, included one homemade self-esteem inventory in Appendix B to give you some idea of what is typically included in such instruments.

Because of the many problems involved in evaluating the higher level objectives of programs for the gifted and talented, and in view of the great deal of individualization that usually characterizes such programs, alternative approaches to evaluation must be considered. One such approach, developed for the Alpha Project for Able Learners in the State of Washington, involves the use of an anecdotal recording system which is presented in Figure 17. This system is designed to provide a continous chronicle of student growth by documenting several aspects of the learning process. The system focuses on specific "learning segments" for individual students. A learning segment is defined as any series of related activities directed toward the accomplishment of predetermined objectives.*
A learning segment may require a day, a week or several months, and it is conceivable that a youngster may be working on several learning segments at one time. The system is mainly designed for individual documentation; however, if several students are working on a project together, and if their objectives are the same, the anecdotal record can very well be used for groups. There may, of course, be differences in the degree to which group members accomplish specific objectives and these differences should be recorded by individual rather than by learning segment.

The instrument presented in Figure 17 provides a structured approach for recording evaluative information. Before discussing how the instrument can be used as an evaluation technique we should point out a few related features. First, the instrument encourages teachers and students to be a little more "objectives-oriented" in planning learning activities. Second, the students themselves can participate in planning and in so doing, begin to learn the differences between various types of objectives. In places where versions of this instrument have been used students did much of the planning and record-keeping themselves. This involvement has caused students to become more responsible for their own education and has helped them to think more carefully about what they are studying and why they are studying it. Finally, in places where versions of the instrument have been used as a reporting system to parents, there have been very favorable reactions to questionnaires dealing with the degree to which parents have been informed about the program and the progress of their own children.

When the instrument is used for evaluation purposes, the major task is analyzing the content in terms of the *differences* that characterize gifted programs. The objectives for each learning segment are listed and classified according to their cognitive and affective levels. As the evaluator reviews the anecdotal records he should attempt to ascertain whether or not there is appropriate emphasis on higher level objectives. His judgment should be guided by the general goals or policy statement which underlie the program. Thus, for example, if the program places heavy emphasis on the development of creative thinking, the records should show a heavy concentration of objectives and activities that promote this type of mental process. The evaluator should study the objectives in relation to other information included in the record and attempt to determine if congruence exists between the Activities, Resources, and Products on one hand and the objectives on the other.

The Areas of Study section will help to point out such things as inter-disciplinary studies or topics that do not fall into one of the traditional curricular areas. In a similar fashion, the Activities, Resources, and Product sections will help to reveal whether or not educational experiences and outcomes are generally different from those that occur in the regular school program. As information begins to accumulate, the evaluator must examine each section of the anecdotal record in terms of factors such as diversity, opportunity for self-expression, unusualness, and originality. He must constantly ask himself the question: "Would this student *ordinarily* have the opportunity to do these things in the regular school program?"

Admittedly, this approach to performance evaluation places a great deal of reliance on (1) the accurate portrayal of information and (2) the experience and judgment of the evaluator. Nevertheless, it offers an alternative means for systematically describing and analyzing *what actually goes on in a program*, and in this respect it may have certain advantages over tests. Boards of education and funding agencies frequently ask: "What is different about the program for the gifted?" and "What do students actually do in the gifted program that isn't being done in the regular classroom?" The answers to these questions require descriptive information rather than test scores, but the descriptive information must be carefully analyzed in order to call attention to the differential nature of experiences. As the evaluator prepares a written analysis of anecdotal information, he should constantly focus attention on the quantity and quality of learning experiences and products which, in his judgment, represent relatively unique departures from the regular curriculum.

---

* Note: I do *not* believe that a gifted youngster's *total* program must be rigidly planned and predetermined. All students need an opportunity to explore randomly, to play around, and to spend some time just being themselves. This type of exploration may very well lead to the development of certain objectives, but I would like to emphasize that I do not advocate the use of anecdotal recording systems such as the one in Figure 17 for every single thing that a child does in the gifted program.

1. PLANNING

Another approach that has been developed to provide information about what is going on in a gifted program is the Classroom Report (See Figure 18). Stake (1970) describes this report as follows:

> The purpose of the Classroom Report is to assist the teacher who desires to tell various people about her classroom. We are acquainted with many teachers who want to tell parents or townspeople or administrators more about their student group and curriculum and teaching techniques than they can in informal conversations. Usually the writing chore is too great a burden.
>
> In developing this form, we have assumed that reporting on students as a group (rather than individually as you do with a report card) is a sensible thing for teachers to do. We believe that schools

have a responsibility to keep the community informed, and we believe that the work that goes into the preparation of a report like this helps the teacher put a number of important responsibilities into perspective. Furthermore—with increasing demands for evaluation and accountability—we feel that by making evaluation reports that are sensible to teachers and parents we can better resist irrelevant evaluation requirements.

A bit of advice for using the Classroom Report: (From the Manual for the Classroom Report).

1.   Think of this as an opportunity to improve your communication with parents, administrators, townspeople—and even your mother. We're serious. Think of people you have been telling, or whom you would like to talk to, about what you are doing in your classroom. Then think of how you might use this form to get a good conversation started, or to improve an already-good conversation.

2.   Think who your readers will be. Parents, students, school board members, the Junior Chamber of Commerce? Will your Report be included in a project evaluation report? Different readers think that different information is important. Usually there won't be time to write up a different Classroom Report for different readers, but you probably can make *one* report relevant to a large audience.

3.   Use the form the way you want to. Change or add words as needed. Note that the report comes in three sheets (making 12 pages) but some teachers use only one or two sheets. You can add your own sheets as inserts—but don't plan a grand report that never gets done.

4.   Recognize that it is hard work to collect information— but that often the hardest-worked-for information is the best. (Ask any newspaperman.) You have good information already. Some of it would be better information if you used a special instrument or procedure to collect it. This manual will suggest some possibilities.

The central idea of the Illinois Gifted Program is that the special talents of all children should be given special opportunity in school to develop. Each participating school district decides how it will use the limited funds it gets. The following objectives have been set forth for the program in this classroom.

CLASSROOM OBJECTIVES:

CLASSROOM EMPHASES:

Emphasis given in this classroom

. . . to develop . . .	Extra	Usual	None
Better ability to learn	_____	. _____	. _____
Problem solving abilities	_____	. _____	. _____
Humanistic values	_____	. _____	. _____
Creative ideas	_____	. _____	. _____
Artistic performance	_____	. _____	. _____
Vocational skills	_____	. _____	. _____
Social criticism	_____	. _____	. _____
Self-awareness and esteem	_____	. _____	. _____
Content understandings	_____	. _____	. _____
Sense of responsibility	_____	. _____	. _____
Respect for authorities	_____	. _____	. _____

ACCELERATION or ENRICHMENT

We attempt to have the students

_____ learn the same things that other students do but learn it faster.

_____ learn additional things that other students don't get much of a chance to learn in school.

MAJOR CLASS ACTIVITIES:

Figure 17

ALPHA PROJECT — EVALUATION OF STUDENT GROWTH

NAME _____ GRADE _____

TEACHER _____ SCHOOL _____

AREAS OF STUDY (Check all that apply)

___ Language Arts/Humanities ___ Science ___ Personal and Social Development

___ Social Studies ___ Music ___ Other (Specify)

___ Mathematics ___ Art ___ Other (Specify)

Brief Description of The Content of The Study _____

Beginning Date _____ Ending Date _____ Number of Days _____

OBJECTIVES (List in order of importance)

1.
2.
3.
4.
5.

COGNITIVE OBJECTIVES — Check the highest level for each written objective

#	
6	Evaluating , Judging
5	Synthesizing , Creating
4	Analyzing (breaking down into component parts)
3	Application (of learned material to concrete situations)
2	Comprehension: Translating, Interpreting, Extrapolating
1	Knowing / Remembering

AFFECTIVE OBJECTIVES — Check all that apply

C	Developing attitudes and values toward ideas, causes, social issues , etc.
B	Developing skills that lead to better relations between people.
A	Developing interest in and commitment to a topic, area of study or learning in general

ACCOMPLISHMENT OF OBJECTIVES

In the spaces below please indicate the degree to which you think each objective has been accomplished by:

1. Placing a check mark (✓) in the appropriate space for the cognitive objective.
2. Placing the corresponding letters (A,B,C) in the appropriate spaces for each of the affective objectives.

Not At All	A Little	About Half	A Great Deal	Completely

ACTIVITIES (Briefly list what the student did to accomplish these objectives. Underline any activity that you consider to be relatively unique)

RESOURCES (Reference Books, Films, People, Etc.)

PRODUCT (Briefly describe any projects, stories, plays, filmstrips, etc. that resulted from this study. Attach samples if available.)

Sponsored by; Superintendent Of Public Instruction - State Of Washington

Prepared by: Dr. Joseph S. Renzulli - The University Of Connecticut Bureau Of Educational Research

USE OF SCHOOL TIME

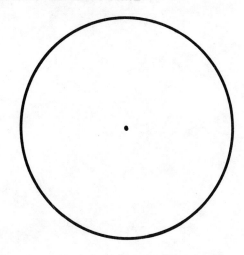

I.   Individual Student Work
         Assigned reading
         Work on projects
         Exercises, tests

II.   Teacher Explanations

III. Exchange of Ideas
         Recitation
         Inquiry
         Discussion

IV. Social, recreational

V.   Administrative matters

The pie-chart above indicates approximately how time is spent in this classroom. The activities for any one day, of course, would not necessarily look like this.

AN ILLUSTRATION OF STUDENT
ACCOMPLISHMENT THIS PROJECT
WOULD LIKE TO TAKE PARTIAL
CREDIT FOR:

Scholastic ability, similar to what many people call IQ, was measured by the _____ on _____

                        (test)   **(date)**

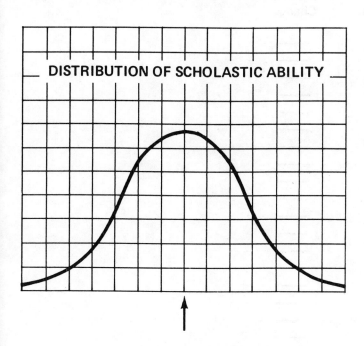

The bell-shaped curve at the left indicates the spread of scores of students this age across the nation. Each little box in the bar graph represents the score of one student in our classroom.

The scholastic giftedness of our group is indicated by the clustering of scores to the right of the arrow.

1. PLANNING

STUDENT PROGRESS

The following items are examples of the kinds of performance this project emphasizes. Note the progress of the class during the period.

VIEWS OF THIS CLASSROOM

Recently we tried to find out what others have been thinking about this classroom. Their views can give us a better idea about what is needing change and what is important to keep.

Views were gathered from:

	Classroom's Best Features	Features Needing Change
Work on Thought-processes	———	———
Subject-matter coverage	———	———
Clarity of teaching	———	———
Student motivation	———	———
Relevance to "real world"	———	———
Utility for later schoolwork	———	———
Pace of work scheduling	———	———
Workload	———	———
Chance for self-determination of work	———	———
Facilities; materials	———	———
Class activities	———	———
Group atmosphere	———	———
Acceptance of individuals	———	———
Teacher competence	———	———
Student competence	———	———
Evaluations of students	———	———
Project self-evaluation	———	———
Administrative support	———	———
Community support	———	———

STAFF EVALUATION OF THE CLASSROOM

Several staff members associated with the Gifted Program have discussed the strengths and weaknesses of this classroom. Their views are summarized here. The marks at the right indicate what they think needs change and what is important to keep.

Views were gathered from _____ persons. Each was asked to name the best three things about the classroom and the three things most needing change.

	Classroom's Best Features	Features Needing Change
Work on Thought-processes	▬	▬
Subject-matter coverage	▬	▬
Clarity of teaching	▬	▬
Student motivation	▬	▬
Revelance to "real world"	▬	▬
Utility for later schoolwork	▬	▬
Pace of work scheduling	▬	▬
Workload	▬	▬
Chance for self-determination of work	▬	▬
Facilities; materials	▬	▬
Class activities	▬	▬
Group atmosphere	▬	▬
Acceptance of individuals	▬	▬
Teacher competence	▬	▬
Student competence	▬	▬
Evaluations of students	▬	▬
Project self-evaluation	▬	▬
Administrative support	▬	▬
Community support	▬	▬

Adapted from Stephen Lapan

1. PLANNING

Which Describe Our Classroom Best?

☐ Students move freely in and out of the room, taking much responsibility for the use of their time.

☐ When a student explains something to the class the teacher is likely to praise him for his contribution.

☐ Students learn that growing up means "living by the rules"—and helping others to do likewise.

☐ Strong effort is made to get students to know the answer to questions such as those on standardized tests.

☐ Assignments are made clearly so that school time is used wisely and productively.

☐ When a student explains something to the class the teacher is likely to invite him to discuss it further.

☐ Laughter, small talk, an even occasional outburst are common in this classroom.

☐ Strong effort is made to get students to think through and defend their own opinions.

☐ Most of the important work we do is in individual study and homework.

☐ Our test scores are less important to us than what a student does in working with others.

☐ We make an effort to relate what we do in school to what adults do in their work.

☐ Students compete with each other. It is important to them to get good marks.

☐ Most of the important work we do is in group projects in the classroom.

☐ What a student does on our tests is the best indication of how well he is succeeding.

☐ We emphasize that it is important for the students to decide (as a group) what is worth while.

☐ Students tutor each other. It is important to them that their friends learn too.

Comment:

Adapted from Joe Steele

FOCUS. . . .

'Tis a Far, Far Better Thing that I Do*

What effect does a special program for the gifted and talented student have upon that student? Do the bright kids who decide to enroll in the programs benefit more than those who pass up the chance?

And what do the "enrollees" get out of the opportunity? Higher grades and more honors? After being in the program, do they like school better, develop a social consciousness, or have a better self-concept? To answer these kinds of questions, Claire Dugan Tremaine, at the United States International University in San Diego, has made a comparative study of the "Effects of Gifted Programs on

programs and 59 gifted students had chosen not to be enrolled.

The other method of comparison was a 33-question survey mailed to 289 gifted graduates from three high school districts, San Dieguito, Grossmont, and Sweetwater, comprising 16 high schools. This questionnaire measured the students' attitudes toward education, society, peer groups, and self. Students were also asked about school/community activities and vocational/educational goals. The 101 responses, divided for comparison purposes, were from 60 students who were enrolled in the gifted programs and 41 who were not.

(8) attribute more influence to curriculum and teachers when assessing personal cognitive growth; (9) express similar attitudes toward peers; (10) be equally comfortable with competition; (11) indicate an equally wide range of friends; and (12) engage in equal numbers of school and community activities.

"The hypotheses 6, 7, and 8 were rejected although there were differences in the responses of the two groups," the researcher said, "because the differences weren't significant. No negative affects of the gifted programs were revealed by the study; many positive benefits were found."

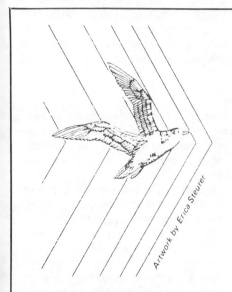

Artwork by Erica Steurer

Sample Questions from Survey Mailed to 289 Gifted High School Graduates—

—What is your present vocational or professional goal?

—In high school, I learned almost nothing. . .I learned in some classes, but not many. . .I learned in about half my classes. . .I learned in many of my classes. . .I learned in almost all my classes. . .

—What is truest about your teachers? None were able to communicate knowledge at all. . .Almost all the teachers were able to communicate knowledge. . .

—List four people who have most influenced your life. . .

—Here are some common sources of friendship. Please check the statements which are true for you. . .We became friends through sports. . .We became friends in one particular class. . .

—Within the last four years, what was the most memorable time you learned something new? Please describe the event and how the learning took place.

—If you have won any honors or scholarships during high school, please list them:

—What do you see yourself doing in ten years? Why that?

their Participants."

"Most program evaluation," she said, "has been informal and sketchy, describing the accomplishments of gifted participants but leaving unanswered the questions of whether they might not have done as well in regular, *unenriched* classes."

Two methods were used to compare the gifted enrollees with the gifted non-enrollees. Tremaine obtained grade point averages, IQ and SAT scores of 1976 graduates from ten high schools in San Diego County. She also listed the number of scholarships and honors they had won. In this group, 74 were enrolled in gifted

Tremaine, who is now MGM Coordinator at Grossmont Union School District, said the study tested criticisms which are frequently made about gifted programs.

The following are the study's hypotheses that the enrolled gifted students will (1) demonstrate significantly higher grade point averages; (2) exhibit significantly higher test scores; (3) receive more honors and scholarships; (4) express more favorable attitudes toward school and teachers; (5) select higher and more definite vocational goals; (6) express more awareness of and respect for needs of society; (7) reveal higher self-concepts;

Why didn't some of the gifted students choose to be in the gifted programs? "Non-enrollment reasons," Tremaine said, "included lack of interest, program conflicts such as band vs. honors English, and the fear of hurting their grade point average." Yet the study indicates their grade point averages and test scores would have been significantly higher and the students would have received more honors and scholarships, among other advantages, if they had enrolled. Gifted students, their teachers and parents can profit from such research.

* "It is a far, far better thing I do, than I have ever done." Charles Dickens, *A Tale of Two Cities.*

From the ITYB, Intellectually Talented Youth Bulletin, Published by the Study of Mathematically Precocious Youth (SMPY), The Johns Hopkins University, Baltimore, Maryland 21218. Professor Daniel P. Keating, Editor

SPINOFF BENEFITS FOR OTHER STUDENTS

by George Banks
Consultant, MGM Program, San Diego USD

In 1950, San Diego Schools had a standardized curriculum which stressed heterogeneous groupings, and Procrustean courses in which all students used the same textbooks (with rather low vocabulary levels) and progressed through the grades at the same rate.

Gifted Program Evolves

In 1951 the superintendent and school board initiated a program for gifted students. Two teacher-consultants were selected, one for elementary and one for secondary schools. To provide direction and design studies, a committee for the gifted was organized with members representing administration, teachers, psychologists, parents, and research staff.

With testing in full swing, attention turned to the problem of enrichment. In the Fifties, enrichment generally meant more of the same, whether spelling words, algebra exercises, or all the problems at the end of the chapter. To provide qualitative rather than quantitative enrichment, the teacher-consultants and the committee for the gifted developed exercises which stressed insights and understandings of basic concepts. These exercises were printed and distributed to teachers for use with the identified gifted.

In a practice which was to become common, teachers extended their use to include those students who learned more rapidly than their classmates. This diffusion of the enrichment activities made it necessary to write more and more of them. In addition, these exercises—while beneficial—imposed difficult tasks on classroom teachers planning learning activities for students whose academic abilities ranged from retarded to college level. Realization of this academic spread led to meeting the needs of the more able by providing them more advanced courses rather than enrichment activities.

Since the Sputnik era was dawning, emphasis was first placed on science and mathematics. The advanced track began at Grade 7 with mathematics. Later foreign languages were introduced, making a six-year language program possible. At Grade 10, other languages were added to the standard Spanish and French: e.g. Mandarin Chinese, Arabic, and Japanese. Students who were high achievers were also eligible for these rigorous courses, and from 15 to 25% of students in tenth grade were enrolled.

The MGM program also introduced opportunities for those gifted in writing. At the senior high school levels the MGM program collected the best poetry and short stories and published them under the title *Quest*. The writing also included many articles by non-identified students who were talented.

Many new courses aimed at the identified but open to the able began as summer enrichment classes. This was a real boost for curriculum development by trial. Some have survived to the present: combination art, music and dance classes; great books; marine sciences; and exploratory courses in medicine and computers. One enrichment course, speed reading for the college bound, became so popular it was added to the tenth-grade Advanced English course as a quarter sub-course. Since one-fourth of the tenth grade chose this class, the MGM program again benefitted non-identified students.

At the senior high school level, courses giving college credit were developed; some have continued to date as junior college courses in calculus and political science. Another avenue to earning college credits in high school was advanced placement courses. College credit is given those who achieve a college-level score on the final tests. Some graduating participants have entered the sophomore year of college and several have entered at the junior year.

Present MGM Program

In 1976-77, the program involved 7322 students at both elementary and secondary levels. In all, there were 438 teachers in 45 elementary, 19 junior high and 16 senior high schools. Gifted students participated in either a cluster or seminar/independent study program.

Cluster students are enrolled in classes with average- and above-average-ability students. Seminar/independent study students participate in classes of identified students only.

San Diego schools now provide "qualitatively different" instruction for those identified as gifted by a variety of direct services to schools and by administering funds for use by principals and their faculties in meeting the needs of their cluster or individualized/seminar classes. Some 50 services are provided for all grade levels. These services provide opportunities for using varied learning styles, such as "Structure of Intellect" model; others provide for individualized study, expressive behavior, or creative products. Some are field trips and some bring performers, poets, artists, engineers, and others to the school site or classroom.

Something New—Futures Seminars

One of the latest of the direct services, begun this year, is an example of the innovative programs presently being developed. Futures Seminars stem from *Future Shock* by Alvin Toffler—a book which led to world-wide interest in the study of energy and environmental problems and their future impact on life styles, energy uses, eco-politics, and quality of life expectancies.

Last year Dr. David Hermanson, Director of Gifted Programs, and three consultants met with experts in gifted education to develop objectives for the 1977-78 school year. The following objectives were considered important:

1. The need for MGM to meet people qualified to serve as mentors and exemplars.

2. The need to meet experts from many different professional fields as part of vocational orientation.

3. The need to exercise adult responsibilities in a pre-college situation without classroom supervision and at sites away from their schools.

4. The need to develop social and leadership skills within the peer group.

Approximately 700 students enrolled in eight seminars at which experts considered outstanding statewide or nationally presented their viewpoints. Each of these met with an invited group of 100 students representative of all district schools. After the speaker's presentation, the audience broke into small groups to discuss the main points and organize questions for a final thirty minutes.

As part of their leadership training, students attending the futures seminars reported details to classmates unable to attend the sessions. To assist these students in their reporting, each seminar was videotaped by students from a television production class.

Student response to the seminars indicated high interest and enthusiasm, and the question-and-answer periods at the end of the sessions run overtime. In the absence of a formal evaluation instrument, the effects of the peer group environment are more difficult to assess. MGM students remarked they had enjoyed meeting and working with peers from outside their high school. Leadership within the groupings seemed to be fluid and without bias.

Parents, teachers, principals, and seminar leaders indicate that most consider this a worthwhile activity that they hope will be continued next year. Several of the speaker/mentors came at their own expense and volunteered to return!

Evaluation

Evaluations are made at three-year intervals by the Evaluation Services Department. Over the years, the program has been changed on the basis of these evaluation reports to strengthen weak areas and to extend strong ones. The last MGM program evaluation was reported to the board on July 21, 1977 and is summarized here.

In the "Conclusion" section the evaluators found:

1. That grade point averages exceeded the district's 3.0 criterion level at both junior and senior high school.

2. That in 33 of 34 calculations, the district objective of three years above the norm was attained at Grades 6, 8 and 10.

3. In the 1976 testing at Grade 6, mathematics computation sub-test, the gifted students scored two years and six months above the publishers' norm, but six months below the expected criterion.

4. The teacher rating scales at the secondary level met district criteria in 40% of the selected items, and approached but did not meet the criterion for the rest.

Considerable evidence exists that the changes in curriculum and guidance made to provide equal learning opportunities for the identified have produced significant improvements for the more able and talented, also. In many ways the record indicates that helping the gifted student benefits the upper 25% of the student population to some measurable degree.

In conclusion, this article has reported some of the past and present parts of the multi-faceted San Diego MGM program with special attention to the Futures Seminars option, which may lead to an extra-school enrichment activity for both gifted and more able students.

Rethinking the Issues Regarding the Culturally Disadvantaged Gifted

MARY M. FRASIER

MARY M. FRASIER *is Assistant Professor, Educational Psychology, and Co-coordinator, Programs for the Gifted, University of Georgia, Athens.*

THIS discussion shall focus on issues relative to providing programs that meet the needs of the disadvantaged gifted population. The term *disadvantaged* shall be used generically to symbolize all of the numerous designations that have been used to refer to this population.

That there might be gifted children among disadvantaged populations was relatively unheard of prior to the 1960's. With the exception of a few studies such as Witty and Jenkins (1934) and Jenkins (1948), the emphasis on disadvantaged populations had largely been on their academic and social difficulties. Attendant to this emphasis had been efforts that were primarily directed toward remediation.

Heralded by those who began to suggest that the provision of appropriate educational opportunities indeed allowed students from impoverished backgrounds and racial and ethnic minorities to achieve (McClelland, 1958), the era of the disadvantaged gifted might be said to have begun. Reissman's (1962) writings about the culturally deprived gifted child were symbolic of the discussions that began to recognize that among the disadvantaged population there were those who had above average potential to succeed.

Many questions arose for which answers are still being sought. Who are the disadvantaged gifted? How should they appropriately be designated (e.g., culturally deprived, culturally disadvantaged, culturally different)? In what ways do they differ from their nongifted counterparts and from the advantaged gifted? How should they be identified (i.e., should traditional identification criteria be used with modifications, or should supplementary measures be developed)?

Definition of Population

Numerous writers have suggested various ways to define the populations that would be included in the category of the disadvantaged gifted. Brickman and Lehrer (1972) reflected the feelings of those who have suggested that the interpretation of disadvantaged be broad enough "to include a variety of persons who have not been able to enjoy culture and education to the fullest on account of various disabilities, whether social, ideological, religious, or of any other origin" (p. 2). Thus, this approach represents those who would suggest that this group would include not only racial and ethnic minorities but also women, handicapped individuals, and underachievers.

Frost and Hawkes (1971) summarized the conclusions of those who felt that the common denominator for membership in a disadvantaged population would be that the candidates are poor. Therefore, the economically deprived of any racial group would be classified as disadvantaged.

A recent discussion by Baldwin (1978) suggested a more plausible way of defining this group. Viewing the disadvantaged as those who are deprived of the opportunity to develop their mental capacities, she described three sets of external influences that define who should be in this group. The influences or variables named by Baldwin (1978, p. 1) are:

Cultural diversity [as] a condition of racial, ethnic, language, or physical differences from a dominant culture.
Socioeconomic deprivation [as] a condition of legal or *de facto* denial of social interaction combined with substandard housing and jobs.
Geographic isolation [as] a condition of being geo-

graphically located away from the mainstream of society.

In defining the disadvantaged gifted, then, it may be concluded that within any group—be it determined by ethnic group membership, sex, physical disabilities, or economics—external and environmental influences represent a most powerful factor in discriminating between the advantaged and the disadvantaged. However, as these external and environmental factors appear to have more perversely affected Blacks, Puerto Ricans, American Indians, and Mexican Americans, the evidence suggests that the use of the term *disadvantaged* more frequently refers to these populations.

Appropriate Designation

Should the gifted among this group be called culturally "disadvantaged," "different," "deprived," or "diverse"? Several writers (Baldwin, 1978; Passow, 1972; Renzulli, 1971; Sato, 1974) have supported the notion by Frost and Hawkes (1971) that the real war should not be an attack on the jargon but rather a systematic effort that is focused on the alleviation of the problems that are denying large segments of disadvantaged populations the right to be recognized for their potential to achieve.

Despite the valiant efforts of researchers such as Torrance (1974) to demonstrate that differences are not necessarily deficits, Good and Brophy (1977) observed, for example, that "a remarkable number of otherwise well-informed people believe that most of the disadvantaged are blacks and that most blacks are disadvantaged or both" (p. 197).

Differences should be celebrated for their contribution to diversity, the very trait that has brought gifted children to our attention. The challenge in educating disadvantaged gifted youth should be to develop potential, not to wish conformity to one model of giftedness with all else being deficient.

Identification

Identification of disadvantaged gifted individuals is the area that has received the most attention. Some of the more important research in this area has been that conducted by Taylor and Ellison (1966/1968), Grant and Renzulli (1971), Torrance (1971), Bruch (1971), Stallings (1972), Meeker and Meeker (1973), Bernal and Reyna (1974), Mercer (1978), and Gay (1978).

The Alpha Biographical Inventory developed by Taylor and his associates (1966/1968) is a 300 item life experience inventory that has proven to be useful in identifying gifted individuals among the disadvantaged population. Significant among the findings from research studies involving this inventory are indications that there are no racial differences on the creativity index and quite small racial differences on the academic index.

Grant and Renzulli (1971) developed the Sub-Cultural Indices of Academic Potential (SCIAP), now called Relevant Aspects of Potential (RAP) (Grant, 1974). On this inventory students indicate how they feel about themselves and how they would react in situations that are common to their everyday experiences. The instrument yields a profile indicative of high potential among minority group students.

The analysis of results from 20 independent studies of the effects of race and socioeconomic status on performance on the Torrance Tests of Creative Thinking indicated that there was either no difference or difference in favor of the culturally different groups (Torrance, 1971). Disadvantaged groups tended especially to excel on figural tests.

The Abbreviated Binet for Disadvantaged (ABDA) devised by Bruch (1971) yields a score derived from selected items in the Stanford-Binet that are biased toward disadvantaged Black children. Culture specific indications of giftedness among native, Spanish speaking Mexican Americans have been the subject of research conducted by Bernal and Reyna (1975). Gay (1978) is doing similar research with Black children.

Stallings (1972) has developed an instrument that can be used to discover giftedness among urban children whose experiences are limited by an 8 to 10 block radius in their community. Called the Stallings' Environmentally Based Screen (SEBS), the goal is to identify gifted children based on their ability to respond to environmental matters.

Two especially promising procedures have been pursued by Meeker and Meeker (1973) and Mercer and Lewis (1978). In their efforts to find a more appropriate way of interpreting the Stanford-Binet results of disadvantaged Black, Chicano, and Anglo boys, Meeker and Meeker (1973) developed a Test of Learning Abilities that would yield specific patterns of strengths and weaknesses based on Structure of Intellect (SOI) analyses.

Mercer and Lewis (1978) were concerned with the development of a procedure to identify disadvantaged gifted children that allows their performance to be compared with their own sociocultural group. The System of Multicultural Pluralistic Assessment (SOMPA) is based on the notion that one's own sociocultural group is a more appropriate yardstick for determining whether performance is below normal, normal, or supranormal.

Creating an Effective Learning Environment

A problem that still remains is one that relates to the attitudes and values held by teachers of these children.

1. PLANNING

Frasier (1977) suggested that administrators and teachers can work together to destroy this negative association by demonstrating a commitment to:

1. *Accept* the fact that all children from disadvantaged backgrounds are not deficient in their ability to achieve academically; that some *can* be found who deviate upward from the behavior of the nongifted within their groups.
2. *Recognize* observable indications of potential giftedness among this population. Findings from a study by Glaser and Ross (1970) will help with this problem, for they identified several qualities that distinguish gifted disadvantaged children and youth from their nongifted peers.
3. *Search* for gifted children from among disadvantaged populations with a specified goal (e.g., the location of 3% to 5% of a disadvantaged population as gifted).
4. *Plan* educational experiences that allow gifted disadvantaged children to develop skills not provided by their environment such as test taking and study habits.
5. *Develop* appropriate guidance and other ancillary services to help these pupils with affective matters such as peer, family, and [self] attitudes toward them as "being different" and the recognition of options (Passow, 1972, p. 30).

Appropriate Educational Programing

Many factors unique to disadvantaged gifted children should be considered when planning appropriate educational experiences for them. Several writers (Baldwin, 1978; Blanning, 1978; Passow, 1972; Renzulli, 1971; Sato, 1974; Stallings, 1972; Torrance, 1977; Witt, 1971; Wrightstone, 1960) have addressed themselves to the general issue of building on strengths rather than weaknesses.

A combined counseling and instructional approach seems to work best to upgrade academic skills and help develop the personal skills of self direction and control. Such an approach should have among its objectives the development of (a) communication skills of reading, writing, listening, and questioning; (b) skills that enhance the ability to distinguish between relevant and irrelevant information; (c) questing skills for seeking assistance not readily available in the home, the community, and the school; and (d) familiarity with information sources that could provide options not readily apparent or considered.

Two strategies that are especially appropriate in this respect are Decision Making Skills for Life Planning (DLP) (Frasier, 1974) and Future Problem Solving Bowl (Torrance, 1976).

The rational behind the DLP is embedded in Bloom's Taxonomy. However, it begins by combining "knowledge of self" activities with analysis and evaluation activities. The premise is that disadvantaged gifted youth, especially, must be assisted in recognizing and understanding what they know about themselves and their abilities and how this information affects decisions that they make about their future. Through a series of structured steps they are led to the establishment of their own directions. The teacher serves as a supportive facilitator. DLP is based on the fact that at critical junctures during their formative years, the individual learns how to ask: Who am I? Where am I going? How will I get there? How will I evaluate my progress toward a goal? This is the individual who is developing the skills necessary to take charge of his or her own future. This type of approach is critical to helping disadvantaged students examine the options available to them. It also helps them plan how to take advantage of those options without sacrificing either self or culture.

The procedure is as follows:

1. Using the song "I've Gotta Be Me" and the poem *A Dream Deferred* by Langston Hughes, students are led in a discussion of the possible fates of dreams.
2. The next step involves an analysis of the students' present ability to make decisions. They examine their powers within the setting of their home, their school, and their community.
3. Then, using exercises from Simon, Howe, and Kirschenbaum (1972), they are assisted in understanding their personal wishes, beliefs, and values. In addition, they are assisted in describing the kind of person they are and then the kind of person they would like to become.
4. Assistance is given in helping each student develop a goal that might be attained in a short period of time.
5. The plan is put into action after they have developed all of the resources—people and things they need to accomplish their goal.
6. Periodic followup is made to see how well the students are doing in meeting the contract they have set with themselves.
7. Evaluation during a followup session is conducted for the purpose of analyzing the behaviors that caused the goal to be met or determining why the goal was not met.

Through this procedure systematic skills are developed that aid these students in making relevant decisions about and for themselves.

Futuring is the science, art, and maybe even game of trying to learn about the future in order to best cope with and live in it (Agel, 1974). Developing appropriate skills for anticipating and coping with the future is a critical need of disadvantaged gifted children, for often they can quickly be consumed by attitudes of apathy or indifference when the future appears hopeless. Future Problem Solving, an approach developed by Torrance (1976), is a technique that is recommended to teach disadvantaged students the skills they need to anticipate and solve problems of the future.

Future problem solving would allow gifted disadvantaged children to practice the much needed skills for imagining, exploring, and rehearsing both imaginable and unimaginable events related to the problems they may face in realizing goals.

A Final Word

These final points are offered as information that should be followed or considered when developing curricula for the disadvantaged gifted child:

1. The fact that a family is economically disabled does not necessarily mean that love and affection do not prevail in the home. The poor, ragged child may be rich in love and affection, which are significant determinants of school success.
2. Bereiter and Engelmann (1966) pointed out that low income children do not necessarily suffer from sensory deprivation or a lack of stimulation. They are surrounded by sensory stimulation. What they may lack are experiences that have definite educational value and that lay the groundwork for future academic growth.
3. Ginsburg (1972) reminded us that in many fundamental ways poor children's cognition is quite similar to that of middle class children. He maintained that there are cog-

nitive universals or modes of language and thought shared by all children. There may exist social class differences in cognition, yet these differences are rather superficial. One must not make the mistake of calling them deficiencies.
4. According to Labov, Cohen, Robins, and Lewis (cited in Ginsburg, 1972), language is merely one element of a cultural orientation that clashes with the school's values, and it is this conflict, not a deficit in language, which largely accounts for poor performance in school.
5. Finally, Ausubel (1964) succinctly pointed out that "frequently the best way of motivating an unmotivated pupil is to ignore his motivational state for the time being and to concentrate on teaching him as effectively as possible. Much to his surprise and to his teacher's, he will learn despite his lack of motivation; and from the satisfaction of learning he will characteristically develop the motivation to learn more" (p. 17).

Only in recent years have the gifted and talented among disadvantaged populations received the deliberate attention of educators. The problem has been one of identification, and then of appropriate education. Previous remediation approaches exemplify the first part of the old Chinese proverb (cited in Tripp, 1970), "Give a man a fish, and you feed him for a day." Future problem solving and decision making skills exemplify the option expressed in the last line of this proverb, "Teach a man to fish, and you feed him for a life time." Use of these types of approaches would allow disadvantaged gifted children and youth the opportunity to develop commensurate with their above average potential.

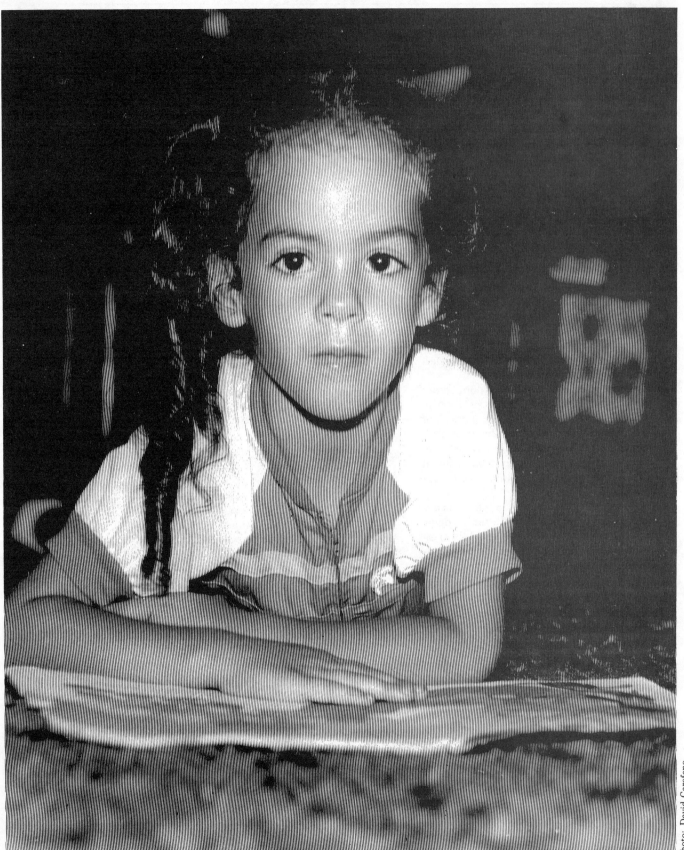

SCREENING AND IDENTIFICATION FOR GIFTED PROGRAM MEMBERSHIP

A plan can facilitate broader understanding of a program; it can provide the basis for a most useful division of labor in which help from many sources if focused on the gifted program. A plan is almost indispensable in devising data-gathering techniques for identifying and selecting students for the program, and for organizing a program evaluation.

Section I offers many suggestions for the development of a gifted program. It is postulated that early identification will make suitable educational planning possible. "A Multi-Level Approach to the Identification of Kindergarten Gifted Pupils," by C.W. Humes, Jr. and D.G. Eberhart concludes that it is possible to identify children in a systematic, sequential manner, using a number of assessment techniques (with certain recognizable limitations). Several other methods of assessment are discussed, including Dr. Renzuli's ideas for "Non-test Measures of Student Growth and Performance."

In the event of setting up a curriculum for gifted students, it should be remembered that there are other considerations besides development of talents. In "Rethinking the Issues Regarding the Culturally Disadvantaged Gifted" we are reminded to take into account the needs of all students. Finally, a gifted program in California showed benefits not only for participants, but for other students as well. A gifted and talented program need not cater to a few, but can, if carefully planned and carried out effectively, be beneficial for the whole school.

IDENTIFICATION AND PROGRAM PLANNING: MODELS AND METHODS

Lynn H. Fox

ABSTRACT

There are two major aspects of program planning for the gifted—identification and the development of alternative educational strategies. In order to best match learner characteristics to specific educational strategies, it is important to assess patterns and levels of abilities and interests. A generalized model for selecting students for specific types of programs, such as special mathematics classes, is described. SMPY has experimented with a number of methods of acceleration for mathematically gifted junior-high-school-age youth, such as fast-paced school-systemwide classes and college courses. Models for alternative matriculation strategies for students who are mathematically gifted are presented. The reader is encouraged to consider how these models might be modified and expanded to meet the needs of students who are talented in other academic areas.

Educators are becoming increasingly aware of the fact that the American public school system has not effectively met the needs of all the nation's children. Over the past decade there have been numerous attempts to correct this situation. Most of these efforts, however, have been concerned only with the children labeled "mentally handicapped" or "educationally disadvantaged" (e.g., Stanley 1972, 1973). What has been overlooked too often is that our nation's brightest youngsters may also be "educationally disadvantaged," because schools fail to recognize their ability and to provide them with appropriate educational experiences. For a number of years there have been excellent programs, such as the Westinghouse Talent Search and the National Merit Scholarship Program, which have identified academically talented students throughout the country and encouraged them to pursue a college education. Unfortunately, these projects do not identify gifted students until after they have completed most of their public school education. If schools are to become more responsive to the needs of their ablest students, then large-scale efforts are needed to identify gifted students at the earliest grades and provide special educational opportunities for them.

The Study of Mathematically Precocious Youth (SMPY) has worked since September 1971 on problems of identifying intellectually gifted youth and developing various strategies to meet their educational needs. The purpose of this chapter is to discuss some methods of identifying gifted students and monitoring their progress through the junior and senior high school years. The first section explains the rationale for focusing on the large-scale identification of gifted students during the early adolescent years. The second section discusses some general considerations in the selection of appropriate tests. In the third section a specific model which school systems or states could employ to identify talented seventh- and eighth-graders is presented. The ultimate success of an educational program for the gifted is dependent upon comprehensive planning that takes individual differences into account and carefully evaluates and monitors an individual's or group's progress. Thus the fourth section describes ways in which long-range planning, including further testing and counseling of students, can be used to ensure the success of programs for the gifted.

The term *program* is used loosely in the ensuing discussions of educational strategies for the intellectually talented child. A *program for the gifted* in this chapter refers to a global approach to education that would encompass a variety of specific strategies. This would include the possibility of subject-matter acceleration, general grade-skipping, special classes, college credit by examination (e.g., the Advanced Placement Program), and college courses used alone or in combination for a particular student. Some examples of the types of strategies used by students identified by SMPY are discussed in the last section of this chapter. For a more detailed account of these various strategies for educational matriculation of the gifted in mathematics, the reader is referred to chapters 6 and 7 of this volume and Fox (1974*a,b* [I:3, 6]).[1]

IDENTIFICATION FOR PROGRAM PLANNING: WHY FOCUS ON THE EARLY ADOLESCENT YEARS?

The need for special efforts to identify talented students and design innovative educational programs for them is particularly acute during the junior high school years, for it is during those years that most schools are the least flexible in terms of individualized scheduling and self-paced instructional programs. It has been noted elsewhere (Fox 1974*a* [I:3]) that subject-matter acceleration is an excellent educational procedure for the gifted. Yet this appears to be the most difficult thing to provide during the junior high school years.

In elementary school very bright children are often allowed to move ahead at their own pace in reading and arithmetic. Recent interest in the creation of open classrooms, team teaching, and small individualized learning centers in the elementary schools are potentially conducive to the fostering of individualized educational goals and programs. In these types of classroom environments, presumably a school could accommodate the educational needs of bright students independent of the number of such students in a given school or age group. Even the more traditional elementary school classroom can often allow for a wide range of individual differences in rates and levels of achievement. Thus, whether or not gifted children receive special attention during the elementary school years in a given school or school system has typically been more a function of the attitudes and philosophy of the teachers and school administrators than of the structure of the elementary school itself.

In most modern senior high schools, individualized scheduling of classes is possible. Usually in large schools there are a number of fairly advanced courses in each subject area from which to choose. Thus, theoretically at least, exceptionally able students can arrange individualized schedules that allow for subject area acceleration and perhaps let them complete high school a year early. In a few school systems it is now possible for students to arrange their high school schedule to include college courses taken for credit at a nearby college during the day, in the evening, during the summer, or by correspondence. (This has been done in a number of individual cases throughout the country. Maryland, for example, is one state that appears to encourage this actively at the present time.) Although few senior high schools are so individualized as to offer opportunities for students to complete a standard course in less than one year's time, there is still greater flexibility possible within the structure of such schools than is usually realized. If high schools are seriously interested in working with academically talented students there are usually many types of special arrangements that they can provide, such as subject-matter acceleration and credit by examination for independent study.

---

[1]In addition to the usual references, citations of chapters in volume I of *Studies of Intellectual Precocity* will be as follows [I:3,6]. The I indicates volume I, and the 3 and 6 are chapter numbers [Editor].

Junior high schools rarely provide the individualized scheduling approach of the high schools with a wide variety of options within subject areas, nor do they typically provide self-pacing programs within the courses they do offer. It is a rare junior high school that can provide adequate subject-matter acceleration for gifted students.

Thus it is at the end of the elementary school years that there is a real need to identify talented students and make special efforts to provide a bridging mechanism for them to span the years from elementary school to senior high school and college. In the area of mathematical talent this is a particularly crucial period. Mathematical reasoning ability is well developed in the upper few percent of youngsters by the end of the fifth or sixth grades. In terms of development of logical thought and reasoning ability, it appears that bright fifth-graders are more apt to be ready for the study of abstract mathematics and physical science materials than are average seventh-graders (see chapter 5 for a detailed discussion of this finding). Acceleration of mathematical achievement for the mathematically gifted is probably best accomplished by having them begin the study of algebra in the sixth or seventh grades.

The fact that many seventh- and eighth-graders are ready for the fast-paced study of mathematics has been well documented by SMPY. Details of the first talent search conducted by SMPY in the spring of 1972 are presented elsewhere (Keating 1974 [I:2]). In 1973 and 1974, SMPY held similar contests for junior high school students in the state of Maryland.

In 1973, 953 students who had scored at or above the 98th percentile on either the numerical or verbal subtests of the Iowa Tests of Basic Skills or another standardized in-grade test were tested on both parts (mathematical and verbal) of the College Entrance Examination Board's Scholastic Aptitude Test, with the cooperation of the Study of Verbally Gifted Youth.[2] The means and standard deviation on SAT-M and SAT-V by grade[3] and sex are presented in tables 3.1 and 3.2. The mean score (551) on SAT-M for the eighth-grade boys who were tested in January[4] was considerably higher than the mean for male high school seniors (510) who plan to attend college. Most, if not all, of the high school seniors had had considerably more mathematics instruction in school than the eighth-graders, who were typically enrolled in algebra I. Two boys, one seventh-grader and one ninth-grader, scored 800 on the SAT-M.

The results of the contest held in January 1974 further confirm the finding that a great number of boys and girls of junior high school age are extremely talented in mathematical reasoning, to the extent that they should receive more challenging experiences than are generally provided in their regular mathematics courses. Of the 1,519 students tested in 1974, 111 scored at or above 640 on SAT-M, which is at the 94th percentile of a random group of eleventh- and twelfth-graders. The means and standard deviations on SAT-M for the 1974 contestants by grade and sex are shown in table 3.3. Clearly there is enough evidence from these three years of testing to warrant some special program planning for mathematically talented students.

Details of the types of accelerated classes that have been initiated and studied by SMPY are reported by Fox (1974b [I:6]) and by George and Denham in chapter 6 of this volume. Recent efforts to replicate this type of program in a public school in Baltimore City are described in chapter 7 of this volume. A number of school systems hope to experiment with their own adaptation of this type of approach to mathematics education for the very able student.

[2]The Study of Verbally Gifted Youth (SVGY) was begun in September 1972 at The Johns Hopkins University, under the direction of Dr. Robert T. Hogan, Dr. Catherine J. Garvey, and Dr. Roger A. Webb. Chapter 8 of this volume summarizes the work of this study during its first year.

[3]A few of the contestants in the talent searches were ninth-graders who had not reached their fourteenth birthday before the contest. Since the number of ninth-graders is small, their scores are combined with those of the eighth-graders.

[4]In 1973 two talent searches were sponsored jointly by SMPY and SVGY. Students primarily interested in mathematics were asked to take the test in January. Students who were primarily interested in the verbal areas were asked to take the test in February.

Table 3.1. Means and standard deviations on the mathematics test (SAT-M) for contestants in 1973, by grade and sex

	January group (math)			February group (verbal)			Combined groups		
	Number	Mean	Std. dev.	Number	Mean	Std. dev.	Number	Mean	Std. dev.
7th-grade girls	88	440.23	66.33	67	396.42	79.56	155	421.29	75.32
7th-grade boys	135	495.41	85.18	52	434.23	90.37	187	478.40	90.68
8th- and 9th-grade girls	158	510.82	62.60	103	445.63	78.11	261	485.10	76.02
8th- and 9th-grade boys	285	551.09	85.24	65	489.85	90.65	350	539.71	89.38
All girls	246	485.57	72.27	170	426.24	82.07	416	461.32	81.73
All boys	420	533.19	89.01	117	465.13	94.31	537	518.36	94.39
All 7th grade	223	473.63	82.67	119	412.94	86.16	342	452.51	88.64
All 8th and 9th grades	443	536.73	80.21	168	462.74	85.69	611	516.38	88.12
TOTAL	666	515.60	82.29	287	442.09	89.19	953	493.46	93.43

Table 3.2. Means and standard deviations on the verbal test (SAT-V) for contestants in 1973, by grade and sex

	January group (math)			February group (verbal)			Combined groups		
	Number	Mean	Std. dev.	Number	Mean	Std. dev.	Number	Mean	Std. dev.
7th-grade girls	88	373.86	73.63	67	392.99	86.34	155	382.13	79.67
7th-grade boys	135	384.74	71.39	52	410.19	76.94	187	391.82	73.66
8th-grade girls	158	441.96	82.90	103	475.73	90.32	261	455.29	87.31
8th-grade boys	285	431.02	89.94	65	476.15	90.15	350	439.40	91.55
All girls	246	417.60	86.02	170	443.12	97.36	416	428.03	91.58
All boys	420	416.14	87.07	117	446.84	90.39	537	422.83	88.63
All 7th grade	223	380.45	72.32	119	400.50	82.47	342	387.43	76.48
All 8th grade	443	434.92	87.56	168	475.89	89.98	611	446.19	90.04
TOTAL	666	416.68	86.62	287	444.63	94.44	953	425.01	89.92

Table 3.3. Means and standard deviations on the mathematics test (SAT-M) for contestants in 1974, by grade and sex

	Number	Mean	Standard deviation
7th-grade girls	222	439.51	67.60
7th-grade boys	372	473.12	84.93
8th-grade girls	355	499.72	70.93
8th-grade boys	533	535.18	80.10
9th- and 10th-grade girls	14	575.00	58.54
9th- and 10th-grade boys	23	648.26	65.83
All girls	591	478.88	76.62
All boys	928	513.10	89.70
All 7th grade	594	460.56	80.51
All 8th grade	888	521.00	78.47
All 9th and 10th grades	37	620.54	77.99
TOTAL	1,519	499.79	86.45

There are two crucial aspects of developing a program to guide gifted students through the secondary school years and into college (usually for such students, college entrance should be one or more years accelerated). The first is the early identification of talented students who need the types of special opportunities mentioned above. The second is the careful monitoring and evaluation of the students' progress through these critical years.

IDENTIFICATION: SELECTING THE METHODS

There are numerous considerations in selecting tests to identify intellectually gifted students. Of prime concern is how well the test will predict success in the type of program that is planned. In other words, is the test a valid measure for the purpose of identifying students who would most benefit from subject-matter acceleration, general acceleration, or special fast-paced classes? Closely related to this issue is the question of what aspects of ability and personality are related to high-level achievement in various situations. Of lesser, but substantial, concern are questions concerning the ease of administration, cost, and availability of the tests to be used.

General Intelligence Tests Versus Tests of Special Ability

In the 1920s the first monumental study of intellectually talented students by Lewis Terman (1925) used measures of global intelligence, such as the Stanford-Binet, to identify students who were extremely bright (IQ scores of 140 or above). The results of this first attempt to systematically study the characteristics of intelligent children and follow their development through adulthood were a major breakthrough toward our understanding of individual differences and intellectual ability (see Stanley 1974 [I:1]). The aim of the Terman study, however, was systematic study of the children rather than educational intervention. Subsequent research by SMPY has shown that program planning and educational facilitation of the gifted require a more comprehensive view of the cognitive abilities of a student, as well as some information about his or her interests (Stanley, Keating, & Fox 1974).

In the half-century since Terman's major longitudinal study of gifted children began, many educators have discussed the problem of operational definitions of intellectual giftedness and their implications for instituting identification procedures in the schools (e.g., Gowan 1971, Pegnato & Birch 1959; Witty 1967). Many have suggested solutions that involve the use of teacher nominations and measures of creativity to supplement intelligence test results (Gowan 1971; Torrance 1968). Few, however, have emphasized the importance of multiple ability testing.

Programs that seek to individualize instruction for gifted students will be better served by tests that provide information about a student's pattern of abilities, current level of achievement, and interests, rather than a merely global estimate of general intelligence. Neither individual nor group tests provide this type of information. Knowing that a student has an IQ of 160 is not adequate information for deciding whether or not the student is ready for a college course in science or mathematics. While it provides an estimate of higher learning potential, it tells little about actual level of achievement in a given subject area or about the relationship between the student's verbal and quantitative skills, nor does it indicate the student's special interests.

Assessing Patterns and Levels of Abilities

In order to assess most effectively a student's educational potential one should employ a variety of measures. Test batteries that show the relative strengths and weaknesses of a student on measures of both aptitude and achievement provide valuable information concerning appropriate educational placement. For example, a student who is unusually good at abstract reasoning problems and scores high on mathematical aptitude and knowledge, but relatively low on verbal measures, may have to proceed at a somewhat slower pace in mathematics than a student who scores extremely high on verbal as well as quantitative measures. Moderate acceleration in mathematics would seem more appropriate for the former, whereas skipping one or more entire grades might be feasible for the latter. No existing test battery will provide all the information useful in counseling gifted students. Thus, the ideal program for identifying gifted students will employ a variety of different tests at different levels.

When one tests very bright students it is particularly crucial to use tests that have enough ceiling to differentiate among them. Thus, in addition to patterns of abilities, one should be careful to assess accurately levels of abilities for bright students. Two students who in the seventh grade score at the 99th percentile on a number-ability subtest of a standardized in-grade test may still be very different in terms of mathematical aptitude and knowledge. One of these students may be so advanced in his ability and knowledge of mathematics that he is ready to study college calculus, whereas the other student may be very able but still lack the basic skills of plane and analytic geometry and algebra II. A single test, particularly a grade-level one, will fail to provide this type of information.

Thus, it is crucial to use tests of a higher level before making decisions as to educational placement. For the ablest adolescents precollege- and college-level tests would be more appropriate than in-grade tests for evaluating knowledge and aptitude. This point is elaborated upon in chapter 2.

Thus, the whole picture of the cognitive strengths and weaknesses of the student should be carefully assessed by using batteries of difficult tests. One might first begin by screening students on in-grade achievement tests, such as the Iowa Tests of Basic Skills. Students who score above the 95th percentile on mathematics or verbal subtests and 95th percentile overall on in-grade norms could be further tested on special tests of ability at a higher level, such as the Scholastic Aptitude Test (SAT), Preliminary Scholastic Aptitude Test (PSAT), Differential Aptitude Test (DAT), or School and College Ability Test (SCAT). These tests should then be followed by other tests of special abilities, such as Raven's Progressive Matrices, Bennett's Mechanical Comprehension Test, Sequential Tests of Educational Progress (STEP) Science, and College Entrance Examination Board (CEEB) achievement tests.

In addition to "ceiling," the "jingle-jangle" problems of tests need to be considered. The actual function of a test may be somewhat different from that which its name implies, and this should be carefully studied. To assess a student's degree of readiness to begin the study of algebra and other more abstract mathematical courses, one should not use a test that relies too heavily upon mathematical computation skills. One should be sure that a test purporting to assess mathematical aptitude and mathematical reasoning ability does not assess mainly computational skills. Readiness to study advanced courses may be somewhat independent of knowledge of specific skills. Some very bright students may be ready to study algebra before they have mastered all the rules of arithmetic operations. Indeed, very gifted students may grasp and enjoy the study of fractions, decimals, and percents more in the context of algebra operations and notation than in arithmetic classes. Similar distinctions should be made when analyzing the results of tests of verbal ability. One should determine whether or not they are measures of general vocabulary, reading level, or verbal reasoning.

Achievement Tests

Achievement tests, particularly those of a specific subject content and of a high level, are extremely important indicators for subject-matter placement. It is somewhat ludicrous to place an eighth-grader in algebra I, when in fact he has already mastered the principles of algebra I and algebra II. Yet this does occur and will continue to occur until more sophisticated testing is employed and the results used to make adequate adjustments in the student's educational program.

One seventh-grader scored 760 on SAT-M in a contest sponsored by SMPY in 1974. His school had not intended to place him in algebra I the next year. After learning of the results of the contest, they decided to test him on algebra I. He made a perfect score. Upon further testing by SMPY on CEEB achievement tests, he scored 800 (the highest score) on CEEB Mathematics Achievement II—a test that most high school seniors find difficult. The final outcome for this student was that he was allowed to take geometry the next year. (He studied algebra II and trigonometry during the summer.) Without the intervention of SMPY that student would have been placed in a mathematics course at least three years behind his ability and achievement level. This type of educational injustice to the gifted can and should be avoided.

Achievement tests sometimes serve another important function—that of indicators of interests. A student with high-level abilities in several fields may develop higher levels of achievement (perhaps by independent study) in one field, such as mathematics or science, than in others, such as languages. This selective acquisition of knowledge in a specific field is a strong indication of interest. For example, two students with very similar scores on SAT-M and SAT-V as eighth-graders may score quite differently on a test of general science knowledge, such as the college-level STEP science test or a test such as CEEB physics. The student who scores very high on such a test is probably more interested in science and mathematics than the student of similar aptitude who has a lower achievement score. Information about interests and career aspirations of students is quite useful in planning educational experiences for them.

Interests, Motivation, and Achievement

While achievement can be an indicator of interest, it is also true that more direct measures of interests and values can be useful predictors of future achievement. Students with similar patterns of cognitive abilities may indeed perform quite differently in different situations and, especially, in different subject-matter areas in school. Knowing a student's interests, as well as his or her level of ability, can make the educational planning process more efficient.

If a testing program or screening procedure to identify talent does not involve the type of self-selection and screening that operated in the SMPY talent searches, it might be wise to include some assessment of interests and values in conjunction with the cognitive testing.

Very bright students with strong quantitative abilities but little scientific or investigative interest may not find the atmosphere of a fast-paced mathematics program to their liking. Programs that ignore the affective components of achievement in their selection procedures are apt to find many students failing to perform well in the classes or be required to slow the pace of the class considerably in order to accommodate those who are not motivated to excel and not stimulated by the challenge of the pace and content. Students who lack the motivation should not be forced by well-intentioned parents and teachers to develop all their abilities at an equally fast pace and high level.

There is, of course, one caution. Students at ages eleven to fifteen, regardless of their intellectual abilities, may have somewhat poorly defined patterns of interests. Interests, particularly career interests, probably can fluctuate greatly during the period of adolescent development. A girl who, because of peer group pressures at age thirteen, may not aspire to an academic career, such as mathematician, could conceivably become more interested in this profession as a result of later experiences.

Thus, one should not require that a student have strong theoretical and investigative leanings in order to participate in a special program in mathematics or science. Information concerning values and interests should not be part of the selection criteria per se, but can be used for purposes of counseling and in the process of careful monitoring of program success. For example, students who are high on aesthetic and social values but low on scientific and investigative interests would probably be less successful working with self-paced geometry texts than in studying mathematics in a small informal class. On the other hand, a girl who is very social might be miserable if she were the only girl in a class of twenty theoretically oriented students. Boys and girls who score high on social values and interests and low on theoretical values and investigative interests are more likely to prefer modified programs of acceleration within subject matter in special classes to an overall grade acceleration, because they are less inclined to want to leave their social peer group. A more detailed discussion of the problems of social interests with respect to mathematics acceleration and fast-paced classes, for girls in particular, is presented in chapter 9.

Schools and school systems are likely to be limited by a number of factors in the number of options they can offer a given student in order to meet his unique needs. The size of the community, the amount of talent that exists in any school and age-grade level, the availability of teachers able to work effectively with very bright students, the geographic proximity of the junior and senior high school facilities, and the existence of a nearby university or community college will all determine the number and types of methods of facilitation that can be reasonably employed. What is suggested here is that the decision-making process for a given student may be simplified if one takes into account indicators of the student's personality, as well as his or her patterns of cognitive abilities.

Test Administration

In any testing program there are important considerations with regard to administering the test itself. Three points are particularly important when testing for the purpose of selecting students for a special program. First, tests of a restricted nature should be used, so that teachers and students do not have access to information about the content of the test in advance. If a test is to be used several different years in a row, it is probably wise to purchase alternate forms of the test, so that the test is somewhat different in specific content in successive years. This prevents leakage of information from one year to the next and avoids the accompanying problems if one needs to test the same students in both years.

Second, the testing should be done under controlled, standardized conditions. This includes testing all the students who are eligible at the same time of year, in similar of not identical testing facilities, with careful attention to exact instructions (especially with respect to cautions about guessing) and precise time limits. On the test for the final screening it would be desirable to test all eligible students at the same time and place.

Third, some tests, such as the SAT, provide practice booklets to be studied in advance. For seventh- and eighth-graders it would be particularly good to have them work with the practice booklets to gain insight into the nature of the test and specific item formats. This probably reduces some unnecessary test anxiety. If practice materials are available, *every* eligible student should be provided with them well in advance of the test and urged to study them carefully. It would even seem desirable to set up special coaching classes based on the practice booklets.

Untimed tests, such as Raven's Progressive Matrices, the Allport-Vernon-Lindzey *Study of Values*, and vocational interest inventories, are more difficult to administer in a standardized way. Special efforts should be made to ensure that the procedures used and explanations of the test given to the students are comparable in every test administration. It is probably wise to emphasize the fact that on "self-report inventories," such as tests of interests, there are no right or wrong answers, as junior high school students are often unfamiliar with these types of tests.

DEVELOPING A MODEL FOR EARLY IDENTIFICATION OF THE GIFTED

Initial Screening

The first step in an identification program for the gifted in the junior high school years is to establish a master list or pool of all children in the school or school system who seem likely to be very gifted. Gowan (1971) terms this a "reservoir" of talent. There are two methods by which this can be done. The first is to scan carefully the latest test results from a standardized achievement test, such as the Iowa Tests of Basic Skills (ITBS). For economic and pragmatic reasons it is always good to take advantage of the existing test records. A master list of students' names and scores is usually available at the school system level. A single criterion or multiple criteria could be used to select students for further testing. One strategy would be to select all students who scored at the 95th percentile or above overall on national or local grade norms. In addition, one could add the names of students who scored below the 95th percentile overall, but who scored at the 98th percentile or above on either the total numerical or verbal subtest of the ITBS or other standardized test.

A second method, which could be used in conjunction with the first, if it is economically feasible, is teacher nomination. Gowan (1971) and others have suggested several types of nomination forms that could be used. This method is time consuming, expensive (if the school system is very large), and not as efficient as the first method. It should never be used as the only method of first screening. Terman (1925) and Pegnato and Birch (1959) found that most teachers are not good judges of intellectual giftedness. They are likely to identify average but dutiful old-in-grade students as gifted and to overlook the brightest child in the class. For political purposes, however, it may be wise to encourage teachers to make nominations. Children who are nominated by more than one teacher and by more than one criterion could then be added to the list of children to be tested further. To avoid testing too many children who are not likely candidates for special programs it might be wise to eliminate any students nominated by teachers who did not score at or above the 85th percentile overall on national norms of an in-grade test. Children who are only moderately above average may find the experience of taking difficult tests such as the SAT to involve considerable stress.

In identifying gifted children for special educational opportunities, it is probably best to err in the direction of over-selectivity. It is better to select children for special programs who have a high probability of success than to take children with marginal probabilities of success and expose them to a situation in which they are likely to fail. At present there are likely to be more children who are in desperate need of acceleration and special classes than can be handled with the limited resources now available. Thus, in the first attempts to break new ground in the area of educating the gifted, efforts should be concentrated where they are most needed. Enlarged programs to work with poorly motivated students and "underachievers" could be tried carefully later.

Assessing High-Level Potential—Second Screening

The second step of identification is to test the pool of the "potentially gifted" on difficult tests of aptitude and achievement in order to identify those who need immediate attention. There are several ways in which this stage can be handled. One is to have a large talent search conducted along the lines of a contest. Details of how this can be done are discussed by George and Solano in chapter 4.

A major advantage of a contest is that it allows for student self-selection. Students who are not eager to accelerate their educational progress can simply elect not to take the test. Self-selection among junior high school students is probably a desirable thing. SMPY has found that students who are not eager for special educational experiences will not typically benefit from them. Parents and schools should not try to force these opportunities.

There are numerous problems with the contest approach. First, it requires some time and effort for proper organization and can be fairly expensive. Unless the contest is given wide publicity, some eligible students will fail to learn about it. If the school system sponsors the contest in conjunction with an outside agency, such as a college, these problems could be minimal.

One method that would seem practical for schools and would avoid some of the problems inherent in a contest is utilization of existing precollege testing services. The Preliminary Scholastic Aptitude Tests (PSAT) administered, scored, and reported under the supervision of the Educational Testing Service (ETS) are given in high schools every fall on the last Saturday in October throughout the country. Although they are primarily taken by eleventh-graders, there is no reason why gifted seventh-, eighth-, and ninth-graders could not also be tested.

The Educational Testing Service has no special restrictions against these tests being given to younger students. School systems could easily use these available testing facilities for the purpose of identification of gifted junior high school students. The work involved for the school system would be minimal. Counselors at the junior high schools could notify eligible students (from the compiled pool) that they could take the test and then help them register for it. The cost to the students is about three dollars. If schools could afford it, they could pay the fees. Otherwise, students could pay the fee themselves, and perhaps groups, such as the PTA, could pay for any students who could not afford the fee. (The PSAT is suggested rather than SAT because it costs less and is given in the fall. The scores on the two tests are directly comparable.)

After the PSAT scores are reported to the schools, they could compile a list of students who had scored at various levels on the tests. For example, all students who scored at least 50 in the quantitative section and above 40 in the verbal section could be eligible for special accelerated classes in mathematics. This group could be tested further by the school system to decide what might be done for each individual.

Program Placement

At first glance the mechanics of placing a student in an appropriate special class appear complex. The strategy used is dependent upon the nature of the program offered and the number of students involved. Program placement can be greatly simplified by first specifying what educational experiences can be offered to a student and then selecting reasonable test score criteria to determine which alternatives can be offered to which students. The identification model as explained above and some suggested criteria and programs are shown in table 3.4.

Total Grade Skipping

If grade skipping is to be an alternative, then it is necessary to specify at what ability level students should be offered this opportunity. For example, seventh- and eighth-graders who score 50 or more on PSAT-V and PSAT-M might be offered the chance to skip a grade. Skipping should only be done by students who are eager to move ahead in all subjects. Some students may prefer subject-matter acceleration in mathematics and science rather than total grade acceleration.

Subject-matter Acceleration

Students who are very advanced in one subject area, such as mathematics, but who are not eager or able to skip an entire grade could be placed ahead by one or more years in just the one subject area. Thus, end-of-the-year sixth-graders who are known to be very talented in mathematics might be scheduled for regular algebra class when they are seventh-graders rather than waiting until the eighth or ninth grade to study algebra. A few very able students might even skip algebra I and begin with algebra II.

Subject-matter acceleration appears less desirable than homogeneously grouped classes for fast-paced instruction. The opportunity for interaction with peers of similar ability and interests is missing. Also, it is unlikely that the regular algebra class teachers will be able to teach such a class at as high a level

Table 3.4. A model for identification of seventh- and eighth-grade gifted boys and girls

---

Step one—First screening

    A. Selection of students on the basis of available standardized in-grade test scores (such as the Iowa Tests of Basic Skills).
        1. 95th percentile overall; or
        2. 98th percentile on a verbal or numerical subtest; or
        3. combination of both criteria.

    B. Teacher nominations—include students nominated by more than one teacher who do not score below the 85th percentile overall on the achievement test used for selection in A. (Suggestions for teacher-nomination procedures can be found in Gowan [1971].)

Step two—Second screening

    A. Testing of the students selected in *Step one* on a more difficult test such as PSAT, SAT, DAT, or SCAT.
        1. Contest method; or
        2. regular PSAT administration.

    B. Criterion scores such as 40 on PSAT-V and 50 on PSAT-M could be used to select students for consideration for program placement.

Step three—Program placement

    A. *Mathematics*: Students who scored above 50 on PSAT-M and were interested in mathematics and science could be placed in a fast-paced mathematics class. Further testing could be done to determine which students were ready to begin with algebra II or geometry, and which ones needed to start with algebra I.

    B. *Science*: Students who scored above 40 on PSAT-V and 50 on PSAT-M could be tested on general science knowledge. Those who scored at or above the 75th percentile on 10th-grade norms and had a strong interest in science could begin to take chemistry, physics, and biology and skip general science courses. Probably, most should take AP level courses in these subjects.

    C. *Social Studies, English, and Languages*: Students who scored 50 or more on PSAT-V who had strong interests in these areas could be placed in accelerated classes or given special advanced classes in creative writing, sociology, anthropology, political theory, foreign languages, and other subjects. This could be accomplished in a variety of ways. Two periods a week for twelve-week periods could be devoted to special topics in English or social studies or both. The courses could be conducted like college seminars. Students who score above 60 on PSAT-V could probably be skipped one or more grades if special courses were not offered in their junior high schools.

    D. *College courses*: Students who scored very high on the PSAT (at least 50 on PSAT-V and above 60 on PSAT-M) might be ready to take some college courses in conjunction with skipping a grade in order to enter high school early. Students who scored at least 640 on SAT-M in the 1974 Talent Search conducted by SMPY were offered the opportunity to take a variety of courses in mathematics and science. These students earned grades of A or B in college courses taken as seventh- or eighth-graders. Clearly this can be done. Whether or not it is a practical alternative depends upon the cooperation of nearby colleges. Some colleges are eager to work with gifted high school students and can assist the schools in planning for the individual course needs of students.

---

or as great speed as special class teachers who are selected on the basis of mathematical expertise. The former, however, may be the best solution when there are too few students to justify a special class—even a county-wide class.

SMPY has found that students who score at least 500 on SAT-M and 400 on SAT-V (this would be similar to 50 on PSAT-M and 40 on PSAT-V) can do well in a fast-paced mathematics class in which three or more years of mathematics are studied in one two-hour meeting a week for a year (see chapters 6 and 7 for details). Students of somewhat lower ability can do one and a half or two years of work in one. The pace of the class and the criteria used for selection will be a function of a number of factors. School-system-wide classes could be highly selective and move at a very fast pace. School-based programs would probably be less selective and slower (see chapter 7 for details).

The success of fast-paced classes depends upon a number of factors. First, the teacher must be very well trained in mathematics at a high level in order to be able to challenge and instruct the very gifted children. Second, good study habits are necessary for success in such a class. Teachers, counselors, or parents may need to work with individual students who have poor study skills. Third, students should never be pushed into attending a class. This type of class is intended for the highly motivated child who is eager to learn at a fast pace.

Advanced Placement Courses

Advanced placement (AP) courses are available in most large high schools for at least some course areas. Students who take such a course may then take a standardized examination. Students who score high on these tests can then earn college credits or be exempted from introductory college courses, or both, at colleges and schools that recognize and cooperate with the Advanced Placement Program. (Details of this program can be obtained from Educational Testing Service, Princeton, New Jersey.)

Unfortunately, high schools typically offer very few of these AP courses in a given year and may restrict participation to seniors. If school systems would conduct special county-wide AP courses and allow gifted ninth-, tenth-, and eleventh-graders to participate, it could be a highly effective program for the gifted. A brief report on such a course in calculus, sponsored by SMPY, is included in chapter 7 of this volume.

College Courses

If college courses taken in the summer or in an evening school class are to be offered as an option, more testing would be desirable to best determine what level course the student should take. SMPY has found that very few students who have not taken high school chemistry are ready for college chemistry, but those who are eager to try such a course could be tested on a CEEB chemistry test, or other standardized high school chemistry test, before making any decisions as to their readiness for a college course. SMPY has found that students who score 640 or more on SAT-M have been very successful in college computer science courses and college mathematics courses. The appropriate mathematics course for a given student depends upon his knowledge of mathematics, as determined by achievement tests in algebra I, II, trigonometry, plane and analytic geometry, and the level of the college courses offered. A very bright student who scores 700 on SAT-M may not be ready for college calculus if he has not mastered most of the precalculus material.

Interests and Maturity

If possible, students should be interviewed or tested on interests before offering them any of the alternatives. The more a counselor knows about the student's interests the better he can help the student select the appropriate program from the available alternatives. Students who have theoretical values and mathematical and scientific career-related interests may be more successful in fast-paced mathematics classes and college courses than students who have other interests and values. Early college admission appears to have the most general appeal for all students.

Students who are immature or who have a history of emotional or social adjustment problems in school should be carefully interviewed. It is possible that their behavior problems are a result of their frustration from being continually bored in school, and that special classes will alleviate the problem. On the other hand, children who have serious emotional problems may be unable to respond to intellectual challenges in a positive way. The experience of acceleration or college courses could be more then they can handle. Great caution should be used in these cases. Fortunately, such cases appear infrequently among mathematically precocious students. SMPY has found that selection of students on difficult precollege level tests in a contest tends to attract students who appear to be unusually mature. Although they may be bored in school they appear to have learned to cope to some extent by studying on their own outside of school subjects that interest them. Students who score well above grade level on tests of mathematical reasoning have personality profiles on the California Psychological Inventory (CPI) which are more typical of older students than do their more average grade-age peers (Weiss, Haier, & Keating 1974 [I:7]; Haier & Denham, chapter 11 in this volume).

TOWARD A MODEL FOR LONG-RANGE EDUCATIONAL PLANNING AND COUNSELING

The initial identification of gifted students is actually the easiest step to plan and conduct. More difficult to implement is a process by which the student and the schools work out long-range educational plans and then monitor the student's progress at each stage of the program. Theoretically, there are almost an infinite number of possible variations by which one could progress from seventh grade to college. The task of the school is to maximize the possibilities for meeting the needs of individuals without becoming inundated with administrative problems. Fortunately, the number of possibilities can be somewhat organized into a manageable number of general strategies that can each be moderately flexible. The nature of the strategies will be dependent upon a number of factors, such as the following: the physical aspects of locations of students, junior high schools, senior high schools, and colleges; the number of students involved; the various talents of the students; the students' personalities; and the parents' and students' goals.

Although each school system will need to generate its own programs, some general guidelines can be provided. Some problems are apt to be almost universal and can be solved. A few general strategies and solutions that have been tried with success by SMPY relative to the mathematically talented student will be presented. Individuals can then decide how these can be translated to meet their own situational demands and extended to cover the area of verbal precocity.

Plan I: Seventh Grade to College in Five Years

This plan is ideal for seventh-grade students who scored at least 40 on PSAT-V and 42 on PSAT-M in the fall of the seventh grade and have strong interests in mathematics and science.

A. *Acceleration.* Students could accelerate their progress through high school by one year. This could be done by formal grade promotion during the course of the five years or by simply allowing the student to fulfill all graduation requirements by the end of the fifth year.

B. *Mathematics.* Fast-paced mathematics classes (as described in chapters 6, 7, and 9) could be organized from the second half of the seventh grade through the fifth year. An example of this would be as follows:

    Year 1: Begin algebra I in January
    Year 2: Algebra II and college algebra
    Year 3: Plane geometry
    Year 4: Trigonometry and analytic geometry
    Year 5: Calculus (advanced placement course)

C. *Science.* Advanced placement (AP) courses in biology, chemistry, and physics could be taken in years three, four, and five, respectively.

D. *Optional Opportunities.* During the fourth and fifth years some students might begin taking college courses in the summer, evenings, or on released time from school, in such subjects as computer science, psychology, astronomy, English composition, or foreign languages. A student's readiness for these experiences could be determined by retesting on the PSAT in the fall of year four.

Plan II: Seventh Grade to College in Four Years

This plan would be suitable for seventh-grade students who scored at least 40 on PSAT-V and at least 50 on PSAT-M in the fall of the seventh grade and had strong interests in mathematics and science.

A. *Acceleration.* Students could be allowed to complete six years of high school in four by taking fast-paced mathematics classes (as described in chapter 6) and beginning their program of senior high school level science, social studies, and English courses a year or more early. In a school system with a three-year middle-school or junior high school program this could be done by completing the three years in two and then moving to senior high school and completing those three years in two.

B. *Mathematics.* Fast-paced classes could be designed for those students in the following sequence:

    Year 1: Begin algebra I in second half of the year.
    Year 2: Algebra II, college algebra, and plane geometry
    Year 3: Trigonometry, analytic geometry
    Year 4: Calculus (advanced placement course)

C. *Science.* Students could take biology, chemistry, and physics in years two, three, and four, respectively. Advanced placement courses would be desirable.

D. *Optional Opportunities.* Students who were qualified based on scores on PSAT taken in years two, three, or four (e.g., 60 on PSAT-M and 50 on PSAT-V) could take college courses in computer science, and other subjects in summers, evenings, or on released time from school. Students who did not desire to enter college full time at the end of the fourth year could arrange a schedule in the fifth year, which combined high school and college courses.

Plan III: Radical Acceleration Alternative

This plan could be used for eighth-grade students who scored 64 or above on PSAT-M and 60 or above on PSAT-V, who showed signs of great interest in mathematics and science and a strong desire for acceleration.

A. *Acceleration.* Students could be placed in the tenth grade at a senior high school the following year in all subjects except mathematics.

B. *Mathematics.* Mathematics could be taken in college courses through all precalculus courses during summer and evenings before, during, and after the tenth grade. An advanced placement calculus course (BC level) could be taken in the eleventh grade.

C. *Science.* Science courses could be arranged to allow the student to take both chemistry and physics during the tenth grade and advanced biology in the eleventh grade.

D. *English.* A college course in English composition and one in literature could be taken in lieu of twelfth-grade English in the summer after the eleventh grade.

E. *Early College Entrance.* Acceptance to college and high school graduation after the eleventh grade with advanced standing in some subject areas such as mathematics and science. Some students could enter college at the end of the tenth grade, if they took calculus and one science course in college during the summer or evening.

Plan IV: Subject-matter Acceleration Only

This plan could be used for students who are very good in mathematics but not interested in or ready for more total grade-skipping or fast-paced classes. Students would need to be identified by the end of the sixth grade. Therefore, tests such as the SCAT or DAT would be better than the PSAT or SAT for identification.

A. *Acceleration.* Students would be accelerated only in mathematics.

B. *Mathematics.* Students could take the regular nonaccelerated school classes in mathematics, but begin one year ahead of the typical schedule. They might wish to take two regular mathematics classes in one year. An example of this would be as follows:

    1: Algebra I
    2: Algebra II
    3: Plane geometry
    4: Trigonometry and analytic geometry
    5: Calculus
    6: College algebra, computer science, and/or statistics.

MONITORING THE STUDENT'S PROGRESS

The student's progress through any of the suggested programs can and should be assessed by the periodic use of standardized tests and by success in these courses.

Special Classes

When the teacher of a fast-paced accelerated mathematics class feels the students have completed the study of a subject such as second-year algebra, an algebra II test such as that in the Cooperative Mathematics Series published by Educational Testing Service can be administered. (Similar tests are available for science courses.) Students who score at or above the 75th percentile on national norms on this test can then proceed with the next course. Students who do not reach that level of mastery could return to a slower paced algebra II class to finish the algebra II and not continue with the accelerated program. SMPY has found that students who have a high score on tests such as the SAT have little difficulty mastering the material for most courses in less than half a year, meeting two hours a week, unless they are poorly motivated, in which case they should not strive for acceleration.

Advanced Placement Courses

The Educational Testing Service offers examinations in a variety of courses in May of each year. Students who score three to five on a five-point scale are considered to have mastered the material at a high level. Colleges and universities have varied policies with respect to these examinations. Some give college credit and allow the student to waive the first basic course in that field and begin with a second-level course. Other colleges give college credits, but do not waive basic course requirements, and vice versa.

Readiness for College Full Time

Students who have participated in any of the program alternatives can be evaluated for readiness for full-time college entrance by the same processes of examination used for all college-bound high school seniors. They should take the SAT and CEEB achievement tests and the appropriate Advanced Placement Program examinations and apply for college admission in the regular way.

SUMMARY

It is important that gifted students be identified sometime between the beginning of the fifth grade and the end of the eighth grade in order that they and the schools can develop an appropriate course of study to aid each such student in the transition from junior and senior high school to college. The degree of acceleration involved will be a function of the ability and motivation of the student and the program options available.

Efforts to identify intellectually able students at the junior high school level will be most effective if they involve difficult tests which assess breadth of special abilities rather than merely global measures of intelligence. A suggested identification plan that would involve minimal cost to schools in time and money was outlined in table 3.4. This method takes advantage of existing achievement testing programs at the school level and precollege aptitude testing at the national level.

Formulas for inclusion in various types of programs were presented based on three years of research by SMPY. Some examples of the types of long-range-planning models that could be used by school systems were discussed. These included different degrees of acceleration and amount of use of outside support agencies, such as colleges and the Advanced Placement Program course guides.

The models for identification and long-range programs discussed in this chapter were based on strategies used by students identified as mathematically talented by SMPY. More research is needed to determine what types of programs would best meet the needs of gifted students who are not especially talented or interested in mathematics and science. It is possible that programs for the gifted in more verbal subject areas will involve less acceleration and special classes of a radically different type than those used in mathematics by SMPY.

Although planning will take time and effort, there is no reason to delay programs to identify and help academically talented youth. The methods and technology exist now. Early identification is possible. The time has come to provide suitable program options for intellectually talented junior and senior high school students.

Teacher Nomination
of
Intellectually Gifted Students

by

Don Nasca

Intellectually gifted students are defined as individuals scoring two or more standard deviations above the mean on an individually administered I.Q. test. The expense, however, of administering individual I.Q. tests to all students has been so prohibited that alternative methods of first narrowing the population to a manageable group of potentially gifted students have been sought. The process of identifying the potentially gifted has relied primarily on standardized group testing and teacher nomination. Limitations of both procedures are well documented with some evidence that training can increase the efficiency of teacher nomination.

Although there are frequent cautions that group administered achievement and I.Q. tests will miss up to 50% of truly gifted and talented students, this caution generally applied to the notion of giftedness prior to the designation of the six categories of giftedness now generally in use. It is true that creativity, leadership, and visual and performing artists were not adequately identified by standardized tests. When dealing with the one category of intellectually gifted however, the percentage of students missed by group administered standardized tests will be substantially lower. There does remain however, the possibility that group administered, paper and pencil tests will miss some intellectually gifted students, that is, students who would normally score 130+ on the WISC and 132+ on the Stanford Binet. Misidentified students may also include another group, the so-called "overachievers", individuals who are not gifted but score very well on standardized paper and pencil tests.

Truly gifted students may fail to demonstrate their ability on group administered tests for one of three reasons:

1. They may have a greater store of information than the population on which the test was normed and can often justify more than the one correct answer. They may become quite frustrated with multiple choice formats frequently found on group tests.

2. Intellectually gifted students are often more interested in processes and causes than with "fill in the blank" type questions and see little significance in low level cognitive questions so they treat these tests with indifference.

3. Intellectually gifted students may be bored with traditional knowledge - oriented courses of study and may fail to accumulate the standard set of knowledge sampled on popular group administered tests.

Truly gifted students may exhibit one (or more) of several observable behaviors that indicate intellectual giftedness. They may display an intense curiosity in some specific topic and develop a high level of familiarity with the topic. This topic may more often than not be unrelated to the curriculum and can remain undetected unless teachers are sensitive to the possibility. They frequently seek causes and explanations for facts, decisions and processes. In fact, they can be tenacious in asking about the why and how of things and may disrupt didactic presentations. Their questions are often insightful, clever, and go beyond superficiality. Their quest for *why and how phenomena* is often of little interest to less gifted agemates and may create a dilemma for the teacher trying to maintain interest of the entire group. They often have several alternatives to any process or technique suggested by the teacher. The more verbal and outgoing student will make these alternatives known. They can be bored with the factual and knowledge based courses of study frequently found in many schools and may reflect this boredom by being inattentive in didactic settings. They can master basic skills quickly and may reject opportunities to complete lengthy skill development assignments. This lack of interest in repetitive homework may be manifested in late and poorly done assignments. They can master schooling requirements easily and tend to develop sloppy work habits. These students may offer grandiose solutions that appear totally impractical. Their insight into the essence of a problem simply outdistances their awareness of the limitations of current technology. They may also propose elaborate projects that are often not carried to completion, and finally, the intellectually gifted student may try to hide his "difference" by withdrawing or acting normal.

The second group of misidentified students, overachievers, score well on group standardized tests primarily because they memorize much of the traditional knowledge - oriented courses of study and therefore have a large store of the knowledge sampled by these tests. When faced with higher level cognitive tasks, however, they simply can't handle them. There is probably no need to focus on these students initially. They will tend to find their way out of gifted programs that focus on higher level cognitive processes. The prevailing philosophy appears to be, " . . . include all students with potential and let each have an opportunity." Until some empirical support for excluding overachievers is develop-

Dr. Don Nasca is Director of the Bureau of Educational Field Services at State University College at Brockport, State University of New York. This is his first contribution to our pages.

NOMINATION FORM
POTENTIALLY GIFTED STUDENTS

INSTRUCTIONS: COMPLETE THIS FORM FOR EACH CHILD IN YOUR ROOM. CIRCLE "1" IF THE BEHAVIOR LISTED APPEARS FREQUENTLY, "2" IF OCCASIONALLY, "3" IF SELDOM, AND "4" IF NEVER. THE LOWER THE TOTAL SCORE, THE MORE LIKELY YOU HAVE A CANDIDATE FOR GIFTED PROGRAMMING.

A. *Asks how or why questions.* Not in reference to standard tasks such as arithmetic algorithms or clarification of assignments but rather, questions that get at causes of, reasons for, general abstractions, and/or application of principles.   1.   2.   3.   4.

B. *Offers alternative methods for standard procedures.* Demonstrates insight by offering alternative ways of completing standard tasks. Although you may recognize these as tried and rejected procedures, the student has not necessarily had this experience and his alternative may represent a fresh insight for his level of experience.   1.   2.   3.   4.

C. *Has extensive knowledge in some out-of-school oriented topic.* May possess a sophisticated collection of models, stamps, coins, Civil War momentos, etc. or possess unusual knowledge about sporting events, fossils, gaming techniques, etc. Frequently shared only if pressed.   1.   2.   3.   4.

D. *Suggests grandiose solutions and/or projects.* Often lacks experience in evaluating consequences of certain actions but has the insight to recognize that some unique solution will solve the problem. Plans often exceed an ability to actually carry them out.   1.   2.   3.   4.

E. *Questions arbitrary decisions.* More outgoing students may question wisdom of arbitrary decisions that lack obviously relevant justification. May desire to explore reasons for the decisions and may seek alternatives.   1.   2.   3.   4.

F. *Is bored with traditional courses of study.* May be bored with knowledge oriented programs that lack any real challenge to their thinking capabilities. These students acquire information quickly and seldom need the repetition so often emphasized in many common courses of study.   1.   2.   3.   4.

G. *Withdrawn yet capable when pressed.* Academically gifted students occasionally hide their gifts because of the fear of being labeled, "different".   1.   2.   3.   4.

H. *Alert to stimuli in the environment.* Not necessarily to the point of being easily distracted but rather, observant. Able to handle several variables simultaneously and frequently able to read and listen at the same time.   1.   2.   3.   4.

I. *Fails to complete homework but appears extremely capable.* This student may resist completing low level tasks frequently included in busy work and practice examples included in textbooks and workbooks. These tasks are boring and fail to represent a challenge.   1.   2.   3.   4.

ed, this appears to be as good a policy as any.

The limitations of group administered tests (the specific test appears to make little difference - any one test will miss specific segments of the gifted population) can be at least partially offset by informed teacher nomination. That is, if teachers are sensitized to the characteristics of intellectually gifted students who are likely to be misidentified by group tests, then teacher nomination can effectively supplement group tests and the probability of locating a greater proportion of the population of potentially gifted students is increased.

Students have demonstrated that the limitation of teacher nomination procedures is primarily a function of focusing on good student behaviors as the criteria of intellectual giftedness. The characteristics of cooperation, attentiveness, achievement and positive social interaction tend to serve as the basis for teacher nomination rather than any sense of high intellectual capability. These behaviors, as already noted, are not the typical characteristics of students being sought through teacher nomination. Although the "good schooling" characteristics of these students are occasionally associated with intellectual giftedness, they apparently occur in conjunction less than 50% of the time.

Teachers sensitive to the characteristics of gifted youngsters, particularly under-achievers, will have an increased ability to supplement group testing procedures with a nomination form. It would also appear that teacher nomination procedures that do not duplicate group testing outcomes will be more time-efficient than those procedures that include characteristics normally assessed within the standard testing program. If teachers are expected to seriously consider each student, then a format that

is as short as possible should be used. If teacher nomination is to effectively supplement standardized testing, it would appear important to carefully assess every child who is likely to be missed by group testing. An efficient teacher nomination procedure will therefore:

• Focus on the characteristics of under-achievers

• Be brief, to insure careful scrutiny of relevant characteristics of every student

• Avoid the duplication of characteristics normally assessed by group administered standardized tests

• Provide sufficient information to insure teacher attention to relevant student characteristics.

An example of a form that satisfies these four criteria is included on the preceeding page.

Note that this form is designed to identify intellectually gifted students who are likely to be misidentified by group administered paper and pencil tests. Intellectually gifted individuals missed by group tests may not exhibit desirable schooling behaviors. In fact, they may exhibit disruptive, withdrawn and/or annoying behaviors.

This form, too, has attempted to reduce the number of critical student characteristics to the barest minimum so that you can give each student the fullest consideration possible. It has also attempted to avoid duplication of characteristics efficiently assessed by group administered tests.

Several characteristics commonly found on teacher nomination forms have been omitted from this form because of their overlap with achievement and/or I.Q. tests, e.g. verbal fluency, reading ability, learns quickly, has a broad store of knowledge, large vocabulary, etc.

A second set of characteristics have been omitted because of the lack of relevance to general intellectual giftedness, e.g. creativity, leadership, musical ability, etc.

The purpose of this form is to identify intellectually gifted students who might be missed by group administered achievement and/or I.Q. measures. It is assumed that multiple criteria are being used to select a pool of potentially gifted students and that final decisions will be based on individually administered I.Q. tests. The pool, for example may contain the following:

1. Students who score 115 or better on a group I.Q. test.

2. Students who are in the top two stanines on an achievement test.

3. Students with grade point average of B+.

4. Students nominated by teachers.

This pool may then be reduced to a group of intellectually gifted students through use of individually administered I.Q. tests or, less preferably, through some process of weighting individual criteria that results in ranking students.

G/C/T

IT'S OK   by Ginsberg & Vukson

to shed a quiet tear because gifted children seem to grow up, up and away much too quickly - just when you have learned to enjoy them.

GIFTED IEPS: IMPACT OF EXPECTATIONS AND PERSPECTIVES

ABSTRACT

A description of the components of Individualized Education Programs (IEPs) is provided and the considerations prerequisite to their development for gifted students are reviewed. Specifically, the problems in developing present educational levels, annual goals, and short-term objectives are examined. Consideration also is given to the potential difficulties in screening and identification procedures. The importance of parent involvement in the educational process of the gifted child is outlined as well as the role of the multidisciplinary team. The final section deals with the rationale for and impact of individualzing an education program for the gifted.

CHRISTINE L. LEWIS
Montgomery County Intermediate Unit,
Norristown, Pa.

LELAGE G. KANES
Antioch University,
Philadelphia, Pa.

Special education teachers around the country who worked with exceptional children during 1977-78 have had to cope with a new educational requirement—the IEP. These Individualized Education Programs are required under Public Law 94-142 (HEW, 1977) the Education for All Handicapped Children Act. In addition to Pennsylvania, Idaho, Florida, and North Carolina are currently developing IEPs for the academically gifted (Farr, note 1). As a result, more and more regular classroom teachers are being drawn into the process for the gifted. This is necessary because it has been found that although formal and informal testing contributes to the creation of a total picture of the student, it could not be complete without the experience of the regular classroom teacher. This teacher may be involved to various degrees in the development and/or the implementation of the IEP. This involvement can range from a supportive role where reinforcement of the goal and objectives emphasized in the special class is provided, to the total responsibilities for meeting the child's special needs and abilities.

Whether or not states have mandated IEPs for the gifted, the concept is an interesting one and many concerns peculiar to the situation of the academically gifted become evident. Because there are a growing number of individuals involved in establishing programs for gifted students, a discussion of the process seems warranted.

IEP—What Is It?

An IEP is an Individualized Education Program to be written for each exceptional child, handicapped or gifted (where state law exists), in order to provide the "free and appropriate education" guaranteed by Public Law 94-142. Karnes and Bertschi (1978) describe the application of the process to gifted and handicapped preschoolers.

The IEP is a reflection of the modifications necessitated by the unique learning needs evidenced by the student. For the gifted, the "qualitatively different" adjustments which must be made are geared towards the individual's strengths since this is why the student was identified as exceptional. If a child has demonstrated potential in a particular field, for example, Math, then this is the area in which curricular changes must be made. On the other hand, a student's giftedness may cover all or a combination of academic areas. A much more extensive individualized program would therefore have to be developed to address the multiple needs evidenced by this kind of student.

Other mandates require that the educational program be developed in the least restrictive environment, with assurances that the students be integrated into regular education to the extent that they can benefit. Depending on the nature and degree of the student's giftedness, integration for the academically gifted into the regular classroom may not always be the most appropriate aim.

It should be noted that the term "regular" refers to a class with a curriculum developed for the student functioning within the normal ability range; a class that is not modified for the gifted. Programs for the handicapped, which emphasize remediation, seek to bring the child's level of functioning up to the normal range: that is, to minimize the effects of the exceptionality. In this case, mainstreaming is a legitimate end to work towards. However, it is hoped that the differentiated education provided for the gifted will accentuate the abilities of the pupil; that is, to maximize the effects of the exceptionality. This being the case, the aim of total integration into the regular classroom may not always be appropriate for the gifted.

Regular classroom teachers may lack training in the kind of instructional strategies necessary for the very bright students or they may not have the resource capacity for which many situations call. With the gifted, one wants to maintain or foster the student's exceptionality, not diminish it; and this may not always be possible when a child is placed in a totally mainstreamed assignment. Furthermore, with individualization, gifted children can be expected to move farther from the mean. The regular class, which is the unmodified one, may become less and less able to meet their needs and may, in effect, become the most restrictive environment. Therefore, a *special* class or program, which could take form within or outside of the child's current assignment, may become the *least restrictive environment*.

How Do You Start?

Identification of gifted students presents certain problems peculiar to the nature of giftedness—namely, deciding what descriptors will be used to identify the academically gifted students. Although a number of writers including Witty (1958), Frierson (1969), and Renzulli (1977), have provided definitions for this exceptionality, decisions still need to be made in order to locate assessment devices such as group and individual intelligence, achievement, and creativity tests, as well as inventories, rating scales, and other instruments which sample the selected abilities and/or characteristics.

At the kindergarten and primary levels the results of psychological tests such as the Wechsler Intelligence Scale for Children (WISC) and the Stanford-Binet Intelligence Scale (S-B) reflect the effects of the child's life experiences. Children with enriched experience backgrounds score high, but as they move through the grades they tend to lose this advantage as the other students catch up in experience. Therefore, a true evaluation of these students in terms of giftedness, as well as of the disadvantaged gifted students, may not be achieved. This problem is not restricted to this age level but is manifested throughout the grades; however, as early identification is crucial to assuring the nurturance of the gifted child's abilities, its effects have greater impact.

The discrepancies between test scores and actual ability makes an excellent case for multiassessment procedures. An accurate reflection of a student's abilities can be best obtained by reducing the chance omission of a component which is an important aspect of intelligence. Reliance on a single instrument increases the probability of such error.

Williams (1972) and Martinson (1974) provide suggested lists of instruments suitable for identifying gifted children. Careful consideration of these assessment procedures and devices should lead to a suitable screening and identification process.

Of What Should the IEP Consist?

The IEP has seven components, four of which are the backbone of the program. These are the primary assignment, the present educational levels, annual goals, and short-term objectives. All four involve assessment and planning procedures necessary to develop the child's unique potential. The primary assignment is the statement of the specific special education program to be provided to the child. It also reflects the degree to which the student is integrated into regular education for instruction. The other three components, however, create problems peculiar to those who are developing a gifted child's program.

An appropriate program for a gifted student should take into consideration several aspects. First, the curriculum should be process-oriented. It is common knowledge that an advanced technology promotes rapid changes in information and its applications. Emphasis on simple knowledge accumulation is a futile endeavor and persistence in this direction is very often deadly to a gifted student's desire to learn and to explore. This is not to say that acquiring a baseline of data is not important. Although education for the gifted should be geared toward more complex skills, such as those indicated by Bloom (1956) in the educational taxonomy or by Guilford's (1956) Structure of the Intellect, it would not be possible for an individual to analyze, synthesize, or evaluate if a knowledge base did not exist.

Second, the curriculum must have its foundation in a content area. The development of the ability to think in a critical manner would best be facilitated by working within the context of particular subject areas. This provides the opportunity to sequence and organize the skills rather than approach them in a random or haphazard fashion.

Third, the education for the gifted must take into consideration the interest of the student. Individualized Education Programs call for the establishment of a team of individuals to develop the student's program. In addition to a teacher, a school district representative, a member of the evaluation team, and the parents, the gifted child can and should be involved in this process. Drawing together the information from a variety of professionals and the student should provide the balanced program needed to address the exceptional qualities the child exhibits.

The combination of these considerations creates difficulty when gathering data for present educational levels. The statement of these levels must indicate the current functioning of the child in both the cognitive and affective domains as well as skills that should be learned next. However, much of the educational testing for the gifted is restricted to the administration of standardized achievement tests and group and/or individual IQ tests. These instruments do not provide the kinds of information about process abilities and student interests that the writing of present educational levels require. Achievement tests only tell in what content areas the child shows strength. They do not contain an elaboration of specific skills within these areas. Williams (1972) lists numerous instruments covering both the cognitive and affective domains that can lead to proper development of the student's levels of functioning. In addition, the administration of informal interest, skill, and learning style inventories can be useful. Alternative testing instruments are available and it would behoove school districts to acquire these tests and train staff in their uses and interpretations Martinson (1974) discusses a number of diagnostic procedures which are useful for teachers and counselors.

The IEP must also include annual goals which are statements of progress in particular instructional areas that the student will make in the course of one year's work. This section raises certain questions about the child's modified curriculum. In the case of the handicapped, the program would be remedial in nature since the child's exceptionality creates a barrier to learning. The gifted child's exceptionality, on the other hand, facilitates the learning process. To create an entire program around what may be considered a minor or relative weakness of the student distorts the purpose of the IEP. It is not that these areas should be ignored. However, they might be handled more appropriately by capitalizing upon the child's strengths. It would not make sense to devote a language arts section of an IEP for a gifted child entirely to strengthening spelling and punctuation. This could be better handled by addressing these areas within the context of journalism, for example, or any other area in which the student evidenced special skill and/or interest.

On the other hand, it is important to deal with skills that have been developed only slightly, if at all, and which would assist the child in reaching his potential. For example, working on problem-solving skills, independence skills, organizational skills, and affective skills can help the pupil make full use of his special academic abilities.

Another major concern of those who are to write individualized programs for the gifted centers around the development of short-term objectives. As part of these shorter, more specific steps that will help a pupil reach the annual goal, the mandates of PL

94-142, which were written with the handicapped in mind, call for objective evaluation criteria of the student's behavior. If a teacher has a child working in the areas of critical thinking skills, creativity, problem-solving, and inquiry, which are examples of what might be appropriate, s/he is confronted with the task of designing evaluation criteria which will objectively evaluate a behavior whose basis lies in the abstract.

When a remediation program for a handicapped child is established, that child will most likely be working on the levels of knowledge, comprehension and application as described by Bloom (1956). It is not as difficult to evaluate behaviors at these levels. Identifying, listing, recalling, applying, using, and showing are examples of behaviors which fall into the first three taxonomy levels and are easily evaluated with an accuracy level. However, behaviors such as predicting, assessing, criticizing, generating and justifying, which are higher level thinking skills, cannot be evaluated by similar methods. It would be inappropriate to attempt to attach a percent of accuracy to a skill whose inherent properties make it too complex to evaluate in this way.

The alternatives that educators must find in order to evaluate the work of the gifted pupil may take many different forms. Rating scales can be constructed, student journals kept, peer evaluations employed, teacher observations logged, and self-evaluations designed. These instruments not only help to judge objectively the performance of the student's work but some may also serve as guidelines that the pupil can follow.

It is also questionable as to whether it is valid for the educator alone to assess the student's work. A variety of individuals can and should become involved in this process. Teachers, the student, peers, community experts, and librarians all have the potential for contributing to the evaluation of the student's work. Because education includes experience both within and outside of the school environment, the gifted student's performance should not be assessed by the conventional means of a paper and pencil test alone. Criteria of evaluation can be many and varied as long as they are appropriate to the nature and complexity of the behavior.

The remaining components of the IEP are a statement of the developmental, corrective, and supportive services that the student must have in order to benefit from special education; the dates of the initiation and duration of the program; and the date of annual review.

What About Parental Involvement?

Procedures for parental involvement in the IEP planning process are specified in PL 94-142 as are the due process safeguards for constitutional protections. Parents must be afforded the opportunity, in conjunction with the teacher(s), school district representative, and members of the evaluation team, to help design the special program to be offered to the student. The perspective that parents have on the learning style, abilities, potential, performance, interests, and attitudes of their child are invaluable to the multidisciplinary IEP team of which they are a part.

Because the IEP is an ongoing process, parents will continue as members of the team to assist in the mandated annual review. This review, which may lead to a revision, is required to keep the student's special program as current and as appropriate as possible.

One important result of parent involvement is the awareness that it brings to school and home of the joint responsibility for the education of the student. The experiences of both environments contribute to the development of the child's fullest potential, and the cooperation and understanding fostered by the IEP process go a long way in strengthening this concept.

Why Do It?

Aside from the fact that this is the law, there are professional reasons for the IEP. If one considers that the gifted child is as far away from the normal ability student as is the retarded child, the rationale for differentiated education becomes clear. Neither one could meet his/her potential if forced to work on a level vastly different from where s/he is functioning.

The gifted student, as all other students, should work within challenging, stimulating situations that neither frustrate nor bore the child into underachievement. It must be kept in mind, however, that what constitutes such an environment for a gifted student may be levels above what meets the needs of the normal child. Many educators make the false assumption that the mere addition of work is a satisfactory solution to the concern of individualizing for the gifted.

The programs provided for the academically gifted should be geared towards higher level thinking skills, creativity, problem-solving, and process development. These modifications should mesh with or complement the normal curricula. Gifted students may sometimes find participation in special programs to be a penalty, in that it often means quantitative rather than qualitative modifications in their curriculum, while allowing little, if any, release time to pursue more challenging, independent goals. This arrangement must be avoided at all costs as it encourages the gifted to suppress rather than enhance their talents.

Besides the obvious benefits that IEPs would bring to the students themselves, an important by-product of the process is the impetus it gives to program evaluation. A valuable aspect of writing these programs is the coordination of curriculum which can result. Educators, by necessity, must seek each other out in an effort to establish the levels at which a student functions, the current and upcoming goals and objectives which will be developed for that student, and the reexamination and readjustment of curriculum required by the IEP. The cooperation that the process fosters gives teachers first, an opportunity to exchange ideas and second, the chance to locate and fill in gaps that exist in their curricula not only in particular instructional areas, but in grades, departments, and levels as well.

Individualized Education Programs for the gifted suffer from many problems which are a function of the federal law's being developed for and addressing the concerns of the handicapping exceptionalities. Although it often seems as if a square peg were being forced into a round hole, the advantages of the IEP more than compensate for the stumbling blocks. The gifted child's difference from the normal child is as pronounced as the mentally retarded child's difference. Considering the drastic adjustments that must be made to meet the special needs of the handicapped, it is no less vital to make as great modifications for the gifted. Martinson (1974) underscores this by pointing out that "attention goes first to remedial problems. . . . but the needs of children who are especially capable of outstanding achievement are the last to receive meaningful attention" (p. 12). The IEP brings to light this fact and affords the very bright student the opportunity to also receive the kind of education to which he is philosophically and legally entitled.

REFERENCES

Bloom, B.S. (Ed). *Taxonomy of educational objectives, Handbook I: Cognitive domain.* New York: David McKay Co., 1956.

Frierson, E.C. The gifted. *Review of Educational Research,* 1969, *34,* 25-37.

Guilford, J.P. The structure of the intellect. *Psychological Bulletin,* 1956, *53,* 267-293.

Karnes, M.B. & Bertschi, J.D. Identifying and educating gifted/talented non-handicapped and handicapped preschoolers. *Teaching Exceptional Children,* 1978, *10,* 114-119.

Martinson, R.A. *The identification of the gifted and talented.* Ventura, Cal.: Office of Ventura County Superintendent of Schools, 1974.

Renzulli, J.S. *The enrichment triad model: A guide for developing defensible programs for the gifted and talented.* Wethersfield, Connecticut: Creative Learning Press, 1977.

U.S. Department of Health, Education and Welfare, Office of Education. *Education of handicapped children: Implementation of part B, education of handicapped act.* Washington, D.C.: Author, 1977.

Williams, F.E. *A total creativity program for individualizing and humanizing the learning process* (Vol. 1). Englewood Cliffs, New Jersey: Educational Technology Publications, 1972.

Witty, P.A. Who are the gifted? *Education for the Gifted: Yearbook for the National Society for Studies in Education,* 1958, *57.*

NOTES

1. Farr, J. Telephone communication. June 9, 1978.

IDENTIFICATION AND EVALUATION PROCEDURES FOR GIFTED AND TALENTED PROGRAMS

Ron Rubenzer

Evaluation and Placement
Center for the Gifted

*Teachers College,
Columbia University*

Talent Search: Who Are the Gifted and Talented?

Where our gifted and talented children? Einstein was four years old before he could speak and seven years old before he could read. Beethoven's music teacher once said of him, "As a composer he is hopeless." A newspaper editor fired Walt Disney because he had "no good ideas." These are just a very few of the examples which illustrate how elusive the characteristics of genius can be. Even teachers, who are in close contact with gifted and talented students are only 50 % successful when they are requested to identify whom they consider to be gifted or talented. To aid in the identification of the gifted and talented, the U.S. Office of Education has developed a fairly comprehensive definition of gifted and talented as:

those individuals identified by professionally qualified persons who, by virtue of outstanding abilities, are capable of high performance. These are children who require differentiated educational programs and/or services beyond those normally provided by the regular school program in order to realize their contribution to self and society. (Executive Summary, 1971, p. 3).

Children capable of high performance include those with demonstrated achievement (top 3-5 % on standardized tests) and/or potential in any of the following areas, singly or in combination: (a) general intellectual ability, (b) specific academic aptitude, (c) creative or productive thinking, (d) leadership ability, (e) visual and performing arts, and (f) psychomotor ability.

More operationally defined, children of generally high intellectual ability will function exceedingly well in almost all academic areas. Children who exhibit specific academic aptitudes typically excel in perhaps only one or two academic areas. The child with exceptional creative ability can be described as the pupil who generates unusual, frequent, and high quality ideas or solutions to problems. Children with leadership ability demonstrate consistently exceptional capacity to motivate and organize other children. High ability in the visual and performing arts will often be indicated by exceptionally good aesthetic production in such areas as the graphic arts, sculpture, music and dance. The child with exceptional mechanical reasoning skills or superior athletic ability can be classified as possessing talent in the psycho-motor area of functioning (Stark, 1975).

Approximately 95 % of all children identified as gifted and talented cluster into the areas of intellectual giftedness or specific academic aptitude (Grinter, 1975), primarily as a function of the relatively greater accuracy in the identification of these two talent areas.

It is apparent that with respect to multi-talent identification, psycho-metric techniques are still at an embryonic stage as evidenced by Guilford's (1959) studies of the intellect. He concluded that "there are 120 possible specific high level talents, with over 80 discovered to date" (p. 473). The best conventional tests measure less than one half of these hypothesized specific talents (Gowan and Bruch, 1971)!

Further complicating evaluation by conventional testing procedures are such factors as (a) socioeconomic sampling biases inherent in tests designed primarily for the white middle class, (b) expertise of test administrators, (c) possible effects of test anxiety, and (d) the motivational state of the subject (Anastasi, 1971).

Talent search designs should also take into account the possible masking of talent; that is, a highly creative pupil may not necessarily be exceptional in academic tasks nor may the intellectually gifted child be able to express his/her talent because of a learning or behavioral disability. The child's preschool environmental experiences should also be studied.

Currently, multi-talent identification models which are being employed in California and Illinois utilize the following screening techniques: standardized tests (top 5 %), past performance, teacher and supervisor recommendations, peer identification, and observations. Of course, each talent area differs with respect to ease and accuracy of identification of said talent, and overlap of talents does occur. A classified listing of representative tests for each of the six U.S.O.E. talent areas is provided in the appendix. A description of all the instruments referred to in the text are presented in this test listing. A discussion of identification procedures and instruments utilized for the six talent areas follows.

General Intellectual Ability

Generally speaking, in the area of intellectual giftedness, children equaling or excelling the 95th percentile (Sanborn, 1971) on individual intelligence tests (Stanford Binet, Form LM, IQ - 127, or Wechsler series WISC-R. WPPSI, WAIS FSIQ = 125) are considered intellectually gifted. However, the suggested IQ "cutoff" ranges from an IQ of 115 (Gowan, 1964) to 132 (Gifted Children's Association, 1971). In order to somewhat mitigate the possible effect of cultural biases inherent in most IQ tests it has been recommended that "the top 5 % of the subgroup be treated as talented and gifted" (Tunney, 1972).

Although individual intelligence tests results should not be the sole determining factor in the identification of giftedness, it has been established (Martinson, 1961; Reynolds, 1962; Worchester, 1956) that accurate identification of gifted children through individual IQ tests is possible from as early as the kindergarten level with individual intelligence tests. The use of individual intelligence tests has been proven to be most useful in identifying exceptional ability in problem solving, learning, scholastic attainment, and vocational success (Butcher, 1968).

The chances of accurate identification of the gifted child are much greater with individual intelligence tests than with the use of group tests. In fact, group intelligence testing actually penalizes the gifted pupil (Sheldon, 1954), and is not recommended for screening before third grade. Of the two most prominent individual intelligence tests in current use, the Stanford Binet (Form LM) appears to have advantages over the Wechsler Intelligence Scale for Children-Revised. In comparative studies (Gallagher, 1966), it was found that the Stanford Binet has a higher IQ range than the Wechsler and that the Wechsler scale does not encompass extremes in intelligence as well as the Sanford Binet: thus creating an artificially low ceiling for the gifted. Other comparative studies have indicated that gifted children generally average 10 IQ points lower on the Wechsler series than they do on the Binet (Beeman, 1960). To date, individual intelligence tests have been the relatively most accurate single measure for the identification of the intellectually gifted. The use of individual intelligence tests however, is often impaired by cost and the present assignment of priorities for testing. Furthermore, individual intelligence tests do not adequately cover such areas as creative potential, leadership ability, aesthetic production or psychomotor skills. These tests may also penalize children with language or environmental handicaps (Martinson, 1974).

Specific Academic Aptitude

Successful pilot studies have been conducted with identification devices (Malone, 1975; Moonan, 1973) which suggest that talent searches may eventually rely to a much greater degree on behavioral criteria.

With respect to identification procedures in the specific academic aptitude talent area. Gowan (1967) has developed a viable identification model. An integral aspect of Gowan's identification model is teacher involvement. Indeed the utilization of teacher judgment in talent search has been considered as most helpful and accurate if teachers are made cognizant of common errors encountered when identifying gifted and talented pupils (See *Teacher Screening Devices* in the Appendix). Gowan's "Reservoir Model" (Gowan, 1967, p. 34) follows:

Reservoir Model for Identification of Gifted and Talented

1. Determine the percentage of students to be included in the program (not less than 1 % or more than 10 %).
2. Employ a group test, screen and cut at a point which will give 5 %. Take the top 10 % of this group and put them into the program. Place the remainder into the reservoir.
3. Circulate to each classroom teacher a paper in which he or she is asked to nominate the:
   3.1   best student
   3.2   child with the biggest vocabulary
   3.3   most original and creative child
   3.4   child with the most leadership ability

3.5 most scientifically oriented child

3.6 child who does the best critical thinking

3.7 able child who is the biggest nuisance

3.8 best motivated child

3.9 child the other children like best

3.10 child who is most ahead on grade placement

3.11 brightest minority group child in the class

3.12 child whose parents are most concerned about increasing the enrichment of his educational progress

4. Use an achievement battery and cut at a point which will yield 3 %. Make a list of all students who are in the top 10 % in numerical skills; add both of these lists to the reservoir.

5. Together with the principal, curriculum staff and guidance staff, plus a few teachers, go over and make a list of children who:

5.1 have leadership positions

5.2 achieved outstandingly in any special skills

5.3 are the best representative of minority groups

5.4 have influential parents

5.5 are examples of reading difficulties but appear bright

5.6 are believed bright, but may be emotionally disturbed

5.7 about whom any single individual feels might be in the program

Place these in the reservoir. All pupils in the reservoir should now be ranked as to the number of times they have been mentioned. All children having three or more mentions should be automatically included in the program. All children having two citations should be sent for individual intelligence testing. If possible, children mentioned once should receive testing.

Creative and Productive Thinking

Theorists have concluded that personality variables play a significant role in creative thinking or productive thinking (Andrews, 1930, Chassell, 1916; Taylor & Getzels, 1975). Therefore, many of the screening devices utilized to identify creative individuals have characteristics similar to personality inventories. The Renzulli/Hartman scales for Rating Behavioral Characteristics of Superior Students and the Bella Kranz Multidimensional Screening Device (See appendix). Both include scales for identifying creatively gifted students and can be used to identify gifted students through teacher observations.

Self-rating devices such as the Alpha-Biographical Inventory (Institute for Behavioral Reserach in Creativity, 1968) or the Adjective Check list (Gough and Heilbrun, 1965) contain descriptions of traits associated with creative personalities. These self-rating devices can be used for high school students and adults.

A more direct approach to the measurement of "creative or productive" abilities is the Torrance Tests of Creative Thinking (TTCT) (Torrance, 1966). The TTCT instrument is a widely used device which is divided into two subtests: "Thinking Creatively With Words" and "Thinking Creatively with Pictures". The former subtest measures verbal creativity in the forms of: fluency, flexibility and originality. The latter subtest measures nonverbal creative production in terms of four scores: fluency, flexibility, originality and elaboration. Because performance on the TTCT is influenced by motivation, previously acquired problem-solving strategies and the expertise of the test scorer, the TTCT scores should be interpreted conservatively. Of course, judgment of the creativity of a product or products by an expert in a particular field is a most effective method of identifying creative individuals. Parents and the students themselves should be encouraged to present products which they feel may reflect creative ability. It is suggested that a combination of teacher screening, creativity test performance and expert judgment of creative productions be employed in the identification of creative talent.

Leadership Abilities

The identification of individuals with expressed or latent leadership skills appears to depend almost exclusively on the observation of "leadership" behaviors. *The Scales for Rating the Behavioral Characteristics of Superior Students* and *the Multi-Dimensional Screening Device* both include scales that relate to leadership abilities. Gowan's *Reservoir Model* also contains a listing of characteristics useful in identifying students with leadership skills. The individual interview techniques employed by the University of Wisconsin Research and Guidance Laboratory (formerly the Research and Guidance Laboratory for Superior Students) which are based on 25 years of research with gifted and talented high school students appear to be useful in gleaning personality characteristics which would be reflective of leadership potential.

Visual and Performing Arts

The identification of individuals with artistic, dramatic, musical or other visual or performing art abilities relies almost exclusively on expert judgment on the expression of the talent in question. There are only a few standardized identification devices for this talent area (visual and performing arts) such as the *Seashore Measures of Musical Talents* or the Horn Art Aptitude Inventory. These devices are designed only for high school and college students. However, these devices may be useful for identifying talented junior high school students. Perhaps the top 1-5 % of a local talent search (art, music or drama) could be considered as gifted or talented.

Psychomotor Skills

The identification of exceptional athletic talent has received considerable attention; however, the identification of individuals who possess exceptional mechanical or reasoning skills has been relatively neglected. Group tests such as the *Guilford Zimmerman Aptitude Survey* or the *Differential Aptitude Tests* may be useful for screening students with exceptional mechanical reasoning skills by administering specific subtests of these devices. The nonverbal (Performance Scales) of the individually administered Wechsler Series may be useful in further identifying students with exceptional spatial-reasoning abilities. Again, unusually high quality performance in mechanical tasks would also be an indicator of talent in the psychomotor area.

When Should Identification Occur

In addition to accuracy in identification of gifted and talented, timing is also a critical factor. Previous it was held that third grade was the timeline by which identification of talent had to occur before irretrievable loss of talent would take place (Kagan, 1958). Malone (1975), however, contradicts this contention. In fact, if the effects of intellectual and emotional recession are to be minimized, identification should occur as early as kindergarten.

Trends in Early Talent Identification

Extensive research is currently being conducted in an effort to develop a device which will be accurate, relatively bias-free, inexpensive and not excessively time consuming. One such device entitled, "Charosel" (Moonan, 1973), is a computer program. Qualitative predictors of giftedness and talent at the kindergarten level are selected in the program from biographical, behavioral and life history data.

As the result of other studies, some of the following characteristics have been found to occur more frequently among gifted and talented pupils at the pre-kindergarten level (Syphers, 1972; Terman, 1926; Witty, 1957):

1. Possession of a large and accurately used vocabulary.
2. The ability to read before entrance to school (50 % of Terman subjects learned to read before starting school).
3. The ability to concentrate more than most age peers.
4. Keen observation and retention about things observed.
5. Interest in calendars and clocks.
6. Early discovery of cause and effect relationships.
7. Proficiency in drawing, music, and other art forms.
8. Early walking.
9. Older playmates.

Parental Involvement in the Identification of the Gifted

The role of parents in the identification of the gifted and talented should be increased. It has been found that in general, parents are highly accurate in identifying gifted students (Ciba, 1974). It is suggested that a parent questionnaire designed to obtain relevant information on the gifted should be included in all identification procedures.

Gifted and Talented Program Evaluation

According to Renzulli and Callahan (1978) the major purposes of educational evaluation are to provide feedback on whether "the goals and objectives are being met and the reasons for success or failure in meeting them." (p. 1). The following components for the development of an effective program evaluation design are suggested by Renzulli and Callahan (1978):

1. Identify decision makers who can use the evaluation information to modify the program operation.
2. Specifically define the goals and objectives as they are derived from such sources as project proposals, policy statements curriculum guides, etc. Both cognitive and affective aspects of student development should be considered.
3. Determine the sources of information and develop a timeline for collecting this information. A pretest-posttest design may be

most useful in measuring student progress in a program. However, the students themselves are a valuable source of information regarding student growth.

4. Carefully select the evaluation instruments which are most appropriate for the needs of the program (See the appendix of this paper for a descriptive listing of test instruments).

5. Analyze the data gathered from the evaluation instruments used. The specific nature of the data analysis would be determined by questions asked when the data was being collected. These questions would be directly related to the program goals and objectives.

6. Present the evaluation findings apropos to the intended audience. The evaluation report findings should be presented in such a way that decisions about program success can be made. The use of charts, graphs and other visual aids is suggested when presenting the data.

More comprehensive and detailed surveys of basic program evaluation procedures are provided by Worthen and Saunders (1972) and Renzulli (1975).

REFERENCES

Andrews, E. G. The development of imagination in the preschool child. *University of Iowa Studies of Character*, 1930 *3* (4).

Beeman, G. A comparative study of the WISC and Stanford-Binet with a group of more able and gifted 7-11 year old children. Presentation to California Association of School Psychologists, 1960, mimeographed.

Butcher, H. J. *Human intelligence: Its nature and assessment*, London: Metheun, 1968.

Chassell, L. M. *Tests for originality*. Journal of Educational Psychology, 1916, *7*, 317-329.

Ciha, T. E. Parents as identifiers of giftedness, ignored but accurate. Unpublished paper read at the National Association of Gifted Children Conference, St. Louis, Missouri, February 1974.

Executive Summary. Education of the gifted and talented, Vol. 1. Report to the Congress of the United States by the U.S. Commissioner of Education, 1971.

Gallagher, J. J. *Research summary on gifted child education.* Springfield: Illinois Department of Public Instruction, 1966.

Gifted Children's Association of San Fernando Valley, Inc. San Fernando Valley, 1970.

Gough, H. G., & Heilbrun, A. B. The Adjective check list manual. Palo Alto, California: Consulting Psychologists Press, 1957.

Gowan, J.C. Identification, in *The education and guidance of the ablest.* Springfield, Illinois: Charles C. Thomas, 1964.

Gowan, J.C. Identification, responsibility of both principal and teachers. In Bish, C. E. (Ed.) *Accent on talent.* Edwardsville, Ill: The Committee for the Study of Intellectual Talent.

Gowan, J. C., & Bruch, C. B. The academically talented student and guidance. Guidance Monograph Series. Boston: Houghton-Mifflin Co., 1971.

Grinter, R., Identification processes. Presentation to Wisconsin Council for Gifted and Talented, February, 1975.

Guilford, J. P. Three faces of intellect. *American Psychologist*, 1959, *14*, 469-479.

Kagan, J., Sontag, L., Baker, C., & Nelson, V. Personality and IQ change. *Journal of Abnormal and Social Psychology,* 1958, *56,* 261-266.

Malone, C. E. Kindergarten bliss: Not so-For gifted the beginning may be the end. LaJolla, Cal.: Western Behavioral Sciences Institute, 1975.

Martinson, R. A. The identification of the gifted and talented: An instructional syllabus for the national summer leadership training institute on the education of the gifted and talented. Ventura, Cal.: Office of the Ventura County Superintendent of Schools, 1974.

Moonan, W. J. *Vistas of analysis: Qualitative prediction and decision analysis.* San Diego: Naval Personnel and Training Research Laboratory, 1973.

Renzulli, J.S. *A guidebook for evaluating programs for the gifted and talented.* Ventura, California: Office of the Ventura County Superintendent of Schools, 1975.

Renzulli, J. S., & Callahan, C. *Evaluation of programs for the gifted and talented,* Washington, D.C. U.S. Office of Education, Office of the Gifted and Talented (Contract Number 300-76-0530), 1978.

Reynolds, M. C. (Ed.) *Early school admission for mentally advanced children: A review of research and practice.* Washington, D.C.: Council for Exceptional Children, 1962.

Sanborn, M. P., Pulvino, C. J., & Wunderlin, R. F. *Research reports superior students in Wisconsin high schools.* Madison, Wis.: Research and Guidance Laboratory, 1971.

Sheldon, W. D., & Manolakes, G. Comparison of the Stanford-Binet, Revised Form L, and the California Test of Mental Maturity (S form). *Journal of Educational Psychology,* 1954, 45.

Stark, S. A half-filled cup yearning to runneth over. *Early Years,* 1975, *5,* 45-47 and 62.

Syphers, D. F. Gifted and talented children: Practical programming for teachers and principals. Washington, D.C.: The Council for Exceptional Children, 1972.

Terman, L. M. The mental and physical traits of a thousand gifted children. Vol. 1, *Genetic studies of genius.* Stanford, Cal.: Stanford University Press, 1926.

Torrance, E. P. Torrance Tests of Creative Thinking: *Norms Technical Manual.* Princeton: N.J.: Personnel Press, 1966.

Witty, P. Every parent and teacher a talent scout. *National Parent-Teacher,* 1957, 4-6.

Worchester, D. *The education of children of above average mentality.* Lincoln: University of Nebraska Press, 1956.

Worthen, B., & Sanders, J. *Educational Evaluation: Theory and Practice.* Worthington, Ohio: Charles A. Jones, 1972.

TEACHER IDENTIFICATION OF THE GIFTED:

A NEW LOOK

ABSTRACT

Teacher recommendation as a means of identifying gifted children traditionally has been regarded as ineffective and inefficient, although such conclusions are based upon studies in which teachers were required to make global assessments of students' ability. The present study sought to re-examine the issue through the use of checklists on which the teachers were asked to indicate the presence or absence of certain behaviors. Significant, moderate, positive correlations between teacher rating and IQ were obtained, and the ratings were found to possess both high efficiency and stability. Teacher rating was found to be a better predictor of giftedness for girls than for boys. With IQ as the dependent variable, a main effect for achievement was found, but there was none for rating nor was there an interaction effect. Teacher rating was a better identifier of gifted underachievers than of gifted achievers.

JAMES BORLAND
Teacher's College, Columbia University

As Martinson and Lessinger (1960) have indicated, much of the success of a program for the intellectually gifted is contingent upon sound identification procedures. Unfortunately, the issue of identification is a highly problematical one for this population. While many would agree with Gallagher (1966) that the individual intelligence test is the optimal tool for identifying the gifted, just as many would probably agree that the expense inherent in such a procedure underlines the need for research into "how much would be lost through the use of some more economical alternative" (p. 9).

According to *Education of the Gifted and Talented* (1972), the report to Congress by then-Commissioner of Education Sidney Marland, teacher recommendation is the alternative most frequently adopted by local school districts. This widespread use takes place despite a large body of research (Alexander, 1953; Baldwin, 1962; Barbe, 1964; Cornish, 1968; Jacobs, 1971; Lewis, 1945; Pegnato & Birch, 1959; Terman, 1925; Wilson, 1963) which indicates that it not only fails to locate a significant proportion of the gifted population but consistently results in a large number of "false positives" being referred for final individual testing.

However, a smaller but generally more recent group of studies (Gordon & Thomas, 1967; Keogh & Smith, 1970; Stevenson, Parker, Wilkenson, Hegion, & Fish, 1976; Weise, Meyers, & Tuel, 1965) has offered evidence that teachers can be highly accurate predictors of children's academic performance. In the study by Stevenson et al. (1976), for example, teacher ratings made in kindergarten had correlations of "about .50" with reading and arithmetic achievement four years later, while stability correlations for achievement in these areas were .55 and .50 respectively over the same period. In other words, given the stability of the children's achievement, the teachers' ratings predicted as well as could be expected.

The outstanding feature of this latter group of studies is that they were highly *directive* in nature. Teachers were not requested to make global judgements of their students' potential; rather, they were asked to rate children on specific traits on the basis of observed behavior. In contrast, eight of the nine studies that purport to show that teachers are ineffective identifiers of gifted children employed what could be referred to as *nondirective* techniques. In these cases, teachers were asked either to submit a list of gifted students or to rate each student in the class as to his or her academic potential. In essence, gross psychometric estimations of academic ability were demanded of the teachers. Inevitably, comparisons of such teacher assessments with results obtained from complex psychometric instruments turn out to be highly invidious.

If, however, teachers were to be asked to identify specific students behaviors which are believed to be indicative of giftedness, it is conceivable that their ratings could have more utility and validity for identification purposes. The goal of the present research, then, was to determine the degree to which teacher ratings based upon responses to a behavioral checklist can be used to identify gifted children. The following specific questions were addressed: (1) To what degree are teacher ratings from a behavioral checklist predictive of IQ?; (2) How efficient are such ratings?; (3) How stable are such ratings?; (4) Are there sex differences in such ratings?; (5) With IQ as the dependent variable, are there main effects for rating and for achievement, and is there an interaction effect?; and (6) Does teacher rating predict IQ as well for under-achieving students as it does for achieving students?

METHOD

Subjects

The subjects were 195 students (89 males, 106 females) who were in the third, fourth, and sixth grades of the Middletown, New Jersey, Public Schools in the 1976-1977 school year. All of the children had been identified by school personnel as gifted on the basis of IQ, achievement, or teacher rating. The subjects were drawn from the district's 12 elementary schools which represent communities widely varying in mean socioeconomic status. Although the subjects were predominantly white, there were some black and Hispanic children in the sample.

Instruments

The IQ test used was the short form of the California Test of Mental Maturity (CTMM), and the achievement test was the Iowa Test of Basic Skills (ITBS). The teacher rating scale was developed by the district for the purpose of identifying children for the gifted program. It is *directive* in nature, containing 15 statements describing possible behavior. The teacher is requested to indicate whether the child in question exhibits each behavior frequently, occasionally, or never.

The scale is divided into three weighted sections. The first, which carries the heaviest weighting, describes behaviors which have to do with reasoning and problem-solving abilities. This section appears to tap what Cattell (1963) calls "fluid intelligence." The second section describes behaviors reflective of acquired knowledge and abilities which correspond roughly to Cattell's concept of "crystallized intelligence." The third section, which has the lightest weighting, describes behaviors which relate to personality variables such as imagination, curiosity, adventurousness, and interest in ethical issues. A unitary score was computed for all children recommended by their teachers, and a score of 74 out of a possible 87 was sufficient for admission into the gifted program. (See Appendix A for scale items and scoring.)

Procedure

All data were obtained from existing school records. Rating sheets were collected from teachers in the spring of the 1975-1976 and the 1976-1977 academic years. Since the Middletown gifted program operates only in grades three through six at this time, no ratings were available for those children who were in the sixth grade in the 1976-1977 school year. Further, due to the district's testing procedures, no CTMM scores were available for third grade children, and ITBS scores were available for the 1975-1976 school year only.

Final data were gathered in the spring of 1977.

RESULTS

To What Degree Are Teacher Ratings Predictive of IQ?

In order to determine the degree of relationship, if any, between the teacher ratings and CTMM IQ, the Pearson Product-Moment correlation between each of the year's ratings and IQ was computed. A multiple correlation with the two sets of ratings as independent variables and IQ as dependent variable was also computed.

The correlation between 1975-1976 ratings and IQ was .22, $p < .005$, based upon 164 subjects who were in the third and fifth grades in that year. The correlation between rating and IQ for 43 fourth graders in the 1976-1977 academic year was .32, $p < .05$. When the two sets of ratings were combined for this latter group, the multiple correlation obtained was .33.

Due to the homogeneous nature of the sample, these correlations may be somewhat attenuated. Nevertheless, significant, moderate, positive correlations between teacher rating and IQ were obtained in each case. These correlations compare favorably with that between ITBS achievement and IQ, $r = .35$, $p < .00001$, two variables between which a strong relationship might be expected given a more heterogeneous sample. The negligible increment in the multiple correlation over that between the later set of ratings and IQ is explained by the high correlation, $r = .86$, $p < .0001$, between the two sets of ratings.

How Efficient Are Teacher Ratings?

Pegnato and Birch (1959) defined efficiency as the ratio between the number of students referred by a certain screening instrument and the number in that group who are ultimately identified as gifted. In order to test the efficiency of the rating scale used in the Middletown Public Schools, all students with a teacher rating of 74 or higher, the cutting point for admission into the gifted program, were considered to have been screened by the scale. The criterion used to judge the efficiency of the scale was a CTMM IQ of 125 or higher, a score which would place the student in the top five percent of the population, a common definition of giftedness.

The results of this test are shown in Table 1. Seventy-six children were given ratings of 74 or higher in the 1975-1976 academic year. Of these, exactly half, 38 children, achieved a score of 125 or above on the CTMM. This compares most favorably with the results obtained by Pegnato and Birch (1959) who found a higher efficiency for only one of their screening measures, a group IQ test with a cutting point of 130. If the criterion in the present case is raised to a CTMM IQ of 130 or higher, the efficiency is still a respectable 35.5 percent for the 1975-1976 ratings.

Table 1
Efficiency of Teacher Ratings (%)

Year	n	Criterion IQ>120	IQ>125	IQ>130
1975-76	76	75.0	50.0	35.5
1976-1977	19	89.5	47.4	42.1
Combined ª	16	93.8	43.8	37.5

a. Student was required to have a rating of 74 or higher in both years.

The 1976-1977 ratings fared equally well. With a criterion of 125 IQ, the efficiency was 47.4 percent; with a criterion of 130 IQ, the efficiency was 42.7 percent.

Curiously, combining the two ratings and requiring that the student achieve a rating of 74 or higher on both occasions did not result in a higher efficiency. A criterion of 125 IQ resulted in an efficiency of 43.75 percent, while a 130 IQ criterion produced an efficiency of 37.5 percent, figures consonant with those for the single ratings.

How Stable Are Teacher Ratings?

The stability of the teacher ratings over two years and two sets of teachers was tested by computing the Pearson Product-Moment correlation between the 1975-1976 and the 1976-1977 ratings. The resulting correlation coefficient was .86, $p < .001$, indicating a high degree of stability for the ratings. This figure was based upon the 74 cases for whom there were two sets of ratings.

Are There Sex Differences in Teacher Ratings?

The question of sex differences in teacher ratings was raised by the fact that in much of the literature surveyed there were reports of higher ratings for females. Thus, the following null hypothesis was tested: There is no significant difference between the mean rating for females and that for males on the 1975-1976 ratings.

The mean rating for females (n=89) was 68.26 while that for males (n=75) was 67.62. The resulting T-statistic, .246 with 163 degrees of freedom, was not significant at the .05 level. Thus, the null hypothesis was not rejected, and no evidence was found to suggest that teachers gave higher ratings to their female than to their male students.

However, when individual correlations were computed between rating and IQ for the two sexes, interesting differences arose. For males, the correlation between rating and IQ was .16, $p<.10$, and that between achievement and IQ was .55, $p<.001$. Thus, for the males in this sample, teacher rating was not a good predictor of IQ. If IQ is to be the criterion for giftedness, achievement would appear to be a better screening device for this group.

For females the story was quite different. The Pearson r rating and IQ for this group was .29, $p<.005$, while the correlation between achievement and IQ was .16, $p<.10$. Thus, for females in this sample, teacher rating is a markedly better predictor of IQ than is achievement.

In this case, at least, teacher ratings are more accurate identifiers of gifted females than of gifted males. Since there was no significant difference in the mean ratings for the two sexes, and since there was no significant difference between the mean IQ's, $(t(163) = .09)$, the difference between the predictive power of the ratings for the groups cannot very well be attributed to bias. Rather, teachers apparently were more sensitive to manifestations of giftedness in their female students than in their male students, perhaps because nearly all the teachers involved in the rating process were female.

With IQ as Dependent Variable, Are There Main Effects for Rating and for Achievement, and Is There an Interaction Effect?

The subjects were grouped as to high, middle, or low teacher rating and achievement, the middle group being composed of those whose rating or achievement placed them within .5 standard deviations of the group mean. This produced nine subgroups in a 3x3 two-way analysis of variance design. A two-way analysis of variance revealed no main effect for rating, but a significant F for achievement, $F(2,155) = 11.90$, $p<.0005$, was obtained. No interaction effect was found.

Table 2

Analysis of Variance

Source	SS	df	MS	F
Rating (R)	318.79	2	159.40	1.43
Achievement (A)	2654.95	2	1327.48	11.91*
R x A	101.26	4	25.31	0.23
Error	17280.00	155	111.48	
Total	20355.00	163		

* $p<.01$

Using the method of Scheffé (Miller, 1966) to construct confidence intervals for contrasts between means, it was found that the mean IQ of the high achievement group differed significantly from the average mean IQ of the middle and low groups at the .05 level. No other significant contrasts were found. Thus, those students whose achievement test scores placed them more than .5 standard deviations above the mean for the sample scored significantly higher on the CTMM than did the rest of the group. No similar effect was found for rating.

Does Teacher Rating Predict IQ as Well for Underachieving Students as for Achieving Students?

The significant contrast between the mean IQ for the high achievement group and the mean IQ for the rest of the sample prompted an inquiry into the relative efficacy of teacher ratings for underachievers and achievers. The problem of locating underachieving gifted children is a perennial one, and it is rendered especially difficult in districts and cities, such as New York City, where group IQ tests are proscribed or discouraged. It is conceivable, therefore, that teacher ratings may aid in the identification or screening of gifted underachievers.

Using the three achievement groups composed for the analysis of variance, the predictive power of the teacher ratings was compared for the high and low achievement groups. The high achieving group (n=75) consisted of those who scored in the top five percent compared to the national norms for their grade. The mean IQ for this group was 128.2 which placed it in the top three percent of the population. Obviously, this group was achieving up to the high potential suggested for it by the IQ test. The Pearson Product-Moment correlation between teacher rating and IQ for group was .03 and was not statistically significant. Thus, for high achievers rating was not a good predictor of IQ.

The low achievement group (n=34) had a mean IQ of 118.7, a score at about the 90th percentile in the population. The mean achievement test score for this group was only at the 58th percentile, far below what would be expected based upon the potential defined by the IQ test. For these students, the correlation between rating and IQ was .27 (p<.062). Thus, for this group, rating was positively related to IQ, whereas this was not the case for the high achievers. Teacher rating, therefore, may be of differential value depending upon whether the target group is composed of underachievers or not.

DISCUSSION

Based upon the results of this study, teacher ratings appear to have a great deal more utility as devices for the screening or identification of gifted school children than has generally been ascribed to them. Consistent significant positive correlations between ratings and IQ were found, correlations that were strengthened somewhat when ratings over two years were used as predictors.

Moreover, these ratings were shown to have a high degree of efficiency, a finding that contradicts conventional wisdom. These results, in conjunction with the discovery of high stability for the ratings over two years and two sets of teachers, point to a tool of acceptable validity and reliability for the screening and identification of the gifted, especially as more traditional devices are discarded.

The use of the group IQ test has been prohibited for the purposes of student classification in some areas. If giftedness is defined in terms of intellectual ability as revealed psychometrically, teacher rating appears to be as efficacious a screening device as is available to fill the gap left by the demise of the group test.

Teacher ratings were more predictive of high intellectual ability for girls than for boys, a result indicating a possible need for separate scales for use with males and females. The question of whether the sex of the rater had an effect upon the ratings was not investigated due to a paucity of male teachers. This is an issue worthy of further study.

The finding that teacher ratings were good predictors of intellectual aptitude for underachieving gifted children is one that also demands further investigation, especially in light of recent emphases upon the location of underprivileged gifted students. It also underscores the value of teacher ratings as opposed to achievement tests in locating the gifted, since quite obviously the latter will not alert one to the existence of a gifted child who is working below his potential, whereas a teacher is unlikely to overlook a child who is a high achiever.

Clearly, teachers are in a position to observe certain behavioral correlates of intellectual giftedness in their day-to-day interactions with children. That they do so with less than perfectly valid results is undeniable and to be expected when the multiplicity of potential interpersonal mediating variables as well as the typical vagueness of the task are considered. Happily, however, there is some evidence to suggest that teachers may not be as imperceptive as has been previously asserted.

The fact that teachers are not able to make accurate global assessments of children's intelligence upon demand, assessments which compare favorably with results obtained from complex psychometric instruments which have undergone 60 years of research and development, should not be surprising. Yet, this is what they have been required to do in many studies in which *non-directive* rating scales have been used. When presented with a *directive* checklist of behavioral correlates of giftedness, these seemingly imperceptive teachers turn in a creditable performance as identifiers. This study shows that differential results can be obtained from teacher ratings. But it also shows that these ratings are a potential source of information and knowledge about who may be gifted.

APPENDIX A

TEACHER RATING SCALE USED BY MIDDLETOWN, NEW JERSEY, PUBLIC SCHOOLS FOR IDENTIFYING GIFTED STUDENTS

Indicate by checking "Frequently," "Occasionally," or "Never" how often the student exhibits the following behaviors:

A.

1. Is intuitive; understands with little or no apparent effort

2. Has rapid insight into cause and effect relationships

3. Has a ready grasp of underlying principles and can make valid generalizations with ease

4. Reasons things out independently

5. Generates a large number of ideas or solutions to problems using imaginative methods

B.

6. Has an unusually advanced oral, written, and/or reading vocabulary

7. Reads a great deal, usually well beyond grade level

8. Has quick mastery and recall of factual information

9. Possesses a large fund of information in a variety of areas

C.

10. Uses imagination ("I wonder what would happen if . . . ?"); manipulates ideas (i.e., changes or elaborates upon them)

11. Tends to show more than usual interest in ethical values and broad philosophical issues

12. Adapts readily to new situations; is flexible in thought and action

13. Is willing to take a chance on an unusual question, answer, or activity; enjoys a challenge

14. Shows a great deal of curiosity about many things

15. Possesses unusual depth and breadth of knowledge about a specific area, namely —————————

Scoring: Every item checked "Frequently" was awarded three points, every item checked "Occasionally" one point. Point total in Part A was multiplied by three; point total in Part B was multiplied by two; point total in Part C was left as is. Point totals were summed over the three parts to arrive at the total rating score.

BRAVE NEW WORLD OF INTELLIGENCE TESTING

BY BERKELEY RICE

Researchers are experimenting with measurements of social intelligence, coping skill, cognitive style, learning potential, audiovisual perception, and electrical responses of the brain. Though still on the drawing boards, the tests promise to change the way we think about intelligence.

In the current turmoil over intelligence testing, critics are calling for ways to measure mental ability that will be fairer, more precise, and more relevant to real life than those now in use. Fortunately, these demands come at a time when research into intelligence and its measurement has produced dozens of innovative approaches. Future test-takers, for example, may be:

☐ listening to clicks in earphones while electrodes taped to their temples send brain responses to be analyzed by a computer;

☐ held, as infants, by their parents while they watch toy cars roll down a ramp and—sometimes—knock over toy dolls;

☐ tested on mental abilities that may be influenced by watching television regularly;

☐ describing whether or not they prepare their own lunch, and relating how many pupils in their class they know by name;

☐ deciding, at age three-and-a-half, how they would respond if they were in a game with three children and only two wanted to play.

Definitions of intelligence have eluded social scientists since at least 1921, when the *Journal of Educational Psychology* boldly asked a symposium of "leading investigators" to define the concept. The vigorous debate that ensued produced no agreement, prompting psychologist Edwin Boring's ironic conclusion that intelligence is merely "the capacity to do well in an intelligence test."

More than half a century of research later, agreement scarcely seems closer. When I asked researchers in the field to tell me about new tests of intelligence, they often replied, "What do you mean by intelligence?" Obviously, I wasn't sure. In fact, that's exactly why I was calling. But years of research into increasingly numerous and narrow categories of mental ability seem to have made experts touchy about talking to laymen who don't know the difference between Poe's raven and Raven's Progressive Matrices.

The new approaches are alternatives to the dominant trend in cognitive psychology in the past few decades: the attempt to break into separate mental abilities what previously was thought of simply as general intelligence, as measured by an IQ score or some other single measure. Known as "factor analysis," this research produced various lists of mental abilities, as well as models of how they fit together. The abilities include verbal fluency, spatial perception, analogical reasoning (reasoning by analogy), series and sequence manipulation, memory, and creativity. Their number threatens to reach unmanageable proportions. For example, a commonly used system involves tests of 23 supposedly distinct factors, although many experts find the distinctions among them hazy.

An increasingly important alternative is called "process analysis" or "componential analysis." Including such influential researchers as Robert Sternberg of Yale, this school attempts to obtain distinct measures of the separate steps in the reasoning process and how different people handle them. (See "Stalking the IQ Quark," page 42.) But others fear that process analysis also runs the risk of telling us more and more about smaller and smaller steps in the reasoning process until the information becomes practically unusable. "I don't think Sternberg's work will pay off for years," says William Turnbull, a psychologist who is president of Educational Testing Service. "It's been great for psychological understanding about the way the mind works, but not for real-world application."

Some psychologists who follow cognitive research doubt the eventual utility of either factor-analysis or process-analysis theories, because both postulate models of intelligence and then treat the various components and

"Brave New World of Intelligence Testing," by B. Rice, *Psychology Today*, Vol. 13, No. 4, September 1979. ©1979 by Ziff-Davis Publishing Company. All rights reserved.

A new computerized brain-potential test uses EEG readings and 30 other measures of electrical activity.

processes of their models as though their reality were well established. Ulric Neisser, a cognitive psychologist at Cornell, admits that "cognitive research may indeed be successful in identifying the processes, and such research is certainly worth pursuing." But he feels that "we must be wary of believing that it will enable us to define intelligence itself. Otherwise, we may find ourselves acting out a new version of Boring's scenario in the year 2000, when someone defines intelligence as what the models model."

What follows is a highly selective field report on some of the most interesting and promising new approaches to assessing intelligence. Some have already lead to actual tests; some remain in the experimental stages of research. Together, they promise to broaden and alter the way we think about the concept of intelligence.

Neurometrics

For many years, researchers have been measuring the electrical activity of the brain to test the extent of retardation or brain damage in children. But new techniques of measuring the brain's "evoked potential" now promise to develop a uniquely accurate test. Edward Beck, a psychologist who is one of the pioneers in evoked-potential research, describes the results of this test as "a fingerprint of the brain."

The basic technique consists of monitoring brain activity with an electroencephalograph, or EEG, to measure the brain's response to such sensory stimuli as sounds or flashes of light. Recent advances in computer technology have enabled neurophysiologists to sort out the minute changes that occur when a repeated stimulus suddenly stops or fails to continue in a predictable pattern. For example, a loud click normally followed by a soft one might suddenly be followed by another loud one, or by si-

lence. The brain gradually disregards a regular sequence as it loses its novelty. The interruption, however, recaptures the brain's attention until the sequence returns to the normal pattern. The brain's response to such interruptions, or its evoked potential, gives a distinct measure that can be statistically compared with the response and IQ data of normal children (see "Brain Potentials: Signaling Our Inner Thoughts," by Richard Restak, *Psychology Today*, March 1979).

The Brain Research Laboratories at New York University Medical Center, under neuroscientist E. Roy John, recently developed a sophisticated "Quantitative Electrophysiological Battery," which includes not only EEG readings, but about 30 other measures of the brain's electrical activity as well. The computerized brain diagnoses might someday be used for testing the intelligence potential of schoolchildren. It could be particularly useful for those too young to take written exams, or those whose poor command of English or late verbal development hinders their performance on written or oral tests.

The new brain-potential techniques have limits as measures of intelligence, however. They can only assess a modest range of mental abilities, like reaction speed. And their accuracy thus far has been confirmed largely by correlation with IQ scores, whose own validity is open to considerable debate. While some psychologists have hailed the measurement of evoked potential as a major breakthrough, others remain dubious.

A similar new method uses heart and other muscle responses to measure mental processes in infants. Like evoked-potential work, it was developed initially for use with the handicapped. Richard Kearsley, a pediatrician and developmental psychologist who is codirector of the Center for Behavioral Pediatrics and Infant Devel-

opment at Boston's New England Medical Center, came up with the method because he was dissatisfied with existing tests of infant intelligence. He describes them as "woefully inadequate to assess the cognitive status of infants and young children in general, and the mental abilities of handicapped children in particular." Most of the standard tests rely largely on measures of neuromotor skills that are easy to test—such as stacking blocks—and that are presumed to develop parallel to mental abilities.

But studies have accumulated that show these skills to be inaccurate predictors of later intellectual competence. In fact, as Kearsley has discovered in his own studies, in physically handicapped children motor and mental abilities can develop independent of one another. When such children score poorly on conventional infant-intelligence tests, they frequently are labeled mentally as well as physically retarded. This often puts an end to serious attempts at their education.

Kearsley tests children from three months to three years old. To skirt biases introduced by their neuromotor handicaps, Kearsley has the children sit—often on a parent's lap—in a darkened room resembling a puppet theater. Electrocardiogram leads attached to the child's chest feed into a cardiotachometer that records changes in the heartbeat during the test. Meanwhile, two hidden observers watch and record the child's facial and physical responses. The 45-minute test centers on three auditory and two visual episodes, each lasting about four minutes, and similar in principle to the interrupted stimuli used in measuring evoked brain potential.

In one of Kearsley's episodes, a small car rolls down a ramp and knocks over a styrofoam doll. After four seconds, the child sees a hand stand the doll up and then roll the car back up the ramp. The sequence is re-

A child's cardiac response to an interrupted routine provides a limited measure of mental ability.

peated six times, by which point the child has had an opportunity to build up a reasonable expectation about the event's predictability. In the seventh trial, when the car rolls down the ramp and hits the doll, the doll does not fall over, thereby violating the child's expectation. After two more trials in which the doll remains standing, the sequence returns to the original pattern for the last few trials.

While individual children differ to some extent, the cardiac response and behavior pattern usually indicate a child's reaction when the car/doll sequence is interrupted, and again when it returns to "normal." In addition to registering a slight speedup in heart rate, for example, a child might frown when the doll remains standing, and smile when it finally falls down again. The speed with which the child responds to such changes in routine, Kearsley believes, provides a relatively uncontaminated measure of mental ability. Although limited in scope, Kearsley thinks such tests promise a way to measure intelligence unbiased by physical handicaps or social, economic, and cultural background.

Testing the Technological Generation

The steady decline in the scores of students taking the College Board's Scholastic Aptitude Tests (SATs) has prompted numerous unproven explanations. The drop may in part be due to lower academic standards in public schools, or to increasing numbers of college applicants from a "broader"

(read "lower socioeconomic status") range of society. But many educators point to television as the cause, arguing that the decline in scores parallels the passage through college age of this country's first TV generation.

While social critics bewail this situation, a number of psychologists talk seriously about a new "visual" generation growing up not only with television but also with electronic toys, hand calculators, home computers, and audiovisual aids, who are learning to receive and process information differently from those reared in the print age. If true, this theory could mean that testing a visually oriented generation with tests like the SAT that have been designed for print-oriented people, puts them at an unfair disadvantage.

At a jammed symposium called "Intelligence Testing in the Year 2000" held recently by the American Education Research Association, John Horn, a cognitive psychologist at the University of Denver, said that the influence of television and computers may change the distribution of mental abilities in the population, as new methods of receiving and processing information require increasing reliance on visual, auditory, and manual aspects of intelligence. "Do you program the computer," Horn wonders, "or does the computer program you?" Other psychologists look forward with enthusiasm to the use of audiovisual testing ("cinepsychometrics"), because the method can deal with skills like listening and perception that are not easily measured by the

standard paper- and-pencil tests.

Many experts dismiss the idea of the "visual" generation with a disdain bordering on that they reserve for television programming. Solid evidence on both sides of the debate has been meager. But testing for skills related to computers will undoubtedly seem more reasonable as computer technology becomes increasingly common in everyday life. Harvard's newly revised curriculum will now require all undergraduates to demonstrate proficiency in the use of computers. The U.S. Navy has developed a computerized Graphic Information Processing (GRIP) battery of tests in which trainees who are destined for electronic communications assignments can demonstrate specific abilities such as the visual processing of information or the tracking of a target on a radar screen.

Countering Cultural Bias

Generations of black, Chicano, and other minority children have been measured by intelligence tests that seem to assume everyone grows up exposed to the same white middle-class culture. Similarly, any written test in English discriminates against those for whom English is a second language, or against black children whose normal "street English" differs markedly from that customarily used in middle-class society, in schools, and in intelligence tests. The tests are used to predict school performance, but minority-group children generally score lower than they might on a more neu-

The U.S. Navy's GRIP battery of tests measures visual abilities like tracking a target on a radar screen.

Having given up on "culture free" tests, researchers are coming up with "culture adjusted" tests like SOMPA.

tral, or "culture-free" test.

The quest for freedom from cultural bias has proven as troublesome in intelligence testing as it has in civil rights. The major problem with the culture-free tests developed so far is how to evaluate their accuracy. Most have been measured against IQ scores, which completes an absurd circle, since no one has yet developed a culture-free IQ test.

The frustration met by those who have tried to come up with culture-free tests has given rise to an entirely different quest—for the "culture specific" test, aimed at measuring the special skills of minority cultures. One attempt is BITCH, the "Black Intelligence Test of Cultural Homogeneity," a vocabulary test that uses black street slang like "dig it." But while black children do score higher on BITCH than on standard tests, many educators question its value as a meaningful test of intelligence.

Diane Ravitch, an educational historian at Teachers College, Columbia University, readily admits that intelligence tests are biased to the extent they depend on knowledge of a particular language. But she fears that tests like BITCH stress factors that are not relevant to educating children for most significant roles in U.S. society. "Language is part of a culture," she points out, "and schools are expected to teach the English language to the children who are going to be part of an English-speaking culture." John Horn adds, "In our society, intelligence must involve good reasoning with the contents of our culture. If this is lacking, then a vital component of intelligence is lacking."

Other attempts to make testing fairer to people from minority cultures have involved "renorming" data on traditional standardized tests to create separate statistical profiles for minority groups from which "adjusted" scores can be derived. The best-known

attempt at such cultural adjustment is Jane Mercer's "System of Multicultural Pluralistic Assessment," known as SOMPA.

A sociologist at the University of California at Riverside, Mercer has developed an interlocking battery of measures for children from five to 11 years old:

☐ A Wechsler IQ test gives a measure of the child's mental ability within the "dominant" school culture.

☐ In a one-hour interview with the child's parent, the examiner fills out a complete health history and a "sociocultural inventory" of the family's background: "How many persons live in the household? What was the highest grade in school that you [the mother or father] completed?" An "adaptive-behavior inventory" taps the child's nonacademic performance in school, at home, and in the neighborhood: "How many pupils in her class does she know by name? Does she prepare her own lunch?"

☐ A complete medical exam gives details on the child's physical condition, manual dexterity, motor skill, visual and auditory ability—all of which, if impaired, might affect school and test performance.

Nine-year-old Bernice, for example, is a black child who ranks at the bottom of her school population in academic performance. Her score of only 68 on the Wechsler IQ test would make her eligible for placement in a class for the mentally retarded. But her scores on the SOMPA sociocultural scale reflect her impoverished cultural background in a family living on welfare in an urban ghetto. Compared with other children from similar backgrounds, her IQ score of 68 is only 9 points below the mean for that group—not a significant difference. Her scores on the adaptive-behavior inventory show that for her age, she is unusually capable of taking care of herself and getting along in her com-

munity. Her estimated learning potential, or "adjusted IQ," of 89 means she belongs not in a class for the retarded but in a regular class that takes her background into account.

Advocates of SOMPA call it the first and only nondiscriminatory assessment battery. Because of a 1977 civil rights law requiring states to use nondiscriminatory testing in the schools, SOMPA has appeared on the market at an opportune time. The states of California and Louisiana have already adopted it for determining student placement in special-education programs, and others are likely to follow. More than 3,000 school psychologists and guidance counselors have already taken one of Mercer's $150 workshops on how to administer the system.

While SOMPA seems like a promising and comprehensive way to measure mental ability among minority-group children, its introduction into the California school system has provoked a major controversy. Critics express outrage at the fact that the Psychological Corporation actively sold the test battery for more than a year before publishing the technical manual containing validity and reliability studies. Such studies normally accompany the release of a new test, and without them, no one can really judge its value. Some black psychologists reject SOMPA because it uses the Wechsler IQ test, which they consider too biased to be used even as a baseline measure.

In addition, by emphasizing potential rather than current ability, SOMPA may create unreasonable expectations among parents and teachers, who must still contend with present reality. SOMPA could also leave children who really do need special educational help in classes where overburdened teachers will not be able to give them the attention they need.

Mercer dismisses most of her critics as backward and narrow-minded.

One important index of "social intelligence" is knowing when to be assertive and when not to.

"People in the universities have tremendous emotional and intellectual investments in IQ and intelligence tests," she told me. "They see my work as a threat to the whole field of psychometrics. For 75 years, they have been confusing ignorance with stupidity. It's about time they stopped."

Social Intelligence

The adaptive-behavior inventory developed by Jane Mercer is typical of a growing number of attempts to measure what, for lack of a better phrase, can only be called social intelligence or social competence. However it is defined, social intelligence has attracted the attention of a growing number of researchers in recent years. One reason is that many psychologists, educators, and parents have begun to wonder about the relevance of most traditional measures of intelligence to the demands of everyday reality. Numerous studies, most recently Christopher Jencks's (see "Who Gets Ahead in America," *Psychology Today*, July 1979), have found only slight correlations between IQ scores in school and successful performance in later life. Since so much of life involves getting along with other people, interpersonal skills may be just as crucial for testing as spatial ability or analogical reasoning.

Researchers have identified a number of useful coping skills for children: getting attention from adults and peers; using other people as resources; expressing affection and hostility; recognizing these emotions in other people; being willing to accept substitutes for things they want; perceiving awkward or embarrassing situations; being sensitive to verbal and facial expressions.

As with more conventional forms of intelligence, defining such traits and skills is difficult. For instance, try distinguishing—intelligently—between "coping" and "adapting." One federally funded conference amassed a bewildering total of 29 different indicators of social competence, each of which required lengthy debate and refinement. Even worse, traits like assertiveness or independence that might be appropriate in one situation would be inappropriate and even counterproductive in another. In fact, one index of social intelligence is knowing when to use certain skills and when not to. Measurement with any degree of precision presents awesome problems, not to mention the problems of evaluating what is measured.

At Educational Testing Service (ETS) headquarters in Princeton, New Jersey, research psychologists Irving Sigel and Ann McGillicuddy-DeLisi have been asking three-and-a-half-year-olds what they would do during a game if there are three children and only two want to play. The researchers ask groups of children how they would solve the problem, whether they think their initial strategy would work, and what their fallback strategy would be.

"I would play his game if he would play mine," said one child. "If he won't play," said another, "I'll have to hit him." Overall, the research has shown that girls are more optimistic than boys in predicting that their strategies will succeed. But if their first strategies fail, the girls tend to give up, rather than develop alternatives. When boys' civilized requests fail, they are more likely to adopt aggressive strategies like hitting.

In another pilot test of three-year-olds' interpersonal relationships, the researchers asked questions about friendship: "Are you still friends if your friend is playing with someone else?" "Are you still friends if your friend hits you?" In this test, girls are more willing to say they would end friendships than boys, particularly if the friend hits them. While their research is still tentative, Sigel and McGillicuddy-DeLisi have discovered that children's social behavior tends to reflect not only sex, but family structure and parental beliefs as well.

Further along the age spectrum, ETS researchers are working on tests of interpersonal skills that might become part of exams for professional schools. A prototypical test for medical school students measures "human dimensions" such as sensitivity using simulated patient interviews and medical history-taking. Another research group is exploring the use of a test for business school students in which the students would respond as "supervisors" to videotaped "employees" who present problems like requests for raises or promotions. The students' responses—spoken into a tape recorder—would test both their knowledge of what to do and their ability to do it.

Cognitive Styles

Most of us do better on tests of certain mental abilities than of others, and not necessarily because we are more intelligent. Over the past two decades, researchers have discovered that people tend to have distinctive and relatively consistent patterns of thinking, perceiving, and problem-solving. These tendencies, known to researchers as "cognitive styles," include such dimensions as:

☐ *Convergent versus Divergent.* Convergent thinkers tend to reach logical conclusions based on conventional reasoning, and generally do well in scientific activities. Divergent thinkers tend to be more creative, coming up with original and novel responses that can lead them into artistic careers. Convergent minds do better on multiple-choice tests that require finding one correct answer; divergent minds are better suited to open-ended questions that allow a number of alternative possibilities.

☐ *Field Independent versus Field*

The ideal way to measure intelligence would be to combine separate dimensional ratings into one overall index.

Dependent. Some people characteristically concentrate on the big picture, others on the internal details. Researchers in cognitive styles call the first type "field independent," because they tend to think independently of the surrounding context or "field." They, too, are generally more capable at tasks requiring logical ability, and may be somewhat impersonal and insensitive to social surroundings. People of the opposite type, called "field dependent," tend to be less analytical, more socially perceptive, and more subject to external influence. Psychologists use the "Embedded Figures Test" to differentiate the two types, because it measures the visual ability to distinguish figures from similarly textured backgrounds.

Some cultures seem to encourage one style more than the other. For example, apparently because their present culture values social interaction more highly than analytical ability, Mexican-American children tend to be more field-dependent than Americans. In Western cultures, boys tend to be more field-independent than girls.

☐ *Scanning versus Focusing.* Scanners tend to go meticulously through all the details of a situation—including incidental ones—with uniform awareness. Focusers tend to fix their attention on only a few key details, ignoring peripheral cues that occasionally may be important. If all relevant cues are immediately perceptible, however, focusers will do well. To discriminate between scanners and focusers, researchers use written descriptions or videotaped portrayals of complex social situations in which one must evaluate a variety of disparate details in order to form a correct impression of the situation.

☐ *Right Brain versus Left Brain.* Nearly every literate person must be familiar, if not bored, with the "split brain" fad that has dominated much recent writing in popular psychology.

According to an oversimplified version of brain "lateralization" theory, each half or "hemisphere" of the brain is responsible for certain mental abilities, the left side generally handling the logical and verbal functions, the right side taking most responsibility for intuitive, emotional, and spatial abilities. While the distinctions are only relative, many people tend to be predominantly one-sided in their responses to a variety of problems and situations. For example, writing a letter, reading a poem, or fixing a watch seem to rely more on left-brain activity, while the right brain is generally more active in humming a tune or drawing a picture.

☐ *Masculine versus Feminine.* Wary of sexism, researchers are nevertheless finding differences in cognitive styles between men and women. These may be due in part to child-rearing and culture, and in part to differences in brain-hemisphere dominance. Whatever the cause, men tend to have better spatial ability, women better verbal ability. Women seem better able to focus attention on one particular task, while men perform better on tasks requiring simultaneous use of more than one mental skill. These differences in cognitive abilities tend to increase as children mature into adulthood, although at all ages, the differences are a matter of degree, and often slight.

Cognitive styles influence most human activites, including social behavior, and are linked closely to our personalities. As such, they are not easily modified by training, unlike specific abilities such as memory. But people who become aware of their own cognitive styles may be able to learn to use problem-solving strategies—and pick careers—that capitalize on personal style, or to try less congenial strategies that would be more effective for a particular task. Standard tests of verbal and mathematical abilities might in-

clude items specifically designed for people with various cognitive styles; specific tests measuring styles alone might be useful in career guidance.

For all the promise of this field, few definitive tests that reveal differences among people on the basis of their cognitive styles exist as yet. The principal reason is that the styles that have been identified thus far overlap, and are not predictable enough to warrant solid judgments about their presence.

Learning Potential

All intelligence tests are implicit measures of potential for learning, but one branch of psychometrics has appropriated the term "learning potential" for the capacity measured by a particular kind of test. The approach involves giving children unfamiliar problems and measuring the number of "prompts" or the amount of coaching the children need before they can solve them.

In the Soviet Union, where standardized testing has never been as popular as it is in the U.S., much of this research is based on the work of L. S. Vygotsky, who conceives of the "zone of potential development" as the difference between a child's actual or baseline performance on a standardized intelligence test and the degree of competence the same child could achieve on the same test with proper training. The zone is measured by the number of prompts a child needs to solve problems of various degrees of difficulty. Children who are learning disabled generally need fewer prompts to achieve satisfactory performance than do brain damaged or truly retarded children.

The best-known researcher in the field of learning potential is Reuven Feuerstein, an Israeli clinical psychologist. Feuerstein has developed a test-teach-test method for children aged 12 and older using several relatively

Tests of cognitive styles might help people pick careers that capitalize on their usual way of thinking.

culture-free measures of nonverbal ability:

□ Raven's Progressive Matrices, generally considered one of the better tests of general intelligence, which require the completion of matrices (like tic-tac-toe boards) in which all but one square is already filled in according to a certain sequence or pattern.

□ The Organization of Dots test, which reveals the child's ability to draw lines between dots that define geometric shapes, within a mass of other dots.

□ The Stencil Design Test, which presents a drawing of a design constructed by superimposing two or more stencils. The child looks at a range of separate stencil shapes, and must identify the stencils used.

In Feuerstein's technique, called the "Learning Potential Assessment Device," the examiner first administers a pretest to achieve a baseline score, and then conducts a teaching session on the principles and skills involved in the tests. A final test on a series of increasingly difficult tasks gives a measure of the child's learning potential, or "modifiability." For future remedial work, the examiner also tries to isolate particular cognitive processes that cause the most difficulty.

"Individualized" Testing

Tests that diagnose the problems that impede learning are becoming more common as many educators call for less use of tests for the purpose of comparing and sorting students. At the Educational Development Center in Boston, an independent institute devoted to innovative teaching methods, a group of researchers has designed an assessment battery for grades one to six called "Tests of Reasonable Quantitative Understanding of the Environment," or TORQUE. Although TORQUE measures only quantitative

abilities, such as computation, estimation, and measurement, project members hope to be able to adapt their approach to language and social science tests as well.

TORQUE probes each ability with a variety of different contexts and formats, such as games and puzzles, thereby giving students a wide range of opportunity to demonstrate each skill. By encouraging open discussion between examinee and examiner about the test items, TORQUE intentionally blurs the line between testing and instruction. The tests are not timed, because they are designed to help the teacher find out how well a student can perform the tasks, not how fast. Students correct their own tests, thereby avoiding the aura of secrecy common to traditional testing. The drawback, of course, is that such one-to-one testing is far more expensive than standardized group testing.

Tailoring standardized tests to individuals and analyzing individual responses more sensitively than is now possible may become increasingly feasible with computers. Applicants for drivers' licenses in some parts of New York, California, and Washington, D.C., are punching answers to the written part of their test into computers. Researchers predict that expanded use of microprocessors and computers will enable psychometricians to develop "response-contingent" tests in which the correctness of one answer will determine which of several possible easier or harder questions appears next, a principle used in programmed instruction. Multilevel or "flexilevel" computerized exams could start off with a "locator" test to determine a student's approximate level of ability, and then select the proper main test for that level. This would help prevent the boredom that often afflicts bright students during traditional testing and the frustration that troubles slow

ones. Computerized multiple-choice tests could allow students to assign different values or degrees of correctness to several possible answers. The computer could also handle the data needed to give partial credit on second-best choices, choices that current scoring merely counts as wrong.

John Horn has predicted that technology will soon enable schools to record students' reaction times and responses. Such advances, says Horn, "hold promise for unlocking new understandings of human abilities."

While people of goodwill may differ about the purposes of testing intelligence, everyone doing research in the field recognizes that the task remains exceedingly complex. As Sam Messick, the psychologist who is head of research at ETS, told me recently, "Diagnosing each ability separately doesn't help much, because life doesn't present challenges to only one ability at a time. Most tasks require several different abilities simultaneously. People can have very high scores on individual abilities, but that's not enough."

"The ideal way to measure intelligence," says Cornell's Ulric Neisser, "would be to combine all the relevant dimensional measurements into one overall index. In practice, however, this ideal is unattainable: many of the relevant dimensions cannot be measured in any standard way." As examples, Neisser lists common sense, wit, creativity, lack of bias, sensitivity to one's own and others' limitations, openness to experience, and intellectual independence.

Even making such lists can lead to confusion and absurdity. For example, the group of experts that tried to identify the abilities that contribute to social competence finally agreed that one essential ingredient had to be "cognitive ability," or what most of us still refer to as intelligence.

EXTENDING THE DEFINABLE GIFTED:

PSYCHIC CHILDREN

by Mary Meeker, Ed.D.
President of S.O.I. Institute, California

Researchers have found that about 1/3rd of *identified* gifted children are creative; about 1/3rd are academically talented; about 1/3rd are leaders (school and social). (Meeker, M., 1966) As is the custom with definitions of any kind, there is discord among experts. We have struggled with the term gifted; we have struggled with the definition of creative. There is less struggle with the definition of leadership since this is an easily observed behavior. We are still struggling with the term talented and this will continue until we resolve the traditional issue of the concept that an IQ score defines giftedness. Educators who have slipped away from the traditional concept of giftedness know and can document that some children who do not score at 132 or higher on a test of intelligence are indeed talented and some are gifted in particular SOI dimensions. And educators who use the SOI analyses of a Binet can certainly document and validate such findings with an SOI (Structure of Intellect) profile of the child's intellectual pattern.

So, as if we do not already have enough problems, for me to suggest that some small portion of the 2% of gifted children are psychic, and that some unknown percentage of children are psychic and are therefore gifted in an as yet unidentifiable dimension, adds another burden to our 'definition' of giftedness.

Among the 69 identified gifted students I have been following since 1962, and among the 1/3rd of that group who are also identified as creative, I have gathered case histories which include such information as the following:

GIRL A: Her mother reported that on two occasions the girl had dreams which were unsettling and so she told them to her mother. One dream centered around a friend of the mother's of whom the girl, 13, was very fond. In the dream the young woman and her husband died. One week later the wife was diagnosed as having cancer and was given six months to live; a month later the man was found to have brain cancer. The couple died within one week of each other. In psychic terminology such dreams (and not all all are so negative) are labelled pre-cognitive dreams, for the dreams seem to foretell reality. An inquiry later to see whether the girl continued to have pre-cognitive dreams proved futile. The girl refused to discuss dreams and simply reported that she did not remember her dreams' any more. This might be interpreted as selective forgetting. (IQ 181; now involved in a doctoral program in languages.)

GIRL B: Mother reported this incident: "She was sitting in her bed and playing. She was around two years of age. She suddenly said as though in a moment of comradeship with me as I was working in the room, 'You know, mama, my father is not my real father and my sisters are not my real sisters. I come from far away and and that is where my real father is and I have many sisters there.' She did not say anything about her real or other mother nor did she seem at all surprised that she could remember other people, if indeed she did." This child also played alone most of the time and often ascribed personalities to her toys. She did not have imaginary playmates, instead her fantasies were so real that she did imagine herself to be a cat and for months wanted to drink her milk from the bowl on the floor. She meowed and aptly copied kitten mannerisms such as licking paws, etc. She had never been around cats at all. She read at 18 months and understood numbers at 19 months, repeated the pledge of allegiance at 2 years by heart, drew and cut out tiny figures by 2 1/2. (IQ 219) She had unusual sensitivity to people and people's thoughts. The mother reports that she never thought of the youngster as psychic although she feels the child can 'read' other people's faces unusually well. This is the heightened awareness, of course, that many psychics admit to and cultivate.

There have been many instances reported by children in the study where they 'knew' something was going to happen, both good and bad, before it actually did. They say this matter of factly as though everyone had the same ability to 'know'.

BOY A: A sophomore in high school, he discussed with me that he always saw and always had seen colors (auras) around people. When asked what colors and how far they extended he replied, different colors and different distances. He did not attribute any significance to the colors nor did they give him any other information. He did say he had discussed this with his chemistry teacher and his chemistry teacher seemed to feel that many children had the same ability — it was something people just did not talk about. After this conversation I searched out some books on auras. They were few, but Dr. Patricia Diegele's book is available from her in Honolulu or from Box 957, West Sacramento, CA 95691. It seems that auras change in color and size, but that in and of themselves they are signifiers of the soul's evolvement. This youngster (IQ 154) had such severe problems with his relationship with his father that he dropped out of school and did not continue his education. As is often the case, the gifted potential is lost when home conditions and interpersonal relations are too negative.

Girl C reported to her mother that only her black and white dreams came true. It is obvious that we know little about the population of psychic children. We do not really know how 'psychic' is defined in children. We do not know the approximate percent of gifted who may be psychic; nor do we know the percent of children, non-gifted, non-creative, who are also psyhic. In surveying the field of gifted research, one would have to acknowledge that there is no information to document additional gifts of 'knowing'. Nevertheless, many gifted children and adults report having received inspirations, or even whole and complete poems and stories. We have tended to think of these children as being 'creative'. Psychologists know, as do neurologists, that there is no explanation for the process we call thinking, or ideas. How it really happens in the brain is a mystery; even the ability to use language to express thought, as well as the ability to have thoughts is not directly known.

So when we discuss creativity, creative inspiration, then we are labelling behaviors which are observable, not necessarily explaining them.

For assessing the larger realm of defined creativity* I selected characteristics which are personality descriptors rather than product descriptors. I think this is more necessary when we discuss children because children are in the process of being creative and what is creative for the child may not be a creative product judged by adults to be creative. For example, the first time a child rhymes moon and June, that is for him creative production. It is not creative for the adult.

The inspiration, or the new awareness is what is important. Thus in the Meeker Creativity Scale* the behavioral discriminators to be rated are:

ACUTE SENSITIVITY TO PROBLEMS, PEOPLE, PERCEPTUAL STIMULI (hearing, seeing)
High Originality
ACUTE FLUENCY MOTOR AND IDEA
Ability to organize, to abstract and to synthesize

Any of the above, and they are only a few of the behaviors to be rated in the scale, fall in the RECEPTION BLOCK OF ABILITIES rather than in Memory Evaluation, Convergent Production. That is, if we were to cycle the intellectual processes in handling information, we can look upon psychic abilities as an extension of divergent production, or creativity in this manner:

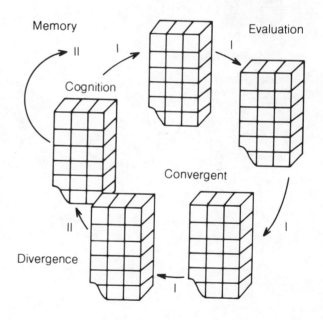

Thus the heightened sensitivity in awareness either auditory (clairaudient) or visual (clairvoyant) may be a second level in the spiral of intelligence in which the circle from divergent or creativity processes further enhance the ability to cognize at a more keen level. Two investigators, Ralph Blum and his wife, are at present writing a book for parents of psychic children. They are concerned with documentation. If increased documentation is a fact, then we need to develop a schema for describing the various psychic descriptors and begin to gain some notion of the numbers of children fitting these descriptors. We should not leave to chance this documentation of extensions of the human development.

PROGRAM EXAMPLES

Programs for the gifted are found in all parts of the country, in many subject fields and socially-valued pursuits, and for children and youth of several age levels. What seems to be missing, however, is even one example of an elementary or secondary program which can be accurately described as comprehensive in that it serves several kinds of talents at several age levels.

A welcome feature of existing programs is that they may be found in public and private schools, on colleges and univer-sitites, and being offered by community-based organiza-tions. Thus many patterns of organization and sources of support are being used.

This section offers not only sample programs, but some of

the potential difficulties one encounters in running them. For those not able to begin such comprehensive projects, a number of articles are included that focus on specific techniques and shared activities that may be effectively used in the classroom.

One of the options for schools that are near Universities is to send the gifted students out for special classes. "A Unique Learning Opportunity for Talented High School Seniors" describes a program based on this experience. Another option is acceleration. Debate often centers around the maturity of the student and their "loss" over not being able to share high school with their peers. The focus beginning on page 142, "Student Speak Out" lets the students of accelerated programs speak for themselves.

THE CATSKILLS SATURDAY SEMINARS UPDATED

Robert M. Porter
State University College, Oneconta, N.Y.

"Saturday is the day I looked forward to more than any other," said seventeen year old Evelyn Fairbairn, president of the Margaretville (New York) Central School Student Association. Singer in the school chorus and fine flutist, she was a member of the first mathematics seminar in a then unique program to provide intellectual stimulation for high schoolers in several upstate New York counties.

"She was interested in everything under the sun," the instructor recalls. "Among other things we touched upon Boolean algebra, in which one deals with collections of abstract things instead of numbers. We talked about set theory, which usually is reserved for graduate students, introduced calculus, and had some fun with number theory. Like the other high school youngsters at the seminar, Evelyn was head and shoulders above most of my college students as a mathematician" (1,p. 191).

Evelyn was a participant in Saturday Seminars for Able and Ambitious Students, set up in the fall of 1958 by sixteen central schools in three adjoining rural counties of the Empire State with Ford Foundation seed money. The years that followed provided proof that such a program, given this impetus, can sustain itself. In describing this program Elizabeth Pascal, writing in a Fund for the Advancement of Education publication, noted that "special provision for gifted students need not be limited to large city systems, to private schools, or to wealthy communities. The staffs of rural high schools may be limited in size, but ingenuity may more than compensate for that limitation" (2,p. 58).

And the village and towns came in two sizes. Small and very small. 1973 Census Bureau estimates list Cherry Valley at 1167, Edmeston 1640, Laurens 1898, Milford 2494, Morris 1716, Worcester 2013.

The largest municipality and only city contributing its students to this program is Oneonta, population 15,871; hometown of Collis Huntington (Southeran Pacific R.R.), S.S. Van Dyne (mystery stories), its Main Street store, Konstanty's, means Jim, the National League's most valuable player in 1950. Six and one-half miles from the center of Oneonta is Daniel Patrick Moynihan's 600 acre dairy farm. For use of the land a tenant farmer pays Moynihan $350 and 23 gallons of maple syrup yearly (3).

People in the small towns of the Catskills environs are interested in their children's education. The firing of the Soviet Sputnik I on October 4, 1957, had its effect here too. According to Bricknell, "The rate of instructional innovation in New York State public elementary and secondary schools more than doubled within 15 months after that date" (4, p. 8). One Sputnik spin-off was this small schools rural enrichment program in upstate New York.

This article is an update of this writer's report on this program in THE GIFTED CHILD QUARTERLY, Autumn 1964, and his presentation at the 11th Annual Meeting of the National Association for Gifted Children at Springfield, Mass. in 1964.

Who likes to get up at 6:30 A.M. on a cold winter Saturday morning, after a busy week, ending with a Friday night basketball game? Not many people. But 17 high schoolers from Hancock, New York did it this past winter to ride 50 miles to a college campus. 8 Oneonta students walk three blocks from their homes to the same campus. 50 miles -- and three blocks, - these are the extremes from which come 175 or so teenagers each semester to seminars. (The high point was Spring 1967 when 280 students enrolled in eleven seminars).

The schools are small, all right. They vary in size from 300 to 2900, K-12. Many have graduating classes of 15, 25, 35. The New York State Board of Regents and the State Education Department for years have been urging such schools to merge. Some have; more have resisted.

The first sponsoring group for these seminars was the Catskill Area Project in Small School Design, funded by the Ford Foundation, 1957-61, to experiment in improving rural education. Later, the name was changed to Catskill Area School Study Council (CASSC), but the ingredients remained the same, i.e., about 40 area school districts.

From a small start of 35 juniors and seniors from 11 schools in 2 seminars - math and science, - the idea caught on so that over the years 40 schools in a four-county area around Oneonta have sent their able and ambitious to the State University College at Oneonta (SUCO), a member of the State University of New York (SUNY), for Saturday classes. Some schools have merged. Some send students during certain years. In any one year about 20-25 schools are involved. There are 10 sessions in the first term (September-December) and 10 in the second term (January-May). They run from 9:30 a.m. until 12:00 noon, with a 15 minute break at mid-session.

The Saturday Seminar Program has received national recognition through references to it in such books as *Schools of Tomorrow-Today* (1) and *Encouraging the Excellent* (2), and through articles in such publications as *Farm Journal* (5, p. 70A-70H), THE GIFTED CHILD QUARTERLY (6, p. 128-133, 139), *New York State Education* (14, p. 21-23), *The Superior Student* (7, p. 15-16; 8, p. 57-58), and *The Bulletin of the National Association of Secondary School Principals* (9, p. 25-38). Educators from eighteen states have visited the Catskill area to secure first-hand information about the seminars. It has served as a pilot project for several similar programs elsewhere.

How Does the Program Work?

Each semester I send memos to each college department asking for proposals for seminars for the next term. I may receive 20 or 25 such proposals. 75-word descriptions are sent to our participating schools. If 18 youngsters sign up, a seminar becomes economically viable and is given. We usually present 6 to 10 seminars each term. In the Spring 1976 we offered ten: Science, Society & Technology; Bicentennial Arts & Crafts; Psychology of the Self; Principles of Athletic Training; Jazz & Modern Dance; Music Theory; Still Photography; Computer Programming; Creative Writing; Lessons in Meditation. 188 students from 22 schools, an average of 8½ per school. Two-third were girls. 90% came from grades 9-12. There were 10 youngsters from grades 7 & 8, and 2 post-graduates.

We usually get a foreign exchange student or two. (Postcard from India: "I remember those nice Saturday seminars. Here in India I am studying Economics & Sociology at college." Pankaj).

On one memorable occasion some years ago, Iraq's Said Ahmet was holding forth as guest speaker in a social studies seminar. Spending a year in a local high school, he was telling his American peers of a tempestuous life foreign to rural New York.

"Any questions?" Hands go up. "How were you treated as a political prisoner in an Iraqi jail?" "I prefer Oneonta, New York." "How do you tell the direction of Mecca when you are traveling?" "By a compass on my hotel room floor."

There have been several Rotary exchange students in our program. During one semester there was a Bolivian boy in Introduction to the Theatre. His father's occupation? - a professional theatre director.

Why Do They Come?

The flurry of interest in the gifted in the late '50's and early 60's' changed to mid 60's to interest in the disadvantaged gifted. The children we serve in the CASSC Saturday Seminar Program often come under this heading too. This is not so much because of a poor socio-economic home background - although Otsego county is one of New York State's poorest - but because of the limited resources of the schools they attend. The Mt. Upton Central School District budget for 1976-77 is $682,000; Grand Gorge, $610,952. After paying essential bills for salaries, heat, utilities, maintenance supplies, not much is left for election microscopes or the lush enrollments of an Abington, Pa. High School for instance. So - the basic reason for our program is to augment local high school offerings and facilities.

But Linda & Kevin came for other reasons, too. To see a college campus and college professors in action, to see members of the opposite sex from neighboring towns, "because it sounded fun", "Because I wanted to find out what college would be like", "I wanted to socialize and meet other students", "I wanted to take subjects not taught in high school".

How Often Do They Come?

Sometimes just often enough to get a Certificate of Participation, given for attending 8 of 10 sessions. In the fall attendance averages 80%, in the winter-spring term 75%.

How Much Does It Cost, & Who Pays It?

From $30.00 for a term of 10 sessions at the onset, the cost now is

$40.00. The local school districts usually pay it. The Upper Catskill Council on the Arts pays $10.00 per pupil in 2 Arts Seminars, reducing their cost to $30.00. In recent years they have not been so fast to reach for the check. So now there are several variations on the theme. Some districts pay for both terms; some pay for just one and anyone wishing to attend the second term pays the bill himself. Afton pays $30.00, the student (i.e., the parents) pays $10.00. A school board worried that $40.00 may be wasted on an entrant who won't go the distance may say, "You pay the fee; we'll reimburse you if you finish the course successfully (i.e., get a certificate for attending 8 of 10 sessions)."

Instructional Services

Instructor-consultants receive $40.00 per session. Some teach the whole semester's series of ten sessions. Less often a department, e.g., Biology, Psychology, offers a seminar in which five professors give two sessions each, or ten professors offer one session apiece. $75.00 is allotted for supplies, books and assistance for each seminar.

The Study Council Office prepares materials for the consultants at their request, arranges for audio-visual equipment, purchases the supplies and materials as well as storing materials left over from one semester to the next. For the most part, the money is used to purchase consumable materials.

Instructor-consultants have a great deal of autonomy. Once their seminar has been accepted they are responsible for carrying it out. In one interesting sense the seminars are self-regulating, for if the interest falls off the student attendance will probably reflect it.

Transportation

Transportation is usually provided by the schools. This is often a cooperative venture, with a bus from an outlying area picking up students from other schools along the way. Some come in their own cars. There are several advantages in coming to the college campus. What boy isn't interested in seeing the girls from neighboring towns? Youngsters see a college environment; they experience college instructors; there is opportunity for choice of seminar from among a variety of offerings.

However, on occasion, the seminar goes to the student. During the spring term of 1970, the seminar in psychology was made possible through telelecture and electrowriter equipment, for students from several small towns about sixty miles southeast of Oneonta. For the first session, a SUCO professor appears in person at the Hunter-Tannersville Central School to meet with eighteen students from that school and seven from three small neighboring schools. But for the next eight sessions, he spoke to them from the SUCO campus. A teacher's aide presented films, transparencies, and other material mailed to her by the professor. At the tenth session he again journeyed to appear before them.

Evaluation

This is the most difficult, and most important, aspect of any program. Following Gordon Allport's suggestion that if you want to know how people feel about something, why not ask them, we do this, in two ways. We ask students to fill out a questionnaire at the end of each seminar series (what did you like best? least? how could it be improved?). We also hold a yearly luncheon meeting here at the college to which are invited the chief school officer, a guidance counselor, and a student from each school.

Suggestions for new courses, and new approaches such as indicated above here, have resulted from these queries and meetings. For example, at the start, about a half dozen seminars were offered each semester, and youngsters were placed in them according to administrative judgment based on their standardized test scores. About ten years ago students were given choices. The list of seminars available for choice was increased so that presently about twenty-five are proposed each semester. Most of the increase has been in "non-academic" areas with such offerings as Television Studio Techniques, Film-making and Still Photography, Yoga, Animation in Film, Creative Posters, Writers' Workshop: Song Lyrics, Foreign Cooking, Introduction to the Theatre. In fall 1973, six seminars were of this variety, while only three had a more conventional academic orientation - Anatomy of Marine Invertebrates, Elements of Psychology, and Psychology of the Self. Some controversy has arisen among the administrators of the schools in the program, some of whom favor the so-called "hard" subjects and feel that the term "able and ambitious" is no longer appropriate.

Rationale

There are no examinations, no compulsory assignments, no grades given. In some seminars there are suggested assignments; a written composition in Expository Writing, the reading of *Medea* in Communication in the Arts, for example. Some instructors would like to make mandatory assignments, but the feeling of the Study Council's Board of Trustees has been against this. Our students are already the busiest individuals, the leaders, the get-up-and-go-people of their schools. It is the philosophy of this program that no further burdens should be placed on them. In the words of a recent publication on the gifted, "many highly capable and talented students are overscheduled and excessively programmed in and out of school to the extent that individuality is submissive to adult directed performance" (10, p. 29). No college credit is granted for these seminars. It is recognized that there are many competing interests, many other demands on these able and ambitious high schoolers. Participation is entirely voluntary. For some eligible youngsters it is no doubt better that they spend their Saturday mornings in other pursuits. They must make choices.

A Visit to Some Seminars

Over the years a visitor to these seminars would have seen many varied sights on a typical Saturday morning. He would have seen a humanities group doing choral reading of Vachel Lindsay's "The Congo"; groups of two or three were reading special parts. Another humanities section would have been looking at architectural slides and hearing a discussion of the Golden Mean, or listening to the "Requiem Mass" as conceived by Mozart, Cherubini, Faure, Berlioz, and Verdi.

A few doors away, the participants in the social studies seminar who were studying the Middle East were seated around a large table covered with shawls. The instructor, whose years of teaching include time at Robert College in Istanbul and the American University of

Beirut, is asking, "Where do you think these were made?" After guesses of Iran and Iraq, he comments, "These are frauds! They were made in Paisley, Scotland! Not all copying these days is by East from West!" To a question, "What do Middle Easterners think of America?" his reply, "They hate you!" may open the eyes of youngsters whose horizons need some expanding.

Then we came to the mathematics specialist. Non-Euclidian geometry was the topic. Through a given point, can only one line be drawn parallel to another line? "Not at all," says Lobachevsky, and the icono-clastic instructor explains, "You name a law and we'll find a place where it fails. One plus one doesn't always equal two; the parts sometimes total more than the whole." You could feel the stimulation, thrill of new ideas in the pupils' minds.

In the science classroom were large maps and the conversation reflected the course theme of meterology. The group was planning a field trip to the weather station at Griffiss Air Force Base, with transportation provided by one school at a very nominal cost to students involved.

A current visitor might look in on the long-running Psychology of the Self Seminar. Things you may never have thought about until now was the essence of the instruction the students were receiving.

Item: "There's a low but positive relationship between height and intelligence, and between birth weight and intelligence (the instructor recalls that the *Reader's Digest* labeled this the "fat chance" theory).

Item: This is an unfair world! The better you are in one area, the better you are in other areas. Positive correlation, not compensation, is a law of life. For example, one of the clearest relationships in psychology is that between social class and I.Q.

Students might be discussing their values. "Your values are your preferences," the instructor is saying. "I am going to give you a famous instrument which will provide you with some insight into yourself." Whereupon he hands out copies of the highly-regarded Allput-Vernon Lindzey Scale of Values.(Data collected over the years indicate that this is the rank-order of the values held by students in this seminar: social, aesthetic, political, theoretical, religious, economic). After explaining what the terms mean, he says, "How well do you know yourself? Jot down now your guess as to the order in which you hold these values most highly. Take this instrument home and fill it out. See what it says. Next week we will discuss your guesses and the instrument's findings." Next week's class session will include an explanation of Spearman's correlation method for comparing rank orders.

Or the instructor might be handing out paperback copies of *Dibs* by Virginia Axline. "Students in my college courses find this the most interesting of all the books I recommend to them. I think you will enjoy reading about a little boy being skillfully helped to find himself". And so the enrichment, the augmentation of their high school courses goes on for these youngsters. Tomorrow's classes today.

3. EXAMPLES

On-the-job, hands-on training is the keynote of the popular seminar Television Studio Techniques. The students produce their own shows. Everyone has an assignment in using the excellent equipment of the College's Instructional Resources Center. Each of the three cameras is manned by an eager learner. Before them is the "talent" on a panel discussion on high school athletics. A small girl is flanked on one side by a much larger school soccer hero. On the other side, a distaff athlete from another school. The countdown, and then the tape rolls. Behind the cameras on the set and in the control room, the director, technical director, floor director, audio engineer, production assistant, and video-tape operator are learning by doing. The visitor has difficulty in tearing himself away to continue his rounds.

Across the college quadrangle Introduction to the Theatre students are being shown a variety of equipment. They see that the lip of the stage can descend to form the orchestra pit, that behind-the-scenes equipment includes an item usually found in a Broadway theatre, the circular staircase leading down from the floor above, that work has long since begun on scenery for next month's college production and that many yards of hanger space are needed for yesterday's costumes waiting for use again in tomorrow's shows.

After the tour of facilities in the ultra-modern theatre complex, the instructor will begin class sessions on such topics as what are the elements of theatre (language, actor, audience)? What are some types of theatre (Proscenium, Arena, Thrust)? Subsequent sessions will see discussions of dramaturgy, Contemporary Theatre, Black Theatre, types of acting, and production problems of two current SUCO offerings, *Blithe Spirit* and *South Pacific*.

The Bill of Fare

In the past 19 years we have offered a wide variety of seminars. Examples: Genetics, Astronomy, Aviation Ground School, Meteorology, Biological Lab Techniques, Mathematics, Organic Chemistry, Expository Writing, Thinking About Literature, History of the Black Man in America, Earth Science, Date Processing, Communication in the Arts, Current Economic Problems, Modern Russia, Music Appreciation, Space Science, Conversational German, Psychology of Sleeping and Dreaming, Wood Sculpture and Oriental Philosophy. An innovative offering called Century 21 featured speakers on medicine (organ transplants), banking (instant credit and payment by computer), space exploration (the heavens above), foods (the American kitchen, circa 2000), engineering, criminology, oceanography, transportation, with predictions of things to come.

To quote Dr. Lawrence J. Heldman, SUCO Professor and Executive Secretary of CASSC, "some seminars are trendy". Some have a few years of popularity. Yoga was popular in the early 1970's. Now interest has waned. Some - Psychology of the Self, Still Photography, Computer Programming - seem to go on indefinitely. An Introduction to the German Language attracts enough students for one term per year.

Survival through the only Realty - Change

This, then, is the rural schools enrichment program which Ford Foundation seed money helped set up in 1958. This is an optional learning environment that New York State Commissioner of Education, Ewald B. Nyquist talks about. As he says, "in New York State, the number and variety of alternative learning patterns which already exist reflect initiative and courageous willingness to experiment" (11)

Why has the program survived through all these problems through eighteen years of doubts (Coleman, Jencks, et al) about, and eroding public confidence in, public education? Here are some reasons:

1. Because it offers needs fulfillment, and because people will go to considerable lengths to avail themselves of such an offer. Wrote one boy in a seminar evaluation, "What did I like least about the seminar? Getting here. I usually have to walk 4½ miles or so to get to where I can catch the bus which brings me here. What did I like best? The disecting. It's something we didn't do in my biology class at my school and I've learned a lot by it."

2. Because it is self-supporting. Its only support is tuition money. As Dr. Heldman points out, many programs fail when government funds cease. The "seed money" invested here in the first four years has caught on.

3. Because it is innovative, flexible, and changes with the times. Examples:

a) we have offered overseas seminars as indicated above.

b) we have increased the seminar choices available to students. At our springtime evaluation meetings, we invite suggestions. Suggestions in Spring, 1976 included courses in thanatology, (death & dying), genealogy (and a chance to dig up the family tree), agronomy, law and the student. (A local Oneonta lawyer will offer this last-named seminar).

c) Because of a feeling that our program was becoming too unacademic with our offerings in yoga, cooking, photography, for example, we began an honors seminar in Spring '76, open only to very able young people eager for a highly demanding academic offering. In Fall, 1976, creative writing was offered for a chosen (by their schools) very few. Each article produced was scheduled for publication. The instructor was a SUCO staff member, onetime Fulbright Scholar in Italy and Finland, author of 2 books and 40 articles and reviews.

d) We have added more courses in technology - TV production, computer programming, still photography.

3) We use faculty and resources of Hartwick College, a fine liberal arts institution, also in Oneonta. Several years ago we offered a seminar in computer-programming. It was oversubscribed, with too many for SUCO facilities. A phone call to Hartwick found that an instructor was willing and its Computer Center was available. Result - two sections of this seminar with about 20 students in each. Another course - in off-loom weaving - has also been given at Hartwick, and two of its instructors agreed to my suggestion that they propose seminars in thanatology and genealogy ("We can't

tell you where you're going, but we can tell you where you've been"), in fall, 1976.

f) We have enlarged the grades we serve. Originally, in 1958, we took 11 & 12 graders. Now we have students from 7, 8, .9 and 10 grades as well.

As this observer watches these youngsters pouring out of the yellow buses Saturday after Saturday at the SUCO Campus, he is mindful of the long line of able and ambitious persons nurtured in this geographical area. Collis Huntington's nephew, Henry E., an Oneonta native, once owned a large part of Southern California, and he built one of the world's great libraries and art museum at San Marino (12, P. 16A).

George W. Fairchild, who put together IBM, was an Oneonta native and the Bundy time recorder, key feature in IBM's start ($1000 invested then is worth $18 million now) was developed here (13, P. 16A). Fairchild's son Sherman (aerial cameras), also born in Oneonta, died one of the world's wealthiest men.

Isaac M. Singer, Fly Creek, made improvements in the sewing machine so that it would work. Lewis E. Waterman of Decatur devised the first satisfactory fountain pen.

Two famous men were born in Roxbury within a year - Jay Gould, "Wizard of Wallstreet" in 1836, and John Burroughs, Naturalist and author (27 books) in 1837. James Fenimore Cooper lived in Cooperstown, and Abner Doubleday is supposed to have started baseball there, today the home of Baseball's Hall of Fame. 25 miles further northeast is the hamlet Sprout Brook, industrial Henry Kaiser's birthplace. Plenty of able and ambitious predecessors have led the way.

These seminars offer a choice, allow area teen agers to keep their options open, offer them an alternative to the fast-paced mediocrity of America that scheduled them to a Saturday morning of open-eyed, open-eared, open-mouthed but closed-mind boob tube viewing. There can be more to the start of the end of the week than a long phone conversation and a trip to McDonald's.

A mental hotfoot never hurt anyone. Over 6000 teenagers from the Catskills and environs have come to the Saturday Seminars to try one, and they're still coming.

REFERENCES

1. Morse, Arthur D. *Schools of Tomorrow-Today,* Albany, New York: State Education Department, 1960.
2. Pascal, Elizabeth. *Encouraing the Excellent.* New York: The Fund For the Advancement of Education, 1960.
3. *Time,* January 26, 1976.
4. Bricknell, Henry Mr. *Organizing New York State For Educational Change.* Albany: State Education Department, 1961.
5. Davis, Richard C. "Are Small Schools Worth Saving?" *Farm Journal,* April, 1959.
6. Porter, Robert M. "Deeper Involvement For Better Brains Some Current Developments in Educating Gifted High School Students in New York State." GIFTED CHILD QUARTERLY, Autumn, 1964.
7. Porter Robert M. "A Rural Enrichment Program", *The Superior Student,* the Newsletter of the Committee on the Superior Student, published at the University of Colorado, Boulder, February, 1960.
8. Porter, Robert M. "Saturday Seminars in the Catskills," *The Superior Students,* November-December, 1963.

9. Porter, Robert M. "Saturday Seminars For the Able & Ambitious", *The Bulletin of the National Association of Secondary School Principals.* (54 - 348), October, 1970.

10. *California Project Talent.* Compiled by Paul D. Plowman and Joseph Rice, Co-directors, Sacramento, California: California State Department of Public Education, 1967.

11. Nyquist, Ewald B. *Optional Learning Environments.* An Address to New York State Council of School District Administrators, Grossinger's, October 7, 1973.

12. *Daily Star,* Oneonta, New York, Bicentennial Edition, July 3, 1976.

13. *Ibid.*

14. Porter, Robert M. "Saturday Seminars Stimulate Students", *New York State Education,* January, 1962.

A MODEL COUNSELING LABORATORY FOR THE GIFTED AT WISCONSIN

Nick Colangelo and L.R. Pfleger
Research & Guidance Laboratory
University of Wisconsin, Madison

INTRODUCTION

One of the significant trends in education today is the increasing concern in gifted and talented students. On the federal level the U.S. Office of Education now has a department for gifted and talented and federal funds are allocated under the Special Projects Section P.L. 93-380. These monies are available to state and local districts interested in establishing programs for gifted. Furthermore, many state departments of education are designating a state coordinator for gifted and talented.

Founded by Prof. J.W. M. Rothney, for the past 19 years, the Research and Guidance Laboratory has served as a development and demonstration center for innovative practices designed for gifted and talented students. It is the most comprehensive resource available to local school districts in Wisconsin as they attempt to provide appropriate experience for their gifted and talented students. Recently, the Laboratory has received increased national attention. In response the Laboratory is in the process of expanding its resources and scope to serve educators in school districts across the nation. For further description of the laboratory see Rothney and Sanborn 1966, also the annotated bibliography in this issue.

BACKGROUND

The research and Guidance Laboratory was organized in 1957 to conduct longitudinal research-through-service activities with gifted and talented high school students. To date, it has worked directly with over 3,500 students in over 95 school districts in the state of Wisconsin. More than 100 research projects on the gifted and talented have been completed at the Laboratory. Efforts have been focused primarily on identifying characteristics of gifted and talented students, on developing practical methods for working with such students in school, and or questions related to educational and vocational development of the gifted and talented. A published resume of the research findings is available from the Laboratory.

"A Model Counseling Laboratory for the Gifted at Wisconsin," N. Colangelo and L.R. Pfleger, *Gifted Child Quarterly*, Vol. XX, No. 3, Fall 1977. Copyright 1977 by the National Association for Gifted Children, all rights reserved.

The Laboratory is unique, for it is the only organization of its kind in the country that has carried on longitudinal research with populations of gifted and talented students for nineteen years. Of particular interest is that schools in the Laboratory program have provided an excellent cross-section of school systems, ranging in size from those with fewer than 20 teachers to those with several hundred in both rural and urban settings. This background places the Research and Guidance Laboratory in a unique position to assist school systems in developing and maintaining a meaningful and realistic program for its gifted and talented students.

LABORATORY

Administrators, counselors and teachers of cooperating schools select students on the basis of multiple criteria suggested by the Laboratory staff. These students come to Madison for one-day visits at least once a year during their period of high school attendance. A full day of activities is arranged for them, including testing and evaluation, analysis of written and oral performances, visits to classes and laboratories, and conferences with University staff members in any area of interest. These procedures are designed to:

a) broaden their horizons with respect to educational and vocational opportunities.

b) develope realistic self concepts about their own strengths and weaknesses.

c) foster plans for suitable educational programs

d) discover methods for overcoming limitations.

e) encourage development of personal and academic strengths

f) provide counsel on any matter which may influence fullest development of the individual student.

Findings are interpreted to students and the implications are considered in individual counseling sessions. Highly individualized adaptions to particular characteristics and needs are emphasized throughout.

Students' visits to the Laboratory are followed closely by visits of Laboratory staff teams to schools they attend. At the schools, conferences are held with parents of each participating student. Laboratory findings are interpreted to the parents and are supplemented by information parents give. Suggestions are made to parents regarding ways they may facilitate their child's growth. The conferences are designed to:

a) inform parents about characteristics of their children they may not know

b) stimulate action of parents to meet developmental needs their child shows.

c) facilitate communication between the parents, the school, and the student.

d) discover points of view and other parental characteristics which affect the student's development.

On the basis of activities and performances at the Laboratory, a written report regarding each individual student is sent to the school he/she attends. These reports have been received and circulated among teachers prior to the visit in the school by Laboratory staff. Ordinarily, reports contain information about the student's

3. EXAMPLES

performance, interests, and needs, along with suggestions the school may implement to provide desired educational and personal experiences. After parent conferences are completed, a teachers' inservice training program is held. Specific suggestions to the school are discussed, and general principles for guidance and education of gifted students are emphasized. Usually by means of a case approach, attempts are made to solve problems encountered in educating gifted students. Objectives of these training sessions are:

a) stimulation of and assistance with the processes of identification of gifted students.

b) encouragement and assistance in making special provisions for development of gifted students, and stimulation to do so for other students.

c) provisions of information about educational and vocational requirements and opportunities particularly applicable to gifted students.

d) encouragement of innovation and experimentation in school procedures for gifted students as well as for other students.

e) demonstration of appropriate guidance services for high school students.

NEW DIRECTIONS

The Laboratory staff has been focusing on new directions for the gifted. Under the direction of Dr. Phillip Perrone, who will become the new director of the Laboratory, the following five areas have been identified as foci for generating knowledge regarding superior performance.

1. Nurturance --early development--pre-school.
2. Self-identification--ultimately the individual must recognize and accept his / her superiority although superiority may need to be recognized by significant others first (family and teachers).
3. Educational development--nurturance and stimulation of the school-age child in school, home and community by the individual and the planned interventions of significant others.
4. Direction/Focus/Application--psychoeducational (value clarification, decision-making, creative expression, etc.) directed toward goal setting and implementing goal-directed behavior.
5. Selfstimulation for growth and development.

Each of these five areas has been broken down into subareas which will be researched by teams consisting of the Counseling and Guidance faculty at the University of Wisconsin-Madison and the Laboratory staff. These people are undertaking a comprehensive and extensive search into these areas:

1) to determine and summarize the significant research available to gifted.

2) to assess the most valid and reliable measures of the characteristics of giftedness.

3) to apply this research material to further knowledge about gifted students.

The Laboratory personnel will publish the results and these will be available to all interested educators.

SUMMARY

The Research and Guidance Laboratory is an established center for research and service to educators in the area of the gifted. The founding philosophy of the Laboratory has been to provide individualized attention to any school district expressing an interest in developing programs, or practices appropriate to their gifted student population. In the past, the Laboratory has served as a guidance program development model for gifted students in Wisconsin schools. The Laboratory is presently engaged in expanding its services to all educators in the nation. In addition to its past activities, the Laboratory is expanding into additional research areas on gifted. Educators are encouraged to contact the Laboratory for more information and printed materials.

Research and Guidance Laboratory
THE UNIVERSITY OF WISCONSIN-MADISON
Education Science I Bldg., 10th floor
1025 West Johnson Street.
Madison, Wisconsin, 53706

REFERENCES

General information on the Laboratory programs was taken from the following Research and Guidance Laboratory Publication:

Pulvino, C. J., Colangelo, N., & Zaffrann, R.T. *Counseling and Program Development for Gifted.* The Research and Guidance Laboratory, 1976.

Rothney, J.W.M. & Sanborn, M.P. "Wisconsin's Research through service program for superior students" *Personnel & Guidance J.* 44:694-99, 1966. For other descriptions see also the annotated bibliography appended below.

Sanborn, M.P., Pulvino, C.J. & Wunderlin, R.F. *Research Reports: Superior Students in Wisconsin High Schools.* The Research and Guidance Laboratory, 1971.

Career Education for Disadvantaged, Gifted High School Students

Barbara A. Moore

Brian is a fifteen year old sophomore. Last week he learned how to operate a large commercial movie camera and develop a variety of color film. Three weeks earlier, Brian was working with several commercial artists drawing layouts for advertisements. Next week, Brian will accompany a roving newspaper photographer.

What makes these activities unusual? They are part of the "Professional Career Exploration Program for Minority and/or Low Income, Gifted and Talented 10th Grade students (PCEP)". A major objective of PCEP is to provide disadvantaged students, identified as gifted and talented, with professional career exploration activities to help expand their range of possible occupational careers in the future. Funded by the U.S. Office of Education, through Purdue University, the PCEP is currently operating in Elkhart and Columbus, Indiana. Two PCEP programs under the direction of a full-time PCEP Coordinator operate in each school corporation.

Brian comes from a single parent, low income Black family. Brian, up until last year, had few educational and/or occupational goals. Yet, he has been identified as gifted and talented, a fact which was difficult to determine because of his background. Through participating in the PCEP, Brian is researching possible careers in art which require advanced education. He will have opportunities to reevaluate his current high school program to ensure the necessary foundation for advanced education. PCEP has created an awareness of further opportunities such as the Upward Bound program in eleventh and twelfth grade. Before Brian leaves high school he will have an in-depth exposure in a variety of educational and occupational possibilities.

The Need for PCEP Programs

Typically, gifted and talented students who are, in addition, minority and/or low income, face several unique problems in making occupational choices (Sanborn and Wasson, 1966; Ward, 1965). First because they are gifted and talented, these students show qualities of multi-potentiality. That is, the gifted and talented can succeed in many areas and usually show interest in a wide variety of things. Unique to the gifted and talented is also the need to have time to intellectualize educational experiences in order to make effective decisions. Secondly, the factor of being minority and/or low income often contributes to low self concepts, lack of parental support and/or expectations and fewer past occupational experiences. These conditions can hinder these gifted and talented students from making wise choices.

Career education programs for the gifted must differ in several ways from career education for other segments of the population (Hoyt and Hebler, 1974; Riessman, 1965). Career education for the gifted generally stresses challenging occupations, scholarly professions, and independent types of employment. In addition, career education programs should contain specific components which can help make the career education program an optimum experience for the minority and/or low income gifted and talented students. These special provisions, as defined by researchers, are:

1. Exploration opportunities in actual community settings (Gallagher, 1975; Stalling, 1972; Gallagher and Kinney, 1974).

2. Active professional role models (Bandura, 1970; Pressey, 1955; Stallings, 1972; Gallagher, 1975).

3. Special time allotted for sharing and intellectualizing experience (Rothney and Sanborn, 1968; Gallagher and Kinney, 1974).

4. Opportunities to examine their own self concepts and values (Sanborn and Niemiec, 1971; Hoyt and Hebler, 1974).

5. In-depth views of the career ladders and lattices for each profession explored (Hoyt and Hebler, 1974; Kintgen, 1973; Tuckman, 1967:46).

6. Individual guidance and counseling time (Pressey, 1955).

7. Sensitizing time to analyze professional lifestyles, values, ethics, and goals (Hoyt and Hebler, 1974).

Career education programs, specifically designed to attend to the occupational choice problems of the minority and/or low income, gifted and talented students, are needed. Hoyt and Hebler (1974), report "efforts to locate career education programs for the gifted and talented have, for the most part, been unrewarding." The U.S. Commissioner of Education, in his landmark report to Congress on *Education of the Gifted and Talented* (1972), reported the "low priority level being given to programs for the gifted by all the States and by local schools."

The PCEP in Action

Basically the PCEP consists of two major parts. Immediately following the October 1, 1977 starting date, implementation sites were secured and subcontracts were issued to two-full time PCEP coordinators. Under the direction of the coordinators, students were identified using an application selection process. With the help of a PCEP Advisory Committee, the PCEP coordinators began locating community exploration sites. Occupational information and activities were collected in preporation for the second part of the PCEP.

The second part of the operation of PCEP began at the second semester breaks. During the second semester, the students' schedules were revised to permit the students to attend in-class PCEP seminars for approximately four weeks. Then the students went out in the community one day per week for three hours to explore a total of three professions over a nine week time span.

3. EXAMPLES

During the exploration experiences, the students continued to meet in their seminars twice a week. The last four weeks of the PCEP is currently being devoted solely to in-class seminars.. The flexibility of the PCEP Calendar has permitted program operation despite the late project funding date, late negotiations of the coordinators' subcontracts, vacation days, snow days and energy crises days.

Selecting the Implementation Sites
and the PCEP Coordinators

Two sites were selected for the implementation of the PCEP. The Bartholomew School Corporation in Columbus, Indiana operates two PCEP programs. They are at Columbus North and Columbus East High Schools. Memorial and Central High Schools in Elkhart, Indiana, operates another two PCEP programs. These schools were selected on the basis of their desire to meet the needs of this unusual population, their willingness to arrange student schedules and work within the limits of time available, and their enthusiasm in selecting a PCEP Coordinator. Each school corporation identified a PCEP coordinator who had extensive knowledge of the community and experience working with gifted students.

Selection of the PCEP Students

Time constraints modified the screening/selection process as originally designed in the PCEP proposal. One of the major obstacles was working within existing student schedules which did, to some extent, eliminate some students from admission to the program. Each coordinator began by identifying a large pool of potential PCEP students. By consulting student records, the coordinators were able to identify students whose family background information such as socioeconomic status, race, cultural or social limitation indicated a disadvantaged background. Three types of gifted were sought: leadership, artistic and intellectual. In addition the coordinators gathered such information as 9th grade grade-point average and past achievement test and IQ test score results. The coordinators, faculty and guidance counselors began to encourage students to apply for the PCEP. Each application contained the names of two former teachers who were asked to rate the student using the Torrance Checklist of Creative Positives (short form) and Renzulli's "Scale for Rating Behavorial Characteristics of Superior Students." Both of these scales together are used to identify certain kinds of giftedness, especially in minority and/or low income students. Each applicant was also asked to write a short essay arguing for or against his/her own potential for success in the program. The essays were rated on a scale of 1 to 5 based on clarity of argument and writing ability. Finally each applicant completed Torrance's 'checklist of Extra Curricular Interest and Activities.''

The applications were then ranked and the coordinators interviewed each applicant for their respective schools. Approximately twenty PCEP students were selected for each high school PCEP Program.

PCEP Classroom and Exploration Activities

In-class seminar activities included self concept development, values clarification, lifestyles, career planning, the professional work ethic and professional responsibilities as well as occupational and educational information. A variety of instructional media plus community resource persons have been used to help provide students with a realistic view of different occupations.

The PCEP Students experienced a wide array of exploration activities. During the in-class seminar, each PCEP student identified professional areas of interest and then, if possible was assigned to community professionals in those areas. Exploration activities ranged from observation to actual participation in the professional activities. Students spent hectic afternoons in the local hospitals and the emergency rooms. Several students went to court with the Prosecuting Attorney. Others accompanied the Urban League's social workers on community visits. Some of the PCEP students went flying with a local airport designer. Students rotated among these and other professional activities. They explored three professions for a three week period of time each. Exploration plans were developed to help ensure profitable experiences. Each student developed a Professional Occupations Notebook about the PCEP opportunities and information.

Opportunities will be provided at the conclusion of the exploration experiences for the students to share their exploration activities with each other. They will also receive group and individual counseling concerning their career planning.

Evaluating the Program

At the onset of the PCEP all students completed two instruments, the Career Maturity Inventory (parts 1, 3, and 5 plus the Attitude Scale) and the Tennessee Self Concept Scale. At the conclusion of the program students will complete the instruments again. The Career Maturity inventory (parts 1, 3, 5) will be used to measure changes in career awareness. The Attitude Scale will be used to determine if the students' attitude toward work has changed. Finally, changes in student self concept will be determined by comparing P scores on the Tennessee Self Concept Scale. Since the program is still in operation no post test data is available. However, from discussions with students and observation of their activities it appears students are benefiting from the program.

Other types of data other than test scores will also be used in evaluating the program. The attitudes of the sponsors in the program will be examined. The professional occupations Notebook, the Occupational Exploratory Plans, and the Educational Planning Checklist will be examined to determine the quality and comprehensiveness of the exploratory activities.

Conclusions

Our country cannot afford to overlook the professional areas and the human resources of the gifted and talented, minority and/or low income students. In particular, these future leaders should have the opportunity to select the most satisfying and challenging career regardless of past cultural or socioeconomic disadvantages. The Professional Career Exploration Program for Minority and Low-Income Gifted and Talented Students is designed specifically to be an efficient method of expanding the range of occupational career choices for minority and/or low income, gifted and talented 10th grade high school students.

teaching gifted

Can fish talk? Can chickens count? Can guinea pigs tell time? Gifted and talented children in Pennsylvania are finding out the answers to these and other questions in a "Biology Conditioning and Learning Class," offered through College for Kids.

College for Kids offers 36 fast-paced courses for high potential children on five area college campuses. King's College, Wilkes College, Penn State Wilkes-Barre Campus, College Misericordia and Luzerne County Community College cooperate with the College for Kids program by offering their facilities without charge.

Courses range in diversity from criminology, greek mythology and photography to gymnastics, animal behavior and appreciation and understanding of 20th century surrealistic painting.

One of the popular areas of study is "Nuclear Genie," a course covering nuclear reactor safety, carbon 14 dating, counting equipment and how to "tame" the nuclear genie to serve man—all taught in a contemporary nuclear lab.

Courses are taught by college professors or instructors, one evening or afternoon each week for a period of six weeks. No more than 15 students are allowed in one class to assure personal attention to every learner. Average age of children attending the College for Kids varies according to each course. However, most students attending are between the ages of five and fifteen.

Director of College for Kids is Joan Harris, who has seen her idea blossom into 17 courses and 220 students last year. This year College for Kids offers 36 courses. Next session the College hopes to offer 50 courses, with interest noted from 1,000 students.

Says Harris, "Last session we produced one original drama, one dance review, one art show combining art class work from the several colleges (sketches, water colors, pottery and oils) and a play in the French language from our conversational French class."

And the work of College for Kids is not going by unnoticed. Two newspapers have devoted their entire front page to College for Kids, "and also the six o'clock news focused on our human biology class, taught at King's College by Dr. Chin-Chiu Lee," adds Harris.

Nine-year-old Lisa Boback learns how to prepare clay in her course "The Potter's Wheel."

"I am trying to get all areas covered: acceleration, enrichment, physical education and creativity through the arts," Harris notes.

Judging from the interest generated from students and parents, it appears that College for Kids is just what gifted and talented children need.

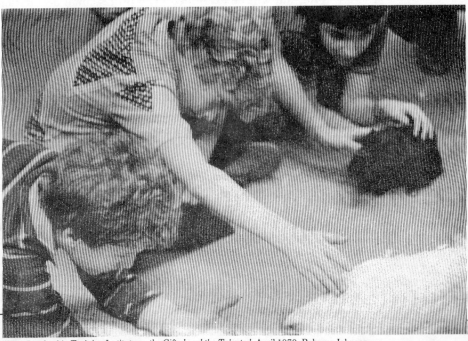

Eric Stull, 10, Robert Boris, 11, and Nickie Democko, 11, learn about imprinting from biology professor Louis Rigley of Wilkes College. Through imprinting a chicken can be made to prefer the company of a rabbit to that of another chicken.

From the *Bulletin of the National/State Leadership Training Institute on the Gifted and the Talented*, April 1979. Babrara Johnson, Editor.

STUDENT GUIDE TO WRITING A JOURNAL

Published by the Northwest Regional Educational Laboratory, a private nonprofit corporation. The work upon which this publication is based was performed pursuant to a contract with the National Institute of Education, Department of Health, Education and Welfare. The opinions expressed in this publication do not necessarily reflect the position or policy of the National Institute of Education, and no official endorsement by that agency should be inferred.

ISBN 0-89354-601-1 Reproduced by special permission of the Northwest Regional Educational Laboratory. This booklet may be purchased for $1.50.

What Is A Journal?

What is a journal? Some people think it's a diary; others that it's a newspaper. It doesn't have to be either. It can be practically anything you like, as long as you're willing to do some writing.

It's About You

The journal reflects the contents of those moments in time that are personal or have special meaning for you--experiences from which you draw some understanding about yourself or your world. They are not necessarily grand or monumental, but they are special in some way to you. A journal is a place to express, on a regular basis, some written record of what you DO, THINK and FEEL.

The one person you need to get to know really well in this world is YOU. The journal can be the most exciting teacher you will ever encounter--for the act of putting into words your experiences, thoughts and feelings will cause you to reflect more on your daily life. Writing about yourself is one way to grow in knowing yourself-- to become more aware of your learning, goals and needs--to understand why you do the things you do.

Whom Are You Writing To?

An important aspect of your journal will be the response you get from your *correspondent*--the person to whom you'll be writing. Your correspondent will be a teacher, a counselor or some other person you've selected who will be responding to your journal entries and helping you communicate better. While on the surface you are writing to your correspondent, underneath you will also be writing to yourself. The correspondent shares in this writing experience, but this does not mean that you must try to please someone else with your writing. It means that someone who is interested in you will be reading and responding to what you write.

Think of your correspondent as another part of yourself, and you will have the key to what is exciting, interesting and important to write about. It is very much like an internal conversation with a part of you that you may not know as well as you would like to.

You are not required to discuss anything in particular. nor are you expected to unburden your soul to the correspondent unless you feel that is what you need and want to do. The journal is YOU--let it say so, but be honest with yourself. Write what *you* think is important. Don't worry too much about style or correctness. Relax and enjoy your writing experience. You will be surprised at the results!

Getting Down to Writing

Remember, what is important is to share ideas, work out your thoughts or create. The journal is not so much a point-by-point description of your daily activities as how you think and feel about them.

Put the events of your life in a context of thinking and feeling, evaluate them a little bit. Did the experience change you, affect you in some way or give you a special insight? How do you feel about the situation? What do you think about it? What effects do you predict the experience will have on your future actions? Learn from what you write. The journal will inform you only to the degree that you inform it. Discover what is interesting to you by writing it down. Concentrate on your reactions, your observations and your judgments about what's happening to you.

What's Expected

It is hoped that your journal will be very much "you," inside and out. The following requirements, however, can help give you a sense of continuity and organization:

1. Use a special notebook or binder which you keep only for journal writing and save all your entries. The notebook will help you keep everything in one place so you and your correspondent can see what you're written before. You should turn in the entire journal to your correspondent with each new entry.

2. You are responsible for your journal. Don't lose it!

3. Turn in your journal each week. While your correspondent has your journal, you might find it important to keep notes to enter when your journal is returned.

4. Remember, your correspondent is another person who is listening to you with an open mind. Try not to waste anybody's time--most importantly yours--with trivia.

5. Your journal entries should cover at least two full pages for each week. Once you become involved with the process, however, you will probably go beyond this minimum.

You can expect two kinds of growth to result from writing regularly in your journal. First, your writing ability will improve, simply because you will be writing often.

Also, your ability to understand your experiences will deepen, both from the regular act of reflecting on and writing about what's happening to you and from the interaction between you and your correspondent. Your correspondent will be reading your journal in a serious attempt to understand what you mean, not in order to criticize or even evaluate your writing. If your correspondent is honestly puzzled by something you write, he or she may sometimes ask you to be more clear in your expression. But the journal should be a sincere dialogue between two people trying to understand each other.

Getting On With It...Hints And Tips

If your mind reaches a blank space and you feel there is nothing to write about, take a look at the ideas on the next few pages...

You may find something there that will turn on your imagination. If not, make something up. You can learn a lot about yourself from the simple process of trying to put words onto paper. That's what creation is all about--taking feelings and thoughts that might be drifting anywhere and finding something about them that pulls them together into something you can give shape to, whether it's just words strung out on paper, stories about what's happening to you or what you dream about. If you put your own time and energy into it, that's creation.

IT IS IMPORTANT THAT YOU DON'T LEAVE YOUR JOURNAL BLANK. Your mind is never empty. Even when you think it is there are things floating in there doing things to you. Ask yourself questions. What's hanging you up? Write about it. You might find out something new . . . .

Form

There are many ways to look at yourself, to show feelings, to react to the world and your experiences. Just because your journal will be mostly in words, don't limit your expression to just one style or form every time you write. If you haven't experimented with different forms of writing before, do it now. Try writing in the form of a poem, a dialogue in which you imagine both sides of a discussion, a play, a speech, an interview or a dream. Try writing as if in the past or the future. You may prefer to write in prose (that's what you're reading right now) or stream of consciousness (writing down exactly what is going on in your here and now without using regular sentence structure, punctuation, logical sequences and so forth).

Whatever form feels comfortable to you, remember your original purpose of reflecting on your experiences and clarifying your reactions to them.

Playing With Words

If you are not sure how to go about writing a poem, read a few poets (maybe your correspondent can help with suggestions) and get a feeling for their rhythms and ideas. Then write a poem of your own.

A dialogue can take several directions. You can hold a conversation with another part of yourself that you don't show to most people, or you can imagine a dialogue with your correspondent. You may report an actual conversation you have overheard or taken part in. Or you can create two imaginary characters and report a conversation. Think of what you would most like to do after you finish school.

Imagine a dialogue between you as a job applicant and an interviewer for that job. Think of the thing you could say that would be most likely to get you hired. Now reverse roles: you're the interviewer--what do you want in a prospective employee? Try doing the dialogue in the form of a cartoon or comic strip. Try writing your own play with setting and directions.

Interview someone about something you are interested in learning about. Be sure to have some questions and ideas ready for the person you're going to be interviewing. It will be mainly your responsibility to keep the interview going. (If you have trouble taking good notes, a tape recorder will be a help here.)

Or you may want to try to pretend you are something. *Be* that thing and write about how you think and feel. Imagine you are the sea, a caterpillar, a cigarette, a garbage can, a tree, a marble. Then describe what you see, hear, feel, do.

Or just set aside a ten-minute period, concentrate on the sounds, thoughts, feelings that come into your mind and write down as much as you can.

See if you can discover other forms of expressing yourself in writing. Experiment! And if you run out of ideas, look on the following pages.

Ideas

YOUR COMMUNITY PLACE

The Place

What is pleasing about your neighborhood?

What is distasteful about it?

Rebuild your neighborhood so that it fits your view of the ideal.

Describe your response to your surroundings at different times of the day (i.e., sunrise, noon, sunset, night).

The People

What do people in your neighborhood believe in? What are they prejudiced about? How do they show these values?

What kinds of work do you see? Which can you do? Which do you like?

Interview some people in your neighborhood. Find out about their past, present, and planned future. Try to describe their lifestyle, their dreams. Discuss why you think they made the choices they did.

What's Happening

What neighborhood activities do you enjoy?

What could you and your neighbors do together to make your community a better place to live?

Then What....

Have you ever worked in your community? What kinds of jobs were you able to find?

Do you think more jobs should be available for youth in your community? What kinds of jobs?

Describe your view of a perfect job. Where would it be? What would you be doing? How much money would you make? What kinds of people would your employers be? How would you relate to your fellow employees?

In your opinion, how does what you are learning at school relate to future employment? Do you feel you are being prepared for getting a job? Are there any suggestions you have which would make you feel better prepared?

Write a story about a person who is unhappy in his or her job. Try to solve the problem in a realistic manner.

How do TV images of careers and life compare to the way people live in your community? What kinds of similarities and differences do you see?

Interview one of your parents and a neighbor about the work they do. How do they feel about their job? How would they change things if they could?

Ideas, Ideas

YOUR SCHOOL PLACE

The Place

Describe how your school looks. How do you think the place contributes to your learning experiences? How would you change it if you could?

The People

Describe someone in your school that you care about

What kinds of problems do you have in school? How did they get to be problems? Who could help? How?

What's Happening

Has some new interest developed for you lately? Are you working on any special projects? How do you feel about them?

Describe a recent day in school. Describe an ideal day.

Then What...

What's worth knowing? How do you know? Why do you think so?

Describe how you would teach a class for a week in a subject you choose. What activities would you plan? Why? Try choosing one class you like and one that you don't.

Discuss the value of the subjects in which you are now enrolled. How does the content of these courses relate to your present and future plans? What would make it better?

List your subjects in order of preference, and discuss why you ordered them that way.

Ideas, Ideas, Ideas

YOUR PERSONAL PLACE

Describe your SELF from as many points of view as you can.

Discuss a response you've had to some recent media experience (TV program, newspaper article, music, movie, etc.).

Discuss your personal reaction to a recent rap session you've had with (a) friends, (b) parents, (c) correspondent, (d) other teachers, (e) a stranger.

Develop a thought or idea you have. Anything goes!

Step outside yourself and describe YOU as if you were a stranger just meeting you.

Get into any kind of emotional response you have experienced (i.e., anger, sadness, happiness, etc.), and describe it with color and life.

Do you like being alone? What do you most like to do when you are alone?

Discuss your hopes and fears, strengths and weaknesses. What relationship do these have to your life?

Write down a dream or a fantasy you've had recently. Analyze its meaning to you.

Do you have a pet? Describe its personality and your relationship with it. Put yourself in its place and describe yourself and a day in your life.

What kind of relationship with nature do you have? If you could spend your time anywhere in the world, where would you go and why? What would you do once you got there?

Discuss something you dislike. Try to decide what it is within yourself that makes you feel as you do about it.

Develop a method for relaxing. Give directions so that your correspondent can try it, too!

Write a story in which you are the hero or heroine. Try to relate the story to future employment you hope to experience.

LET'S START WITH ART

More of a Good Thing

You can start your new program of involvement with your gifted child in the subject area of art. It is one of the subjects which receives less attention these days because of the strong emphasis on reading and mathematics. Some of the exciting art experiences that your child has in school are unfortunately not repeated for the rest of the semester because of time limitations.

Visits to See Art

You and your child are fortunate: art is all around you waiting to be enjoyed. Some of the more common locations the two of you can visit are the following:

1. Museums
2. Art Centers
3. Exhibits at Fairs and Festivals
4. Art Stores
5. Civic Buildings
6. Colleges
7. Universities
8. Occupational Centers
9. Cemeteries
10. Private Homes
11. Restaurants

Simply by visiting places where art works can be found, a mutual bond will develop between you and your child. On these visits, discuss what each of you likes and why.

Develop Some Art Principles

A project involving principles such as line, form, color, and perspective can add to your art growth. Together you can notice how some art utilizes thin lines while other works have both thin and broad lines. In some pieces, thicker lines add force and clarity. Thinner lines have a light and airy dimension in their use. Line can separate parts of art works into more distinct parts.

Form, like line, displays itself in most art works. Shape can make some important figure stand out and catch your eye. It can show a large area in a picture. Sometimes it can be vague and hard to define while other times it is very definite. It can represent a house or tree with only a rough outline.

Color brings out objects. Houses look bigger and more inviting. Animals seem to appear more real. Trees show all of their brilliant features. Some art employs realistic use of color. Other works use color in novel and unusual ways. What happens to objects in the background when light, indefinite colors are used? What do color washes in the background produce? Are the objects in the foreground brighter than those behind them? Can the same color have different shades? Can a small bright object seem as dynamic as a large dull one? What happens to your eye when a color is used in different parts of the same art work?

"Let's Start with Art," H. Kanigher, from *Everyday Enrichment for Gifted Children at Home and School*, sponsored by the National/State Leadership Training Institute on the Gifted and the Talented, January 1977.

3. EXAMPLES

Why is perspective used in art? Notice what happens to objects when they are far in the background. Observe the size of trees in the foreground compared with those in the background. Who is larger, a person in the foreground or one in the background? Can you find an example of a person being shown in a picture larger than a tree, building, airplane, or other large object?

Black and White

The two of you can study black and white photography. How does the photographer use line, form, shape, and perspective to make a work of art out of black and white pictures? How does the local newspaper attract your attention with black and white pictures? What part do the art principles play in this attraction?

Shading

Have some fun with shading. The two of you can draw some simple objects and then shade them to create the illusion of roundness, squareness, rectangularness, and others. You can shade to show that the sun is in front of an object, behind it, near a side of it, or even not shining on that particular day. Shading can show texture: a smooth surface, a rough area, a sunken cheek, a hole in some fabric, a patch of grass, a grassless spot, and many other impressions.

Try Out Some Techniques

You and your child can plan a picture on a piece of paper. One of you can place a center of interest. The other can add background. Foreground can be included. Then colors can be added: interesting colors to make the center of interest stand out; duller, less interesting colors to create the background area. Now, how about some bold lines? Add some fine, thinner ones, too. Shading can show the time of day or night.

This time, cut out shapes from a magazine. Place one shape in the foreground on the left-hand side. Cut another shape and place it on the right. Can you make the two shapes balance? What do you have to do to balance a very large shape on one side with a smaller shape on the other? Can location of the smaller shape make a difference? What happens if you add several smaller shapes on the side across from the large one? Cut out clouds, mountains, buildings, animals, and other objects. Place them in your picture. Cut out background colors. Cut out some foreground ones, too. Does your eye move along from one object to the next? Does your center of interest attract your attention? Are the foreground colors more exciting than those in the background? Does your picture tell some kind of story? Is the picture realistic or on the abstract side?

Buy Some Art

What kind of pictures does your child have in his or her room? Are they ones that the child selected or even likes? Why not change one of them? Here is a good opportunity to have some of the prior experiences that the two of you have had together come into focus. Discuss the room, its furnishings, the color scheme, and other points. What kind of art would add interest to the room? Would you like exciting art or do you relax in the room and want a peaceful atmosphere?

Cement the relationship between your child and you further by spending an afternoon or even longer looking for just the right picture for his room. The purchase doesn't have to be a large one. A nice reproduction can be a wonderful piece of art for the room. All the time that the two of you are looking at different art examples, think of your art principles. See if you can notice the difference between quality art and work that is done in mass production with little attention to quality. Which art pieces have the same characteristics? Are they by the same artist? Does this artist use some of the same techniques over and over again?

If the right piece of art was hard to find today, then this will be a good opportunity to spend another pleasant afternoon together later in the week or next week. Did you discover that certain stores have better reproductions than others? Do some stores display their art more artistically than others?

Photography

With an inexpensive camera, and your art experiences to date well in mind, a camera can turn out another form of art. Begin with black and white film. Decide what the two of you would like to photograph. Be sure that you plan a center of interest. Have some secondary center or centers of interest, too. Try to eliminate a lot of eye-catching details in the background; the center-of-interest should attract the viewer's eye.

Experiment with distance. Photograph each other close up and far away. Photograph houses, office buildings, clouds, ponds, lakes, mountains, animals, and other interesting objects.

Stand above some objects when you photograph them. Lie on the ground when other snapshots are taken. Photograph at eye level. Focus in on a profile. Emphasize a portrait. Do a study of poses: sitting, standing, walking, holding an object in one hand, holding an object in both hands, catching a ball, throwing a ball, and others.

Study shadows: those in the early morning or later in the day, some in the evening, shadows on bright days, those on overcast days or on days when the sun is shining with many clouds in the sky. Photograph objects that cast shadows: trees, buildings, machines, animals, telephone poles, billboards, mobiles, plants, fences, mountains, toys, and others. Try to have your pictures utilize shadows to make them more interesting.

Now experiment with the more expensive color film. A new world should open for you and your child. The all important component of art, color, is at your finger's touch.

Plan each photograph carefully. Intentionally find an interesting object to photograph. Be sure that its colors add interest to the composition of the picture. Plan for an appropriate background. Include a nice, blue sky if you can.

Photograph a group of people dressed in bright gay colors. Snap a picture of bottles with colorful soft drinks. Capture boats on the ocean or lake. Show birds. Photograph trees and colorful plants. A large variety of flowers can add their beautiful colors to your photographs.

Have some of your best photographs enlarged. Notice the effect of increasing the size of the photographs. Have some pictures reduced to wallet size. How are the enlarged and wallet size pictures alike? How are they different?

Start a photo album. The two of you can have an enjoyable experience shopping for the right one. It should have enough pages to hold a large number of photographs. It should have enough pages which can be mounted with snap shots easily and conveniently. Perhaps you will want to purchase one album for special occasions and another for general photographs. Maybe weekend trips will make up one album. Captions above or below each picture will help you remember the dates and events shown. Artistic arrangement of the photographs will add to the beauty of the album.

As the two of you grow in your knowledge of photographic methods, better equipment can be purchased. This is something that can be carefully planned. The advantages and disadvantages of various cameras, in your price range, can be weighed. Information about shutter speeds and lens qualities can be included within the purchase decision. At any rate, you and your child will put your two heads together to make the appropriate choice.

Later, filters can be explored to meet your needs for special snapshots taken under differing conditions.

Photography is a wide-spread interest which can easily establish a sincere interest between you and your child. As the youngster grows and matures, so can the quality of this project involvement grow and mature.

Schools of Art

Following some discussion about the possible development of art, you and your child can visit the local library to find a few books about how art did develop. This investigation can include why early art was used, what art did that language was not adequate to do, how early man prepared and used paint and bushes, and where the painting was done. This is a natural lead-in regarding what types of early animals no longer exist today. The dwellings and clothing are also worthwhile discussion and research topics. Utensils, weapons, pets, food eaten, hair styles, home decorations, numbers in households, bedding materials, tasks of various family members, and an endless list of learnings can be uncovered from a study of this earliest art. It can be experimented with at home. The two of you might compose a picture-story about some exciting thing that you have done or would like to do. The event can be drawn on a piece of paper. Show it in the sequence in which it happens. For example, you might want to describe (in art) a trip to the library to gather information. Draw your home. Indicate how you traveled to the library. Add any special feature that you observed on the journey; a fire station, a hospital, or an amusement park. Sketch a picture or symbol of the kind of day it was: sunny, cloudy, or rainy. Draw the library. Many of these picture-stories can be developed for fun. Take turns drawing stories, like the one described, to tell the other person where you are: at school, at work, at the supermarket, or at the post office. If you're planning to go to several different places before you return home, all the better; the story will be a greater challenge to the other person.

Such schools as the following can be studied by the two of you as a truly educational experience: Classic, Renaissance, Baroque, Rococo, Impressionistic, Modern, Cubistic, and others. Each school parallels important historical developments: discoveries of land, scientific discoveries, events in politics, changes in philosophies, and others. The schools of art have direct relationships to schools of music. In fact, many of the names of schools of art have the same names given to schools of music: Classic, Renaissance, Baroque, Rococo, Impressionistic, and Modern.

It is interesting to discover which men and women were famous for their art during the various periods. Exciting research can uncover the kinds of materials on which people painted and drew. The types of brushes, and how they were made, provide further interesting study. The preparation of paint adds interest and variety to the study.

Sculpture, in its many forms, offers three-dimensional novelty to your project. The two of you can explore single and group sculpture, relief and intaglio, busts and full-size, wood and stone, marble from Italy compared with local stone, and the tools used in this art form. The development of sculpture from its early beginnings to modern time provides other avenues to explore. The change in materials used in this art area add to the versatility of sculpture: stone, wood, metal, plastic, in addition to others.

You and your child can sculpture for fifty cents or less. Purchase a few pounds of plaster of Paris. Mix a small amount of this material with plain water and stir until the mixture is the consistency of thick cream. Pour the mixture into an empty quart milk container. Allow it to dry and harden for one day. Peel the paper off and a block of plaster will stand before the two of you.

With tools as simple as a butter knife, a table fork, a toothpick, a paper clip, and a thumb tack, you are ready to sculpture the block. First, consider what object you wish to craft. Then draw the object in pencil, as an outline. Show what areas will be carved away and which will be untouched. This will be a good way to use the shading techniques which went into your drawings and paintings, earlier. Carve away the shaded parts as much as you wish. After all of your simple tools have been used, smooth the piece with fine sandpaper. The white plaster is beautiful by itself, but you may wish to paint the work with a brush or spray can.

The two of you can do single objects and groups. Show people in action: running, jumping, bending over, reaching with one hand, reaching with both hands, kicking, dancing, and stooping. Show people engaged in outdoor activities: fishing, shooting archery, swimming, riding horses, playing baseball, playing football, playing basketball, and others.

As your skill increases, approach such challenging experiences as carving hair of various lengths, adding clothing of varied styles, adding rings, earrings, watches, and coats.

Purchase or make some of the standard carving tools: V cutters, U gouges, files, rasps, and chisels. Explore the range of these tools. Identify their limitations. Notice the different results from applying differing amounts of pressure on the tools.

Experiment with wire. Use different thicknesses of wire. Form simple figures. Form pairs of figures. Show how these figures interact with each other: dancing, shaking hands, carrying heavy objects, a dentist working on a patient, a doctor with a patient, a sales person and a customer, and other pairs of persons. Show three or more persons. Use wire to show various shapes. Make some shapes common ones and other creative designs. Experiment with modern art. Have some figures and shapes represent everyday things.

When your best wire sculpture has been completed, prepare another mixture of plaster of Paris. This time, however, prepare it a little thicker than water. Cut pieces of old cloth into three inch strips. Dip these strips into the mixture, one at a time, and carefully cover all of the wire pieces. Be certain that you wrap the cloth tightly so the shape of the wire stays the same. When the plaster has dried on the cloth, you will have a sculpture of wire covered with a very hard cover. Tap the sculpture; it really is quite solid. As before, you can either leave the work white or paint it to suit your tastes.

Wood sculpture is unlike carving in a block of wood. In wood sculpture, scrap pieces are cut to varying lengths. Odd shapes and designs are cut from other scraps. A square or rectangular piece is selected to be the base for the sculpture to stand on. The first piece is glued to this base. Another piece is glued to the first. Different lengths and shapes are arranged until the work is complete. Select a different topic and make another sculpture. For modern art, one or two pieces of wood—perhaps of different sizes—can be selected for the complete work. In other more traditional works, buildings, trees, figures, mountains, lakes, rivers, machines, or other objects may be shown.

One medium which always appeals to youngsters is clay. It is readily available for a small amount of money. Many of the topics both of you selected for the other sculpture projects can be chosen for clay forms. Because it is such a flexible medium, it can be rolled, squeezed, cut, added on, scraped off, coiled, and more. It hardens when dry. Scrapes can be put into a little dish with water and brought back to their former flexible state.

Clay can be cut with cookie cutters, dried, painted, and glued onto a board or board covered with fabric. Simple bowls can be formed by long coils or pieces of clay formed and then rounded. These bowls, when dry, can be decorated with paint.

Clay forms can be covered with tiny pieces of newspaper dipped into a watery solution of flour and water. When the clay has been completely covered with newspaper, paper towels can be torn into bigger pieces and dipped into the same solution. These, too, are applied to the figure. When the outer cover is dry, cut a slit along one side of the figure. Carefully pull the clay out. Cover the slit with the same technique described before with newspaper scraps and the paper towel pieces. Finally, paint your art work.

To further increase the value of the study of schools of art, a scrapbook can be kept showing samples of each type of art. Samples of sculpture can be included with drawings, paintings, architecture, and other evidence of the periods of time which they cover.

Architecture

A fascinating area of art study is architecture. Within easy walking or riding distance, in every large or small city or town, is a wide variety of homes, office buildings, factories, civic facilities, parks, museums, and other representative samples of our civilization.

The prior study of the schools of art has developed some background for your pursuit. Throughout history, structures have offered decoration reflecting religious beliefs, the carrying out of commerce, and leisure hour occupations.

A first project might be a study of your own home or apartment. Together, draw your child's room floor plan. Develop symbols for furniture, doorways, light fixtures, pictures, and other elements. Then develop a plan for the entire house. Don't forget to show the exterior as well as the interior.

Next, select a piece of cardboard or other stiff material to serve as the base of your model. Following the floor plan, construct the walls of your house or apartment. Furnish the facility with miniature pieces of furniture. Add pictures, rugs, and other items.

Construct a roof. Be sure that the roof can be lifted off and replaced. Individual pieces of tile (formed from red clay), wood, or asbestos shingles can add realism to the roof and also serve as a good lesson about protection from the elements.

Add landscaping to your model. It is fun to develop miniature bushes, flowers, trees, decorative rocks, and other components in your exterior plan.

If you live in an apartment, your unit can be designed and developed into a cut-away while the other apartment units remain fixed. The landscaping for the entire building can still be considered your exterior.

Other exciting models can be designed: an office building, a museum, a police station, a fire station, a city hall, a church or synagogue, a baseball field complete with the bleachers and club house, a football stadium, a basketball stadium, a swimming stadium, and many others.

Airplanes, trains, buses, automobiles, ships and boats, and other means of transportation can be designed as an extension of your achitecture unit. Futuristic models of buildings and means of transportation can incorporate some very imaginative thinking. This, too, can be a good extension of the prior projects associated with drawing, painting, and photography.

Mobiles and Stabiles

A project which involves the principles of balance and aerodynamics along with art is the design of mobiles. A wire coat hanger on which thread is tied to support objects of different sizes and shapes, along with a piece of string with which to hang the instrument, will have you well on your way with the project. Geometric shapes fashioned from paper, wood, plastic, metal, cork, leather, cardboard, and other materials, provide a simple mobile idea. Planets of the universe placed around the sun make up another theme. Additional themes could include: members of your family (with photographs of each on the respective mobile pieces), kinds of sport activities, animals, airplanes, trains, boats, automobiles, trucks, motorcycles, months of the year, seasons of the year, flowers, trees, buildings, friends of the family, occupations, hobbies, and others too numerous to list.

The stabile doesn't revolve. It remains in a fixed position. Any of the themes mentioned in conjunction with the mobiles can also serve as themes for stabiles.

Both mobiles and stabiles can serve important purposes other than decorating in the home: remind you of important events each week or month, remind you about dental care, motivate you about cleanliness, indicate proper air circulation in the home, provide a test of how much dust is present at different heights, show the resistance of particular colors to fading, and serve to demonstrate which colors attract your eye most.

Art in Your Backyard

The two of you can collect a variety of leaves, twigs, flower petals, stems, roots, and other natural materials in the yard. Many things can be done with these items to increase your fun with art.

Leaves can be pasted between two sheets of wax paper to form a pleasant lamination. This can be hung in the house as a stabile or be part of a mobile. In the latter case, several laminations will be necessary.

Leaf prints are quick and easy. Dip a brush into tempera paint and lightly cover a leaf with the substance. Touch the painted side of the leaf to the paper and a print will appear. Repeat the process using other leaves in your collection. Paint some of the leaves different colors. An interesting picture will result from the series of individual leaf prints. In place of paint, stamp pad ink can be substituted.

A variety of the natural materials can be glued to a piece of paper and then covered with a single sheet of wax paper. The materials can also simply be glued to a piece of paper as a one-step operation. Another alternative is to glue the materials to the piece of paper and paint over the entire surface of the paper with watercolors. This can be done before or after gluing the materials to the paper.

Tissue Projects

Art tissue-paper colors are vast. All of the primary and secondary colors are available at stores where art materials are sold. Tissue paper offers numerous exciting activities.

Paper flowers are going into more and more vases each day. Simply by cutting one or more colors of tissue paper into circular patterns, and poking a straight piece of wire through the center, a beautiful flower can be made. The wire below the flower petals can be wrapped with green tape to add the natural color to the item. Leaves can be cut out of construction paper, glued to the ends of pieces of shorter lengths of wire, and taped to the stem below the petals. A little circle of construction paper can be glued into the center of the flower to complete the project. Different types of flowers can be attempted. The experience serves to provide a good education about the different kinds and constructions of flowers.

Pieces of construction paper, cut out in the shapes of the states, can eventually become a map of the United States.

Pieces of tissue can be cut into various geometric shapes and then glued to white art paper. A moist brush, containing only water, can be swept over the pieces of tissue to induce them to bleed their colors. The result is a mixture of bright hues.

Pieces of tissue can be cut in the shapes of various centers of interest and background objects. The tissue pieces are then glued to a piece of paper. Finally, a felt-tip pen or brush with paint bring the outline of the objects into focus when they are used to trace around each object. The pen or brush can embellish the picture by adding detail to the tissue shapes: eyes can be added to human or animal figures; wheels can be shown on vehicles; ridges can be added to mountains and hills; leaves can be shown on trees.

Cellophane

Circles can be cut from different colors of cellophane. One color can be held up to a flashlight. Another color and even a third can be placed over the beam of light to note the effects of color mixing. The secondary colors which develop can be paired with still other colors to form more colors. The results of mixing light and dark colors will create interesting results. Always, when a number of colors are added together, the resulting color is darker than the original color. When using paint, what happens when white is added to darker colors? What happens when black is added to other colors? Which colors are really not considered true colors? What are the neutrals?

Mixed Media

Remembering your knowledge about line, shape, perspective, balance, and other important art elements, plan a picture using mixed media. Use tissue, leaves, twigs, stems, petals, fabrics, cellophane paper, and paint. Notice the effect of using mixed media. Is the picture as two-dimensional or flat as the pictures you have made using only paint?

Experiment with your various media. Use fabrics and tissue together by themselves. Use leaves and cellophane paper. Use paint and fabrics together.

Hobbies in Art

A variety of exciting kits are available in department stores and other outlets which promise hours of fun. Don't overlook the fun of stringing Indian beads on thread or wire to form rings, bracelets, and necklaces. An incidental history lesson can develop from a study of the patterns that are used by different Indian nations. The patterns are found in their jewelry, blankets, clothing, pottery, and other items.

Other interesting kits which give the purchaser careful directions about their use include woodburning, macrame, paint by number, pastic moulding, and others.

It is a pleasing experience to investigate the experiences of some of these kits. They offer a chance for your child and you to discover the fun of figuring out the directions, planning the art activities, doing the projects, and enjoying the results.

You've Made a Start

Through the art experiences mentioned in this chapter, you and your gifted child have been drawn closer together in purposeful activities. You've seen a side of each other that possibly wasn't there before. You have studied a subject, in depth, which is present everywhere in your lives. You have new-found knowledge which was pleasantly gathered, together. Some of these projects were one-time experiences while others will continue through the weeks, months, and years ahead.

Children Love to Learn Logic

Children want to find meaning in their school lessons, says Matthew Lipman, professor of philosophy and director of the Institute for Advancement of Philosophy for Children. To help students make their education more meaningful, Lipman has been doing research for ten years in the development of philosophy studies for children. His book, *Harry Stottlemeier's Discovery*, represents one of his first experiments in this area.

And who is Harry Stottlemeier and what does he discover? If you remove the *meier* from the name, you will see a resemblance to Aristotle. Ten-year-old Harry, the main character in Lipman's book for elementary students, discovers how his thought processes work. There are no difficult philosophy terms in the book and the story's characters are "real children."

With a National Endowment for the Humanities grant in 1969, Lipman wrote the book and set up an experimental teaching situation in a Montclair, New Jersey, fifth-grade class. He and two graduate-student helpers read the book with the students, asked questions, and played roles from the book. Lipman's 40-minute, twice-a-week experiment, when compared with a control group, showed that the students' mental ages were increased by 27 months. The experience of studying philosophy even affected the students' reading scores two-and-a-half years later.

The young philosophy students also bring their newly-acquired logical skills into everyday reasoning. An example from a 1974 *Time* magazine article on the program follows: "One boy told the teacher that 'All Puerto Ricans are nasty.' Then, looking at the teacher, he suddenly remembered his lesson and said, 'Most Puerto Ricans are nasty.' Almost as quickly, he regrouped and concluded, 'Well, the Puerto Ricans I know are nasty.' "

Another grant under the auspices of the Department of Philosophy, Columbia University, allowed Lipman to write a 14-page teacher's manual to go with his book. Lipman, who has taught philosophy at Columbia University and now teaches at Montclair State College, places great importance on training teachers specifically to teach philosophy in the elementary grades.

From the *Bulletin of the National/State Leadership Training Institute on the Gifted and the Talented*, April 1979. Babrara Johnson, Editor.

Other material developed since that time is a sequel to *Harry*, titled *Lisa*, which covers such ethical questions as what is fair, right, and true, and what are rules. *Suki*, a novel for high schoolers that Lipman wrote, shows how students can make sense of their lives by thinking and reasoning. Five filmstrips have been developed for grades five-to-eight, including *Thinking about Thinking*; a group of 30 essays are under the heading *Growing Up with Philosophy*. Much of this material has been translated into Spanish, French, Danish, and Chinese.

The following chapter titles and formal logic content from *Harry Stottlemeier* give an indication of the scope of the material:

	Formal Logic Content		Philosophical Content
1	Reversing Sentences		A paradigm of discovery; Thinking about Thinking
2		Standardization	The application of logic to life situations
3			The preciousness of thoughts; Logic and fantasy
4			The reality of thoughts
5			The purpose of education; Thinking for oneself
6			Alternative views of the mind
7	Relations		Degree and kind; Culture
8		Syllogisms	Styles of thinking; What is good?
9			Giving reasons; Children's rights
10			Rules and generalizations
11			The contents of consciousness
12	Contradiction		The preciousness of persons
13			Presuppositions; The many ways of thinking
14	Syllogisms		Art and life; Using people as things
15			Description and explanation; Causes and reasons
16	Hypothetical Syllogisms		The nature of hypotheses
17			Perspectives; The objectivity of knowledge

In Lipman's 40-page pamphlet, Philosophy for Children, co-edited with Terrell Ward Bynum, the question is raised as to why the schools do not teach principles of thought. He asks, "Is it because mindlessness is no threat to society?" Lipman believes that if the students are not taught to reason well, the conclusion must be that "we really don't want them to wonder what it's all about."

A Unique Learning Opportunity for Talented High School Seniors

An exploration of themselves and of promising career fields.

Sharon Colson, Christopher Borman, and William R. Nash

SHARON COLSON was principal investigator of the project described here. She is a research associate in the Center for Career Development and Occupational Preparation (CDOP) in the College of Education at Texas A & M University (TAMU). CHRISTOPHER BORMAN is director of the center and is professor of educational psychology at TAMU. WILLIAM R. NASH is associate professor of educational psychology at TAMU. Borman and Nash were co-directors of the project.

An expanded guidance laboratory at Texas A & M University has permitted 20 gifted and talented high school seniors from A & M Consolidated High School in College Station to get to know themselves – and to identify promising career fields.

Participants were selected on the basis of several criteria: general intellectual ability, creative thinking ability, academic ability, specific talent, school success, behavioral characteristics (leadership, motivation, creativity, etc.), and past accomplishments. The 15 most highly qualified students became full participants; the next five became alternates. The 20 participants included 9 males and 11 females.

Each phase of the program directly corresponded to the first, second, and third quarters of the school year. Phase 1, Guidance Laboratory Experiences, combined occupational information, guest speakers, simulations, games, and guidance kits with extensive testing. The Guidance Lab was fast-paced and diversified, because gifted and talented students are easily bored by repetitive activities.

Guest speakers were selected on the basis of student interest. Early in the laboratory experience, each participant was asked to submit three career fields from which guest speakers would be selected. Later, as new career fields were identified and explored, others were added to the list. The students identified the guest speakers as their most worthwhile laboratory experience. The most interesting result was the number of changes in student interests following a guest speaker's presentation. Lack of information or misinformation had given many of the students incorrect perceptions of various career fields. In many cases students changed their career goals after receiving accurate information.

As part of efforts to evaluate the program, we queried high school faculty and parents. Most of them regarded the program favorably. They thought it would ease the students' transition into the college community. Parents reported a sharing of experiences among the participants and their families. The high school principal commented on the improved dress of the students.

"A Unique Learning Opportunity for Talented High School Seniors," by S. Colson, C. Bormon, and W. R. Nash, in *Phi Delta Kappan*, Vol. 59, No. 8, April 1978, pp 542-543. ©1978, Phi Delta Kappa, Inc.

During the last two weeks of the Guidance Lab, the students made first and second career-field choices for the Mentorship Phase of the project. A majority of the students were able to make these selections easily. The information they had received about career fields, their exposure to the decision-making process, and their knowledge of themselves provided by testing had equipped them for this responsibility. Individual counseling was scheduled for those who were unable to decide on a career field. More information was provided in interest areas, and opportunities for departmental interviews were arranged.

Once first and second choices were made, the students individually prepared a study of each choice. These studies included the life-style, working conditions, geographic location, pay scale, training, and degrees necessary for a career in the field, plus the outlook for its future.

Participants in the Mentorship Laboratory Experience were placed with a professor at Texas A & M in a career field of their choice for the second quarter of the school year. Students were placed with a mentor only after a personal interview and discussion between the mentor and the student. If both were satisfied, then an agreement was negotiated between the professor and the project staff.

With the exception of one student, all participants were placed in first-choice mentorships. Mentorship placements varied widely and included physics, civil engineering, psychology, wildlife and fisheries, communications, marketing, entertainment, law, drama, music, education, and electrical engineering.

Overall, mentor reactions to the project were highly positive. A majority of the mentors agreed that their participation in the project caused no significant inconvenience in fulfilling their own jobs.

During the Mentorship Phase each participant was required to keep a daily log of activities. These logs were par-

ticularly helpful to the staff and documented mentorship activities for project evaluation. They also provided topics for discussion during bi-monthly seminars. Most of the students looked forward to the seminars, because they liked the opportunity of hearing about others' experiences and sharing their own.

Although the mentors encompassed 14 academic disciplines and executed their individual responsibilities in different ways, the logs indicated several commonalities among the mentorship experiences, e.g., field trips, experiments, library research, attendance of college classes, operation of equipment or sophisticated machines related to a particular career area, and production of a final product. A majority of the students indicated that their mentors spent a significant amount of time discussing individual student goals and needs.

Parents informed the project directors that exposure to career alternatives, contact with professionals in the career areas, and the providing of specific information about selected career fields were of great help to their children. According to their regular classroom teachers, 51% of the students frequently shared with the class information gained through the career education project.

The Working Internship Phase conducted during the third quarter of the school year provided contact with a professional in the community who was concerned with one or two specific areas of the broader career field. Just as during mentorship, the student was placed in internship with a site supervisor in the community only after a successful interview during which both the student and the site supervisor agreed that the placement was in keeping with the student's career goal.

Internship provided the participants with observations of the life-style required by the career, the disposition and personal characteristics necessary for the career, and the responsibilities that accompany the work. Each participant was paired with an individual from the community who was active in either

business, industry, labor, or a profession. Students worked closely with these site supervisors, gaining firsthand experience. Internship placements were directly related to mentorship placements; e.g., a student in a civil engineering mentorship was placed with a firm of consulting civil engineers; a communications student was placed with a local television station.

Periodically, students were asked to list typical activities that occurred during internship. The experiences varied widely. Students usually had no set routine; they were allowed to sample a variety of activities in order to gain exposure to many facets of the work. However, a few of the students did have set responsibilities: One student had his own radio program; another was responsible for developing a computer inventory system. The following response illustrates the diversity of experiences:

"I have been involved in 'roughnecking' on a core-boring rig and bringing the core soil samples back to the lab and testing them.... I have been surveying all over East Texas using chains, plumb bobs, and transits.... I have been plotting core-boring sites on large maps for a refinery in Louisiana. I have worked side by side with all types of people and have enjoyed the work very much."

In summary, it appears that the project was well received by all who were involved with it. The students, their parents, their teachers, the mentors, and the site supervisors were consistently positive in evaluating the project. The needs of all students involved were not completely met, but all the participants stated they had greatly benefited and would make the same decision again. After completing the internship, 83% of the students said that they had gained insight into the lifestyles of those in their chosen career field; 100% had gained insight into their own needs and interests; 83% were convinced that their career choice was right for them.

FOCUS ...

STUDENT SPEAK-OUT

SMPY counsels its students by offering them a smorgasbord of accelerative options (see the article by Benbow on p. 21) The students is encouraged by SMPY to design a unique educational program that best suits him or her.

The following three articles describe how three students accomplished their goals. These accounts were written by the students themselves. Thus they provide an inside story of how the student perceives these educational options as working.

C.P.B.

A DUAL PERSPECTIVE
Kevin G. Bartkovich°

Being both a protege of SMPY and a chief mentor for SMPY, I am in a unique position. As a student, I have taken advantage of many of the accelerative educational opportunities offered by SMPY. As a mentor, I have had the privilege of facilitating mathematically brilliant youths from all over the country.

My involvement with SMPY began when, while a normal-age eighth-grade student at a suburban Baltimore junior high school, I participated in SMPY's second talent search in January 1973. My score was high enough on the mathematics part of the Scholastic Aptitude Test to be eligible to enroll in an SMPY-sponsored accelerated mathematics class. After 14 months of two-hour Saturday morning classes starting in the summer after eighth grade, we had finished Algebra II, Algebra III, plane geometry, trigonometry, and analytic geometry-a full four years of precalculus mathematics. Thus, I was ready to take calculus in the tenth grade.

During that grade, I participated in an SMPY-sponsored supplemental calculus class as well as attending the calculus class at my high school. The supplemental class provided materials beyond my high school class, so that I was prepared to

take the Advanced Placement Program Calculus BC examination in May of that year. I received the top score of 5 on the 1 to 5 scale, enabling me to receive 8 semester-hour credits of calculus at The Johns Hopkins University.

During my junior year in high school, I took 12th-grade English, thereby fulfilling graduation requirements. As a result I was graduated from high school in 1976, a year ahead of my age mates. I entered John Hopkins in the fall of 1976, already in possession of 24 college credit hours. I accrued these credits through the APP mathematics exam and by taking 5 college courses during my two years of high school, starting with the summer after ninth grade. These credits represent the equivalent of nearly one full year of fulltime college coursework. They gave me sophomore standing.

If I had so desired, I could have graduated from Johns Hopkins after this year, my third. In order to make full use of a four-year National Merit Scholarship, however, I am studying concurrently for a Master's degree as well as a Bachelor's degree. In May 1980, while still 20 years old, I am scheduled to receive both degrees in the field of electrical engineering.

As mentioned previously, since entering John Hopkins I have worked part-time for SMPY. As a freshman, I began by tutoring individual students in mathematics at a rapid pace. During the summer after my freshman year, I served as the teaching assistant for an eight-week, fast-paced geometry course.

During the school years, I have continued as a mentor for mathematically gifted youths. In the summer of 1978, after completing my second year of college, I co-taught with David Meyer[1] a two week accelerated mathematics class in rural South-Central Nebraska. At the conclusion of this unique program, each of our eight students had completed at least two years of high school mathematics. Upon returning to Baltimore, I taught two of the accelerated mathematics classes in SMYP's extremely successful 1978 summer program.

Because of my teaching experience in Nebraska, I was invited back there in November of 1978 to present a two-day seminar to 45 teachers interested in helping mathematically gifted students. This summer, David and I will return to teach another two-

From the ITYB, Intellectually Talented Youth Bulletin, Published by the Study of Mathematically Precocious Youth (SMPY), The Johns Hopkins University, Baltimore, Maryland 21218. Professor Daniel P. Keating, Editor

week class, this time for 17 highly able youths. Also, I will again teach this summer at Johns Hopkins in the eight-week fast-math program sponsored by SMPY.

Through the experiences of accelerating my education under the encouragement of SMPY, I have first-hand knowledge of the types of opportunities which meet the needs of mathematically gifted youths. I also know that educational acceleration need not have adverse social effects, as evidenced by my participation on the Hopkins varsity soccer team and in Hopkins Christian Fellowship. It has been a highlight of my undergraduate career to be able to present brilliant youths with the facilitative opportunities that I was given and value so much.

[1]David Alan Meyer received a B.A. degree, with major completed in both mathematics and physics, and also on M.A. degree in mathematics, both from John Hopkins, on 31 May 1979 at age 201/4 years.

*EDITOR'S NOTE: Mr. Bartkovich is indeed, a most remarkable student and mental. His conducting a two-day workshop for the Nebraska math teachers at age 19 highly successfully is an achievement unmatched even in SMPY's vast experience.

LIFE IN THE FAST LANE
Arlene J. Morales*

When as a tenth-grader I left high school to go full-time to Goucher College, I found myself innundated with people asking, "Don't you feel you'll miss a lot by skipping your last two years in high school?" The answer is an emphatic, No. Rather, I feel I've gained much.

It all started when I participated in SMPY's testing program when I was in the 7th grade. As a result, I was asked to participate in a fast-paced Algebra I course. I had attended a private parochial school since the first grade. I met quite an opposition there when wanting to take Algebra I in the 7th grade. With the help of Drs. Stanley and Fox, I was allowed to. In 8th grade I continued onto Algebra II. The school offered no support, and I had to continue to take 8th grade math in addition to Algebra II. Taking Algebra II was entirely on my own, and even though the other math wasn't difficult made me feel bored and frustrated. The administration would hear nothing of letting me take algebra at the high school; instead my mother had to drive me all the way to the city a couple of times a week. When I asked why I couldn't take algebra at the high school, they said it was just not their policy and it couldn't be done. They told me I wasn't ready, yet I went on to get 99.4 percentile on the national algebra test. I also took a college course that spring in Computer Programming.

In the summer of my eighth grade I took a college algebra course at Goucher, and in the ninth grade I was ready to start Advanced Placement (AP) Calculus. Again, I met with great opposition and thanks to the determination of Dr. Stanley and Dr. Fox, I was allowed to take it. I decided to take an English course at a nearby university during that spring.

The AP course was a very sad course. I felt that, with respect to mathematics, I had wasted the entire year. I wasn't allowed to take calculus at Goucher since our school offered an AP course. There were a lot of people there who shouldn't have been in such a course. That summer I took a placement test at Goucher and placed out of the first semester of calculus. It was in the ninth grade that I realized I would have to leave early. I took physics at Goucher that summer. It was there I learned the prejudice of some teachers against intellectually precocious youths. It served as a good experience, and now I never mention my age since there is no real need to. In my tenth grade, I decided that my school had no more math to offer me, so I started part-time at Goucher. I again received no support or recognition from the high school administration. When I announced my plans for leaving after my tenth grade, they were appalled. They thought it was terribly wrong and thought I should stay through at least my 11th grade and takewhat I call "busywork." I was starting to get bored and knew it was time to leave high school. They wouldn't give me a diploma or let me receive one under any circumstances because, "no one has ever done this before and it is not in our policy to do so." Even though all my sisters and I had gone there since the 1st grade, they wouldn't give me a diploma.

As for my former high school, which is supposedly a very good one, I think it is a pity that they are so restrictive. The administration can deal fine with slow, average, or above-average learners, but they have not yet found a way to help extremely precocious youths. They have not even learned to recognize them, much less support them in any way. Well, it was too bad, but a high school diploma wasn't essential. I went on to Goucher where I was exempted from French (I had been taking it since the first grade) and Spanish (the language spoken at home), I am a math major with intentions of going to medical school. I have finally found a place where I feel academicaly challenged. I found that I even got along better with my high school classmates once I wasn't with them academically. They felt no competition with me once I was out.

It sounds like I have gone through life without taking time for other than academic things. I would like to point out that even though I was accelerated, I did not do so at the expense of extracurricular involvement. High school was a most memorable time for me. I was a cheerleader, played varsity tennis, held positions in the Student Council, was on many committees, and took piano lessons from the Peabody Conservatory, where I had finished all Theory of Music and have been playing for 10 years. I have been swimming competitively since I was five and playing tournament tennis since I was 11. I grew rapidly both emotionally and mentally in those two years. I haven't missed the fun of senior proms, as I was invited by others, I really don't think I've lost anything.

Many people have told me that boys are more apt to skip than girls. I've always felt being a girl the decision to skip would be made more easily in the affirmative. A girl would fit in socially better, since no one "asks a lady's age." Dating was never a problem, because I've always dated people older than me.

This year I am tutoring some 8th graders in algera, teaching piano, and on the executive board of the Commuters as Social Chairman, I participated on the varsity tennis team, was in the Math Club, and worked part-time as a secretary. I'm a big sister for Goucher. This summer I will be working as a mentor for Dr. Stanley in his fast-paced mathematics program. I just want to extend my gratitude to Dr. Stanley and Dr. Fox, who have opened many doors for me. I'm glad that I had the chance to enter college early because of SMPY's program, and I highly recommend it to other young people who qualify.

I feel a little sad when I realize that people who do have the potential but not the means of achieving are being bored by school and may soon lose all interest in academic matters. Let me give you one note of advice: Don't *ever* give up, and don't let people mold you into a form like the "average" student. Fight for your right to be educated to your fullest capacity!

THOUGHTS ON ACCELERATION
*Richard J. Cohn**

I'm sitting here at the table, trying to think of what I should tell you, what could assist you in making those important decisions you must make about your education. First, I'll describe how I've done things, including some mistakes, and then I'll made some observations on acceleration in general. I entered SMPY's talent search in its first year, 1972, as a twelve-year-old seventh-grader. In the eighth grade, I joined a "fast" Algebra II class given by SMPY, skipping Algebra I. The class also managed to learn (through not very thoroughly) college algebra, trigonometry, some analytic geometry, and two-thirds of a gemometry text. This course adequately prepared me for am advanced Placement calculus class in ninth grade. Meanwhile, I began taking courses at night at Towson State University in Baltimore, Maryland.

My favorite aspect of acceleration, more than the "saving" of a year or two of education, was the taking of these college courses. In general, I enjoyed them more than the ones I attend now at Johns Hopkins as a full-time student. None of the courses was impossibly difficult, but unlike most of my high school courses, they were both challenging and interesting. I learned much from my classmates, more of whom were in their mid- and late twenties. These courses also benefited me at John Hopkins by helping make the transition to college smoother with 21 credits from Towson and 14 APP credits (calculus and English). I had quite a hard start on college. These extra credits will enable me to graduate next May with both a B.A. and an M.A. in mathematical sciences. I must note, however, that I seemed to learn the material in some of these courses by the "easy come, easy go" method. When I needed to use the background material I had learned a Towson for courses at Hopkins, I found I sometimes had little or no recollection of it.

Another problem I had at Hopkins was deciding what to do with myself. My parents were preparing for "my son, the doctor". I began my college career as a pre-med student majoring in psychology, but soon switched to mathematical sciences. As long as I did well, that was fine. But combining graduate-level math courses and time-consuming pre-med courses proved to be more than I could take. All along, I knew one day I would have to decide--math or medical school--only it was a little sooner than I thought. It's been a year and a half since my decision, and I have yet to regret it. I now find myself enjoying my courses, doing well, and having time for the truly important things in life like playing racquetball and going to Oriole games.

Almost all "radical accelerants" become very defensive when these magic words "social life" and "adjustment" are mentioned. "Of course, I'm just like everyone else," they declare, occasionally a bit too loudly, as if they are attempting to convince themselves. Some people adjust, but some don't. In freshman chemistry lab one day, someone explained his ex-roommate to me: "You know, he is only sixteen, and it shows: I couldn't stand his immaturity." Two years later, this person is just as immature. But other early entrants seem older than the average student. The kind of social life you have in college is not determined by your age (within limits--ain't no way a twelve-or thirteen-year old will be treated on an equal basis with an eighteen-year old). You determine your adjustment; people who have little or no social life at age 17 or 18 would probably have the same problems if they were older.

Unfortunately, I have neglected to note that I graduated from high school after eleventh grade, a rather important detail. This seems to be a popular method of acceleration for people who feel they've outgrown school socially and emotionally as for those who are bored academically. Many people with whom I've spoken have felt their senior year of high school could have been spent. And of course, they are others, like my roommate, who considers twelfth grade the most rewarding of all his years in school. In making this decision, consider carefully what opportunities, you'll have in high school (Advanced Placement Program (APP) courses, courses at nearby colleges, extra-curricular activities not available elsewhere), as well as the advantages of going on to college. One thing few people mention, until it's too late, is that some colleges do not look fondly upon early entrants (John Hopkins University is not one of these). So, by graduating a year early, you may eliminate yourself from acceptance by a college you want to attend. Thus it is wise to know in advance what the colleges you want to attend think about the age of applicants.

One thing people worry about that should not enter into your decisions on acceleration, except in extreme cases, is knowing what you want to do in life. If you know, that's to your benefit, for it allows you to plan ahead more appropriately. If you don't don't worry you'll find out. Just don't go to a college with a narrow focus (an engineering school, for example). College is a time to experiment, to try things you'll probably never try again. Four years, even three, is ample time to decide upon a major and complet its requirements.

Well, I've tried to avoid the usual pitfalls of this type of article, and I hope I have succeeded to some degree. If you're still reading, I guess I have. Anyway, as a summary of today's lesson, keep in mind the following useful but often forgotten points.

(1) Consider all the alternatives. There are many different kinds and degrees of acceleration. Examine all of them to discover which ones, if any, are most suitable for you.

(2) Always question people's findings and conclusions, including your own. If you feel uneasy, don't hesitate to make changes or at least attempt to do so. Don't be afraid to act.

(3) If possible, do things that interest you, even excite you, since fulfilling other people's goals will often lead to disaster. If you're not doing what you like, you'll often find, whatever you're doing, you're doing poorly.

As a whole, I've found acceleration to be a worthwhile experience. It has permitted me to do things I would otherwise not have had a chance to do, as well as saved me from wasting away in endless high school math classes. Besides, it really impresses prospective employers. I can recommend whole heartedly acceleration to those who feel emotionally as well as academically ready for it.

*EDITORS NOTE: Mr. Cohn, born 29 October 1959, is one of the six highly able students who did spendidly in SMPY's first fast-paced mathematics class and later became full-time students at John Hopkins. That class began in June of 1972 and was taught expertly by Joseph Wolfson. It terminated in August of 1973, after about 120 hours of instruction. Richard entered the class in the fall of 1972 and required fewer hours (about 100) than anyone to complete all of pre-calculus superbly.

Thinking Ahead: Future Studies for G/C/T Individuals

Thelma Epley

Ms. Epley is a frequent contributor to these pages. She is a "retired" California educator who spends her retirement days working to help local California school systems improve their G/C/T efforts. Bob Lamb is an art instructor at Delgado Junior College in New Orleans. His work, too, appears periodically in the pages of G/C/T.

Why Study the Future?

There are two general reasons for studying the future. First, we need to educate the young in ways that will benefit them when they leave school. Second, we need to educate ourselves as well as our young people so that we can maintain quality where it is declining and increase alternatives for dealing with crises, needs and problems as they emerge.

Benefits from the study of the future includes the following:

- strengthening of the ability to anticipate, to forecase and adapt to change through invention, informed acquiescence or intelligent resistance
- understanding and information about the processes of change and how to slow or accelerate it
- group decision-making, clarifying one's own values, knowing better what to defend, to choose, to commit one's life to
- involvement in the real world
- information about strategies, how to generate ideas, ways to search for alternatives
- analytical approach to forces, people and events shaping the future
- widening of the options for thinking about one's own life
- belief in self—the understanding that individuals can affect change—can make a difference

Teachers, parents and others teaching the leaders, the thinkers, the changers and innovators of tomorrow must go beyond the confines of a single discipline to search for new associations—to broaden the scope of thought. Gifted and talented students enjoy exploratory and intuitive thinking which makes future studies, in view of the G/C/T students' potential leadership and influence, a natural emphasis. It may be that the particular role of these young people will be to "image" ways to make future possibilities more real to others.

What Does It Take To Cope With The Future?

Certainly it takes a person who derives pleasure from newness, the skill of matching one's self-image with what is anticipated, mechanisms set up for dealing with distress, a confidence in facing new situations, cooperativeness, curiosity—a healthy productive personality!

As life styles must change to a simpler way of life, it is thought that those who have already faced hardship may persist in their efforts to surmount difficulty and possibly be more inventive about the future. It is important that the greatest flexibility, foresight, initiative and playful approaches to thinking be among the diversity built into individuals through self-esteeming relationships.

The Japanese government has committed $100 million to a study of world problems of the future. Other nations and states are committing money and setting up "think tanks" oriented to the future. Hundreds of courses are being offered across the country. It is believed that the very survival of society may depend upon the study of the future and the diversity we can build into the youth of today!

What Direction Should Education Be Taking?

Education for tomorrow must help young people develop certain new skills. They need to be comfortable with the unknown and willing to take risks. They must study new ways to solve problems. It is important for them to focus on personal development to offset the force of technology. Youngsters need to develop their creative processes. They must transform hunches, insights, cues, and intuitions into action. They should be informed in multi-disciplinary ways. It is essential for them to look upon learning as a life-long process to meet varying changes and needs. Young people must idea-generate as well as learn how to learn and be sensitive to problems. They must accommodate, adapt and cope with changing situations and unforeseen circumstances.

Dr. Robert Glazer, speaking on the future of education, indicates that *"adaptive education" should probably replace straight, cognitive learning.* This form of education capitalizes upon human responses and a variety of cognitive styles. It also helps individuals adapt their capabilities to a variety of situations. In enables people to develop new skills as needed.

Parents, as the first educators of the young, need to help them obtain a good foundation in understanding the universe and their place in it, to find order out of confusion, and to build a strong moral and ethical code. It is suggested that "future thinkers" will be sought among those who have healthy, productive personalities as they will adhere to moral codes and ethical standards.

What Can Teachers Do To Get Started?

Some teachers begin by collecting references and newspaper articles on the future. They help their students evaluate the validity of the printed statements, trends, and predictions. They encourage the selection of those predictions which most nearly align with the value judgments of the individual children. These teachers stimulate their classes to discuss alternative strategies which individuals may bring to bear on the most desirable forecasters. They enhance the feeling of

IMAGING THE FUTURE
A Future Studies Outline

I. SETTING THE STAGE
A. Clip articles from newspapers, magazines and brochures concerning the future and develop a file for writing, building a bulletin board or making a collage
B. Check libraries for other sources of articles about the future.
C. Write to the following resources for information:
1. World Future Society
4916 St. Elmo Avenue
Washington, D.C. 20014
2. Future Studies Program
Hill House, University of Massachusetts
Amherst, Mass. 01002

II. SURVEYING PREDICTIONS
A. Select articles from your file which seem to have the most interest to you.
1. Arrange the articles into positive and negative trends or predictions.
2. Check the articles for changes which are given or needed to support the predictions.
B. List the areas in which you found the most predictions. Did you find some areas in which there were no articles?
C. Arrange interviews with businessmen, editors, college personnel and other interested in the future.
D. Select areas of your interest where predictions are hard to find and contact authorities in that field for their predictions. Other resources may be developed with librarians, authors of books on the future and researchers.

III. MAKING YOUR OWN PREDICTIONS
A. Experts in predicting the future utilize one or more of the following ways to make predictions:
1. Projecting or extrapolating from data, patterns, or trends
2. Extending clues over a number of years
3. Imaging a utopia, then working backwards to define what needs to be done to reach it.
4. Assessing technology and projecting where it will lead
5. Analyzing research in progress or on the verge of discovery
6. Forecasting the implications and effects of legislation, policy making or court decisions
7. Polling the public to see what they are anticipating—for expectancy has a lot to do with how they react to "make it happen"
8. Considering the mystics, extra-sensory perceptionists, the bio-feedback proponents, dream analyzers, hypnotists and others
9. Training in deliberate techniques of creative problem solving—making the strange familiar, paired associations, checklisting of attributes, thinking at right angles, brainstorming and others.
B. Choose a method of forecasting and check your file of articles to determine how many have used that method.

C. Develop a method with a small group as far as possible. Find a group in your state working on forecasting and ask for information or a speaker for your class.

IV. ELABORATING UPON YOUR PREDICTIONS
A. Write a scenario to include the predicted changes you like best, the life style you hope for in the year 2000. Develop the whole scene in all the detail you can accumulate.
1. Include what you will be doing—about your day-to-day life
2. Mention your hobbies, recreation and entertainment
3. Make a sketch of your living quarters—some of the furniture
4. Describe your work, where it is located and your hours
5. Include the transportation system and the communication methods
B. After reading scenarios of all the class members, determine the changes needed in 5, 10, 15 years in order that you may realize your future.
C. What plans can you develop to affect the desired changes? Will you need to consider slowing down undesired changes? How would you accomplish the deacceleration?

V. GETTING IT ALL TOGETHER
A. Visuals are an important asset to any project. Have you ever made your own filmstrip or overhead transparency? The possibilities are fabulous for creating impact. If you should choose this method or slides and a taped presentation, don't overlook the great effects to be gained by music of the future!
B. Another possibility is a "Topic Tower" which is a three-dimensional object with your ideas and quotes placed upon it and embellished with visuals.
C. Visit an antique store and notice the types of things bringing high prices today. Can you select some of the articles in your life today and make a predicition about their value to antique dealers in the future?
1. How about a display of "tools" which you think will be outdated or discarded in ten or twenty years.
2. Exhibit some things which you feel, with modifications which you propose, will survive for some time.
D. The artist and his predictions may also be exhibited with your project. Museums will give you help in finding artists who are "ahead of their time".
E. Architects are another group who must keep ahead of the times. Be sure to explore their ideas or check in architectural publications in libraries.
F. Contact members of the community so they may add to your exhibit. What is predicted in areas such as dentistry, medicine, law, police work, fire control?

power and potential control over one's life which comes from creative ideation and identifying alternatives which can lead to thoughtful action.

Teachers are instrumental in aiding the development of skills in forecasting, planning, decision making and leadership which the young people need to become involved in their future. They help develop sensitivity to problems as well as help with problem definition and the ability to break problems down into manageable parts to offset feelings of helplessness.

Many teachers work with universities, scholars, and authorities in various disciplines to determine the skills and knowledge most worth teaching today for the most mileage tomorrow.

The community is the focus for still another teacher's method in which the class identifies trends in the local community from such resources as newspapers and local agencies. The children make a list of all of the trends. They project what will happen if the trends continue. They brainstorm about the interaction of trends upon each other. The class then uses all of the information to develop scenarios or future images and converts the scenarios into dioramas, slide-sound presentations, plays, books, and the like. The final stage of this teacher's method is to take the results back to the community.

Some teachers start with a flare, asking students to predict what will happen in their community two days hence. Pictures are drawn, everything to load a time capsule is explored, developed and put aside in a sealed box. On the day of the prediction—their future, the materials, articles, pictures, etc. are all taken out and discussed as to the predictions. From this start teachers go in many ways—some teach forecasting, some use newspapers to build more background for a longer forecast of what will be in a newspaper on a certain day.

In a study of the future it is important for the student to know precisely what is expected. He/She must know what has been accomplished when the work is completed. He/She should determine what to do with the work and how to evaluate it in terms of the objectives.

One final note: One task that is inappropriate for future activities is when to get started with your G/C/T children on Thinking Ahead. That should be done *now*. Good luck!

Selected references on Future Studies will be found in the *What Can I Use* section of this issue.—G/C/T

BASIC SUPPORT FOR CURRICULUM: TEACHER PREPARATION AND COMMUNITY INVOLVEMENT

Studies of educational change frequently reflect the central role of teachers in measurable student growth. Through pre-service programs, as well as in-service training, teachers are improving their skills and understanding, and their knowledge of gifted children and youth.

While a teaching staff may have many resources for meeting the diverse needs of the gifted, in most cases, resources to meet some individual needs may be required from the community as well. Mentorships are one practical means of employing community resources.

Often overlooked are the private foundations whose assets are of modest size, and whose service area is geographically limited to a community or metropolitan area. With knowledge of their program, some of these foundations can be induced to help the gifted child. This is an answer for school districts that are pressed by many financial necessities.

An article by M. Frances Klein, "About Present and Needed Resources for Identifying and Evaluating Learning Materials," concludes this anthology of readings. While it is not directed specifically towards te gifted student, the bibliography of reviews and aids for determining quality of materials justify the author's claim that "...No teacher can complain about the lack of available materials any longer."

IN ITS STRICTEST sense, preservice training means the training of undergraduates, those who will be the teachers of the future. For the purposes of this book, however, preservice training means teacher training specifically designed to train teachers who have not been, nor are presently, engaged in teaching programs for gifted and talented youngsters. The reason for this interpretation is that most university based programs for teachers of the gifted and talented may include both graduate and undergraduate students. They also may include both experienced and inexperienced teachers of the gifted and talented, even though their main purpose is to train those who have not yet had specialized preparation.

Programs

An attempt was made to locate various models utilized in the preservice training of teachers of the gifted and talented. Various programs were examined, and although there were variations in methods used, in most cases the training consisted of a sequence of courses leading to a Bachelor's,

while the 1974 survey, which is only a partial listing, shows 11 universities that have degree programs at the Bachelor's, Master's, and Doctoral levels specifically in gifted education. A much larger number have one or more courses dealing specifically with the gifted.

Other trends that seem to have continued are the following:

1. States with established programs and support from the state level have more institutions with course and degree offerings.
2. The majority of the courses admit undergraduates, but the degree programs in most cases are Master's, with fewer institutions offering Bachelor's or Doctorates.
3. Even though titles of courses and the sequence in which they are taken varies, the overall content is similar in institutions offering degree programs.

Although the number of institutions offering training has increased over the past decade, the percentage of total institutions is still embarrass-

Preservice Training

Master's, or Doctoral degree in the education of the gifted and talented. In light of this fact, the following section presents an analysis of these programs and a comparison of the major methodological differences in them, as well as a review of past and current practices. Readers should consult Appendix A for a listing of colleges and universities offering degree programs in gifted and talented education.

Opportunities and Trends

Periodically, surveys are conducted to determine which institutions of higher education offer courses and degree programs in gifted and talented education (The Association for the Gifted, 1974; French, in Hildreth, 1966; Laird & Kowalski, 1972; and Shaffer & Troutt, 1970). Institutions, courses, and instructors are changing constantly, but certain constants seem to remain. One of the most important has been a steady increase in opportunities available, both in the number of courses offered and in the number of institutions offering training. For example, French reports that only four institutions offered four or more courses,

ingly small. Laird and Kowalski (1972) surveyed 1,564 colleges and universities with an enrollment of 500 or more and found that only 13% currently offered courses dealing specifically with the education of the gifted child. Another 12% indicated that they were preparing teachers to become aware of and assist gifted youth to perform at or near potential. The picture presented in this article is not entirely a bleak one, however, as 32% of the institutions not currently offering courses were interested in doing so, and 40% of those now offering courses were interested in expanding their programs. Available data seem to indicate that there is a genuine need for expansion. In a survey of students taking an elective course on the education of the gifted, Lazar (1973) found that 58% indicated a "sincere need to study the gifted as their primary reason for taking the elective course..." (p. 278). In the writer's own experience, at least 60% of the students in an elective course on the gifted had chosen that particular course because of a sincere need. Mohan (1973) who used a six step procedure of (a) a search of literature, (b) a survey of local faculty thinking, (c) responses from researchers and teachers in the field, (d) a survey of student teachers, (e) a survey of classroom teachers, and (f) results of inservice workshops, found that there is a great need for a course in creativity in teacher education programs. More research of this nature may convince institutions of higher education to begin programs.

As previously mentioned, a significant trend has been to offer graduate rather than undergraduate degree programs in education of the gifted. This practice seems to stem from the belief that teachers of the gifted should be experienced teachers who have already shown that they have ability to teach in a regular program. Others seem to believe that this also insures a background of liberal education before the prospective teacher undergoes specialized training (Fliegler, 1961; Hildreth, 1966; James, cited in Hildreth, 1966).

Course Content and Offerings

As indicated in the previous section, the overall content of courses on the education of the gifted and talented is similar in most institutions. In cases where only one course is offered, the subject is usually the psychological and educational characteristics of gifted children combined with an overview of current practices for educating these children. If only two courses are offered, the first usually deals with psychological and educational characteristics while the second usually deals with curriculum and materials development. Institutions with degree programs usually offer a sequence of courses similar to the following:

1. *Nature and Needs of the Gifted.* The content consists of topics such as characteristics, problems, myths perpetuated about gifted and creative children, psychological considerations, and identification measures.

2. *Materials and Methods in the Education of the Gifted.* Content usually centers around the most appropriate instructional strategies and materials to be utilized with the gifted. In many cases, time is spent in designing materials and in developing appropriate curricular units. Emphasis, in many instances, is also placed on techniques for individualizing instruction for the gifted.

3. *Education of the Gifted.* A course of this type is usually concerned with exploring various programs and administrative arrangements currently in use in schools as well as other related issues.

4. *Seminars in the Education of the Gifted.* Seminars usually involve a less structured approach through which students explore topics of interest to them as well as controversial issues

in the field. Independent study and related techniques are often utilized.

5. *Practicum in the Education of the Gifted.* Practica usually involve either a variety of practical experiences with gifted children or one in-depth experience, depending on the interests and needs of the students. Examples of some of the experiences provided are: student teaching in a program for the gifted; internships with consultants, administrators, and other local school district personnel involved in programs for the gifted; visitations to several programs for the gifted; observation of gifted students, including the writing of case studies; and internships in state and federal programs for the gifted.

In many cases, the program also offers separate courses in creativity and its development. In most programs, provisions are also made for students to pursue topics of individual concern and interest through independent study courses, readings courses, research seminars, and workshop courses.

It must be emphasized again that the previous description is a generalization of the content usually taught in a sequence of courses related to the gifted. The topics may be taught in different combinations and sequences and under different titles. The above description is mainly intended to list certain commonalities between programs as an indication of consensus of opinion about the importance of certain learnings.

Staffing

In most instances, one person on the faculty of the special education or psychology departments is responsible for the training program. This person is usually trained in educational psychology or special education, and has both specialized training and practical experience in gifted education. The majority of these professors are also leaders in the field of education of the gifted and talented, since the field is so small. They also serve as consultants to local school districts in program development, consultants to federal programs, and inservice training leaders in addition to speaking at numerous conferences.

Selection of Students

Students accepted for programs are usually those who are admitted through regular university procedures. Additional procedures are established when fellowships or traineeships are offered.

Practical Experiences

In addition to similarities as listed above, significant differences between programs do exist, especially in the specific content and the amount and kind of practical experiences offered. Some of the programs emphasize cognitive learning while others emphasize attitudinal changes. Some are designed primarily for teacher training while others are designed to train researchers, consultants, administrators, and other leaders in the field of gifted education. Since the purpose is different, the emphasis in content and practical experience is also different. For example, in a program designed for leadership development, content will be much more theoretical in nature and include less emphasis on teacher-pupil relationships and day to day teaching techniques. The practical experiences in this situation would include such things as field testing curricula designed for the gifted rather than observation of children, internships with directors of gifted programs rather than student teaching, and so on. Other programs are designed to meet the needs of the student, whether he or she is planning to teach or become involved in other aspects of programs.

John Feldhusen (1973) described practicum activities for undergraduates and teachers involved in his course on the education of gifted children: (a) area schools cooperate in nominating a child for each student in the class; (b) college students arrange to observe the child at home and at school, test and interview him, interview his parents and teachers, and carry out enrichment activities with him; (c) college students spend one and a half days observing in a special class for the gifted; and (d) students make a report to the parents and child, evaluating his talents, and suggesting special educational activities which might be helpful to the child. Evaluations by principals, teachers, parents, and children have been very positive, and college students found the program to be enjoyable and profitable. Parents and teachers evaluated the performance of the college students on (a) ability to interact with parents and teachers, (b) professional knowledge, (c) the quality of reports, and (d) promptness and responsibility. Ratings were on a good-fair-poor scale—7% fair, 1% poor, and 92% good. This type of program has implications for increasing cooperation between public schools and universities as well as developing additional practical experiences for training programs.

Program Variations

One variation on the course sequence model was developed in Illinois when funds were available to assist universities in developing innovative training programs for teachers of the gifted. Conducted at Southern Illinois University at Edwardsville, it combined the training of preservice and inservice personnel. The program was developed for 12 students—five graduate students presently teaching in the area, five undergraduate students, and two full time graduate students serving as graduate assistants. All were enrolled in a sequence of courses which could lead to a degree in special education of the gifted, including between 12 and 28 quarter hours dealing specifically with gifted education. The purpose of the program was to pair these teachers and prospective teachers in teams for the duration of the training, so that in addition to learning together and sharing experiences, a close relationship would be developed between each pair. The two full time graduate students served as assistants to the project director in supervision, demonstration teaching, consultative assistance, and other related tasks. Other students, not receiving fellowships, were also enrolled in the courses. The following experiences were among those provided for participants:

1. Academic courses on the education of the gifted and talented.

2. Work in an inservice teacher's classroom to apply principles learned, including supervision on a regular basis by the project director.

3. Supervision of a preservice teacher with assistance from him/her on prearranged tasks.

4. Selection and/or production of curricular materials appropriate for the gifted.

5. Participation in microteaching.

6. Student teaching or supervising student teaching.

7. Practicum experiences for graduate students at the Area Service Center for the Gifted.

8. Visitation of a variety of gifted programs.

9. Attendance at conferences and meetings on the education of gifted children.

10. Independent study involving research, field study, program planning, and planning program evaluation procedures (Shaffer, 1971).

Unfortunately, funds for this category of teacher training were discontinued the following year. However, preliminary evaluation results did indicate that the concept was successful. Preservice students especially appreciated the interaction with inservice teachers, both in their classrooms and in workshops and conferences related to gifted education. One definite drawback to this program was the fact that most inservice teachers in the program were teaching in regular, self contained classrooms. Most of the preservice teachers felt that they needed more experiences with identified gifted students, indicating that at least part of their practical experience should have been in established programs for identified gifted students with teachers experienced in working with these children (Maker, 1973).

Another exciting variation in programing that utilizes basically a course sequence approach is still in the developmental stages at California State University at Long Beach. This program, supported in part by a grant from the Bureau of Education for the Handicapped, US Office of Education, provides for the inclusion of the gifted with teacher preparation in other areas of special education. The specialist program is entirely competency based, including both generic and advanced specialist training. Specific competencies are listed in the following areas:

- Assessment of physical, intellectual, social, and emotional characteristics.
- Assessment of learning abilities in relation to psychological, genetic, physiological, social, and cultural conditions.
- Assessment of motivational and attitudinal differences.
- Utilization of procedures for individualized instruction.
- Implications of exceptional conditions, for the instructional program.
- Identification of issues and research findings for program implementation.
- Counseling exceptional pupils and their parents.
- Evaluation of instructional systems.
- Analysis and evaluation of program elements.
- Intervention to extend interaction.
- Planning and conducting parent meetings.
- Utilization of ethical practices.
- Self assessment and professional improvement.

Each of these areas is further subdivided into more specific competencies and then further into behaviors. The program guide lists specific competencies to be achieved, the performance criteria and level expected, experiences and instruction to be provided, the learner responsibilities, provisions for informing the student of his competency, and the courses provided. A handbook is currently being devised that will allow for translation of competencies into operational instructional objectives and planned activities to meet these objectives (California State University, 1974).

Also in the developmental process is a large scale validation of the competencies required. A sample of teachers of the gifted will be asked to react to the competencies listed by: rewriting those which are ambiguous or incorrect in some way, eliminating unnecessary competencies or adding necessary ones, and weighting each of the competencies on a 5-point scale of most important to least important.

When the program is operational, other features will include an "entry behavior test" (which may include assessment of the student's performance in a workshop situation) designed to measure skills and attitudes as well as knowledge, an "exit behavior test," program options based on the interests of the students, a system for continual modification and change, and a yearly review process.

Although some of the problems such as what to do with a student who exhibits all the competencies at the beginning of the training provisions for those who need a longer time in the training process have not yet been solved, the program has great potential.

Because of state certification laws, other institutions of higher education in California are also in the process of developing competency based programs.

Evaluations

Few universities have systematically evaluated any of their teacher training programs. It seems that most only employ the required student feedback techniques. These are mainly descriptive, based entirely on the student's perceptions of the course, and limited to one course at a time rather than an entire degree program. The purposes of these evaluations are usually assessment of the instructor and assistance in modifying teaching methods employed by that person. In a search of the literature and calls to directors of university training programs, only four evaluations could be found. Many evaluations of summer institutes and other university based teacher training designed as *inservice* can be found. These are reported in the next section.

The first of these evaluations, conducted by Kooyumjian (1969) was designed to assess cognitive and affective changes in students enrolled in a university course on education of the gifted and the same changes in teachers and administrators enrolled in several summer inservice training workshops on the education of the gifted and talented. The main purpose of the evaluation was directed to inservice, but many of the findings have implications here. Using pre- and posttest data on a diagnostic test of content on teaching gifted children, a test designed to measure adult intellectual ability, a personality inventory which indicates the basic type of structure of a healthy person's personality, and other informational measures, she found significant differences between the groups. Below is a summary of those findings and conclusions which seem most appropriate to this discussion.

4. SUPPORT

1. The main objective of the university course was to increase knowledge about gifted children, and it was effective in doing so.

2. Even though achievement in content on gifted children was an incidental goal for the workshops, to be learned through independent study, seven of the nine workshops showed significant gains in content on gifted. In addition, two of the workshops were not significantly different from the academic course in content gain.

3. There were no changes in attitudes of the students in the university course.

4. There were changes in attitudes of the participants in all the workshops.

5. Individual differences in content gain decreased in the academic course groups, but increased in the workshop groups.

6. Intellectual ability and sex seemed to be irrelevant except to one section of the attitude scale.

7. In the academic course, more than 60% of the participants reported that they gained more information from reading than through discussion and instruction; in four of the nine workshop groups, more than 60% of the participants reported that they gained more information through discussion; and in the other five workshop groups, participants reported a combination of two or three of the methods listed.

A major drawback of the study for the purposes of this book was the lack of information about the methods used in the academic course. Some of the methods utilized in workshops were described, but no mention was made of what actually happened in the everyday classroom situation. One can only assume that methods were very similar to most university courses — a combination of lecture, discussion, reading assignments, papers, and some possible practical experiences. In addition, no part of the evaluation was concerned with actual performance of graduates in their classrooms.

In another evaluation, Maker (1973) attempted to determine the effectiveness of university based teacher training programs which were supported in part by the Office of the Superintendent of Public Instruction. The first of these programs has already been described above on page 23. The second, located at Northeastern Illinois University, consisted of a sequence of four graduate courses on the education of gifted children which could be applied toward a degree in special education. There was no degree in gifted education at the time this evaluation was conducted, but a plan had been submitted to the graduate school. Most of the students were full time teachers, many in gifted

programs, so the majority of their practical experiences were related to the development and testing of ideas in the student's own classroom. Opportunities were provided for visitation, attendance at inservice training sessions, and conferences.

Fellowships were offered to a limited number of students, but others who were interested could take the classes. Selection of fellowship recipients was on the basis of recommendation of administrators or supervisors acquainted with the work of the candidate, interest in teaching gifted children, and academic records. The director was seeking successful experienced teachers who were likely to utilize training received from the program.

The evaluation employed a variety of techniques, including questionnaires to graduates, interviews with students in the programs, telephone calls to administrators of graduates, and a questionnaire designed to assess the instructional climate in classrooms. Results are only reported here for the two universities with a *sequence* of courses that could lead to an area of specialization. Below is a summary of some of the findings that seem most relevant to this discussion.

1. The three categories of responses most often listed as strengths of the program by graduates were: (a) contact with others in the field of the gifted and talented through attendance at workshops and inservice training or visitors to the class, (b) the flexibility of choices within the framework of the program and classes, and (c) the content learned. Students presently in the program also liked the flexibility and chances for pursuing individual interests.

2. The three categories of responses most often listed as weaknesses of the programs by graduates were: (a) too few practical experiences were provided, (b) a greater scope was needed — more courses on different topics as well as different content covered in the courses offered, and (c) a variety of resource people were needed as the same instructor taught all the courses. Students presently involved in the program also felt they needed more experiences with identified gifted children.

3. Most graduates felt they were well prepared for their jobs, but were reluctant to attribute this competence to the training they had received in gifted education.

4. Most graduates and students felt the programs had been successful, and felt prepared to work in gifted education. However, only a small majority of graduates felt that the training was more relevant than the inservice workshops they had attended.

5. Methods most often listed as being utilized by the instructors were class discussion of controversial issues and independent study. However, in one of the programs, students estimated that the instructor talked over 60% of the time while her ideal was 40%. In the other program, the instructor's performance was consistent with her ideal 40%. Students and graduates both listed as important the opportunities to attend training, particularly the inservice offered by the state gifted program outside the university setting.

6. More emphasis was placed on the higher thought processes of application, analysis, synthesis, and evaluation than on the lower thought processes of memory, translation, and interpretation.

A major drawback of the study, however, was that it did not assess the actual performance of the graduates in their classroom or the changes in children. Telephone calls to administrators gave some indication of the success of the teachers, but more information was needed.

The third report (Bruch & Walker, 1973) was not intended to be an evaluation per se, but was designed as a survey of teachers certified in gifted and talented education who had completed an approved degree program at the University of Georgia. A more extensive evaluation is in preparation, but some of the known results are relevant to this discussion, paralleling those in other studies. Many respondents to the Georgia survey agreed, for example, that there should be an increase in real or simulated experiences with gifted and talented students in situ. Other felt needs were for a strengthening of content related to curriculum development, assistance in locating and using different types of media and materials geared to gifted and talented students, and for greater flexibility in the program. (This last was not expressed directly but can be inferred from the respondents' comments.) Those who were in roles involving the coordination of gifted and talented programs expressed the need for training in public relations skills such as public speaking, legislative watchdogging, newspaper publicizing, and program administration. Other such comments emphasized a need for available options for those who would be assuming (or desired to assume) various roles in addition to that of teacher.

The fourth evaluation (Gear, 1974) is a five year progress report on the Teaching the Talented Program of the University of Connecticut, Storrs. This program, supported by the Education Professions Development Act, is designed to recruit and train both prospective and experienced teachers and leadership personnel to work with gifted and talented youngsters from educationally deprived backgrounds. It is concerned with the process of change and the role of change agents in the schools.

Students receiving fellowships were selected on the basis of their potential as future contributors to the existing body of knowledge about the disadvantaged gifted and talented, as evidenced by: (a) their demonstrated leadership and past background, (b) demonstrated commitment to a career in the area of educating the disadvantaged, and (c) potential for graduate work.

The program consisted of three components: theoretical (coursework), practical (internships), and integrative (linking practical and theoretical experiences). Specific objectives were developed, relating to this basic framework, which would be flexible enough to accommodate persons with varying backgrounds and aspirations. The theoretical component included courses in the broad areas of psychology and education of the gifted, talented, and creative; in the sociology of minority groups, Black history, social and cultural dynamics, and urban life; and in the student's professional areas of interest. The practical component involved internships in a variety of locations—urban schools, colleges and universities, community action agencies, state or regional agencies, and suburban schools—and performing a variety of roles—teachers, tutors, counselors, administrators, curriculum specialists, and researchers. The third component, integrative experiences, consisted of seminars, discussions with resource personnel, and on-site visitations to programs for gifted children and youth from disadvantaged backgrounds.

Evaluation of the program has been both formative and summative. During each year data are collected relating to each component of the program, and needed changes are made whenever they become apparent. For example, during internship experiences, students frequently assessed their own progress in relation to their objectives, the staff made on-site visitations, and the staff conferred with cooperating supervisors. Summative evaluations were concerned with perceptions of the program by fellows, the success of the program in preparing fellows to enter various fields, and changes in the organizational structure of the program. Following are some of the results reported:

1. Most former fellowship recipients agreed that the most valuable component was field experience.

2. Other valuable aspects were interaction with peers; flexibility in choosing field experiences, coursework, and field trips; seminars; and problem solving situations.

3. All felt they were more successful in their jobs because of their programs.
4. Everyone found different aspects helpful.
5. Even though this is only a preliminary report, many impressive achievements and honors are listed for graduates and fellows still in the program.

Although this is the most comprehensive of the evaluations, it is only a progress report. It does not measure effects on children or the performance of graduates in their job situations. Such achievements as dissertations, new curricula, present positions, membership in professional organizations, and honors are indicative of the potential impact of trainers, but an assessment of the effects of products and actions are more relevant measures of success.

Summary and Recommendations

Except for variations in content and individual teaching methods, most programs designed to train teachers of the gifted in a university setting are very similar. Some programs have been more innovative than others. It is hoped that the present trend toward more programs will continue.

Continuing Assessment of Programs

If educators are to make progress and adequately train teachers to direct the learning of our most talented students, it is recommended that they must *(a) look more closely at established practices and try to determine if they are the most effective that we can design, (b) try some different approaches to determine if they would be more successful than the old, (c) make changes that seem to be necessary—either add or delete parts of the old models, (d) continually assess the results in our changing society, and (e) make adjustments as they become appropriate and necessary.* It often seems that we have been doing the same things for many years, assuming that these things are effective, but never knowing for sure, and never really attempting to find out.

Only a few programs have been evaluated (usually those receiving state or federal funds), and these evaluations have been limited. They have determined students' and graduates' perceptions of the success of the programs, and in some cases have determined that students did achieve certain content learnings.

Evaluate Programs by Changes in Students

Since the ultimate test of any teacher training program is the success of the graduates in producing desired changes in students, we must *evaluate the success of programs based on changes in students.* In order to evaluate, however, we must establish objectives that can be assessed. Therefore, *directors of training programs should make some decisions related to the knowledge, skills, and attitudes they want to develop in teachers based on how these teacher characteristics actually affect children*

Even though evaluation results are scarce, findings in two areas are consistent students and graduates alike feel that the practical experience they get as part of their training is the most valuable. They enjoy and appreciate flexibility for individual needs within the established framework.

More Practical Experiences

It is recommended that training programs should increase opportunities for practical experiences as much as possible. Some of the following have been provided or could be provided as relevant learning experiences:

- Pair an undergraduate preservice teacher with a graduate experienced teacher for a year or longer.
- Arrange on-site visitations to gifted programs *with provision for interaction with the school staff after an observation period.*
- Provide internships and apprenticeships with master teachers, including experiences similar to student teaching in a *variety* of settings. Most student teachers only have experience with one teacher in one school with one group of students—and for too short a period of time. Lengthen the teaching time by including some of the time that might have been spent in methods courses. For example, several elementary education departments have found that "block" programs are extremely successful. In these programs, sophomores and juniors sign up for a block of three methods courses. They spend two to three weeks in classes designed to give a background of information on methods, then begin to spend one hour a day teaching in a classroom in the area. Since they are taking three of these courses, they spend one-half day teaching three subjects. During the teaching experience, they spend one to two hours per week in class discussing problems, strategies, and other concerns. The last week or more is spent with the instructors again, sharing ideas and experiences with other classmates. Although students complain that they work twice as hard as others in regular methods courses, they feel much more prepared for teaching. Instructors of these courses feel that the program is highly successful.
- If no programs exist in the immediate vicinity, include activities with gifted children (identified by college students) similar to those described on page 15.

- Field test curriculum developed in classes on children and make necessary changes based on these trials. Have students participate in public school curriculum development meetings and projects.

- Utilize the university's microteaching laboratory and if no "real" gifted students are available have the college class role play stereotypes of gifted children, or gifted children they have known.

Although the literature is filled with discussions of characteristics considered to be prerequisites or necessary "entering" characteristics for trainees, students accepted into training programs are not accepted because of having these desirable characteristics — they are accepted mainly because of past grades, that is, performance in academic situations.

Criteria for Entering and Exiting

It is recommended that preservice programs assess the entering attitudes, knowledge, and skills of prospective trainees and then decide either to establish minimum criteria for acceptance into the program based on the relationship of these characteristics to the teaching situation, or accept everyone into an individually designed program to accomplish the needed changes, both in attitudes, skills, and knowledge.

Students are not permitted to leave a training program because of possessing desirable "exiting" characteristics, but because they have fulfilled the course and program requirements (number of hours, reading assignments, and the like). Student evaluations (grades) in too many cases are based entirely on mastery of content rather than possession of desirable attitudes and skills.

Graduation Based on Competency

It is recommended that graduation and grades should be based on competency—possession of needed knowledge, skills, and attitudes—rather than the fulfilling of the traditional requirements of hours, reading assignments, and courses. Some students may already possess the needed characteristics while others may need to spend varying amounts of time in the program.

Kooyumjian's study confirmed many believs that college courses teach content but do not accomplish attitude changes. If this continues, Intuitive children will continue to be taught by Sensing teachers who do not understand or care for their kind of thinking. Teachers will continue to resist changes designed to keep pace with the changing needs of society.

Even though research indicates that experience with programs as well as knowledge of the characteristics, learning styles, and provisions for gifted children produces more positive attitudes toward special programs for the gifted, knowledge of content alone is not enough to produce significant behavioral changes in teachers.

Programs to Develop Positive Attitudes

It is recommended that programs be assigned that will develop positive attitudes toward acceptance of change and the need for development of creativity and problem solving skills in students to help them cope with our rapidly changing world.

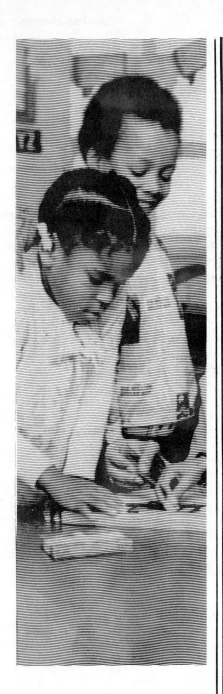

TEACHING STRATEGIES FOR BRIGHT PUPILS

THE CONTEXT

Experiments with training materials and methods for student teachers undergoing initial (PGCE) training are being conducted by the Teacher Education Project to help teachers meet the needs of bright pupils more effectively. The word "bright" is used to indicate a child who might have an IQ of about 130 and wide-ranging talents. "Gifted" is used to indicate an otherwise undistinguished pupil who appears to have one precocious talent (e.g. in music, mathematics, etc.) The Teacher Education Project is a four year (1976-1980) research and development project based at the universities of Nottingham, Leicester and Exeter and financed by the Department of Education and Science.

This article summarises some findings from a research project and suggests some strategies for teaching bright pupils which may help to overcome problems associated with teaching the exceptional child.

THE RESEARCH

In 1976 the Project carried out a small-scale enquiry into mixed ability teaching: its extent, methods, advantages and disadvantages. Using especially devised case-study instruments, 21 effective[1] teachers of mixed ability classes were watched at work and then along with their heads of department were interviewed in depth. A sample of forty headteachers filled in an extensive open-ended questionnaire. The results have been analysed under a number of headings and reported in various journals[2]. The results foreshadowed the findings of Her Majesty's Inspectorate[3]. The sections of the research dealing with bright pupils have been summarised in the following paragraphs.

1. *Identification of bright pupils* in secondary schools was obviously a problem in many schools since, although many devices were used, no clear criteria of identification were discernible. Identification was either reliant upon information gleaned from the feeder primary schools (eg verbal reports by teachers, IQ or reading tests), or it was dependent upon secondary school staff being allowed access to feeder primaries (eg some secondary school staff interviewed possible bright pupils and slow learners before transfer), or it took place at any time in year 1 of secondary education (typically through testing using many different tests — but

by TREVOR KERRY

"Teaching Strategies," Trevor Kelly, *Journal of the Gifted Child*, Vol. 1, No. 1, Autumn, 1979. From the National Association for Gifted Children, National Headquarters, 1 South Adley Street, London Wly 5DQ.

only one kind in each individual school — or through the collected impressions of secondary staff following a pupil's early school performance). Yardsticks of judgement used by teachers tend to be either a bit vague or rather too conventional and subject to discrepancies: 'O' level candidates, 'S' level candidates, IQ 125, IQ 140, top 25% etc.

2. *Special provisions for bright pupils* were available in some schools, but by no means in all. We asked if special provisions were available in maths or the sciences, in English, in music or in art. From a sample of 40 schools no one category of curriculum was specially catered for by more than 15 schools (music), and in the sciences only 4 schools (10%) made special provision. For the rest the weight of opinion was that special provision was made by individual teachers within their classrooms.

3. *Teachers' reporting their own problems in teaching bright pupils* emphasised the confluence of events: fast workers held back → boredom → failure to reach potential. Few solutions to the problem were proposed, but the commonest emphasised the *quantity* rather than the *quality* which could be expected of bright pupils.

THE PROBLEMS OF DEALING WITH EXCEPTIONAL PUPILS: AN OVERVIEW

While recognising the uniqueness of each pupil most teachers would probably accept that learning groups can be relatively homogeneous (the whole 'setting' process in many comprehensives rests on this assumption). In mixed ability groups (23 out of 40 of the schools in our sample used a mixed ability organisation at least in the first year) exceptional pupils bring problems for teachers, whatever the reason for the 'exceptional' tag. In our researches the fast and slow pupils created the problems described below for the teachers in our sample.

1. *Dead time.* This is the time between a pupil finishing one activity and starting another. Often it is spent waiting for a teacher's attention. Bright pupils experience much of it because they work very quickly, slow learners because they work very superficially.

2. *Boredom.* Sets in during dead time and will, if repeated often enough, lead to

3. *Lack of motivation.* The unmotivated child will be bored, and so this can become a kind of vicious circle in which the likely consequence is

4. *Disruption.* The creative mind actively seeks a new occupation when the previous one ceases. The less creative was probably not interested in the first task anyway and is happily distracted from concentration. The bored pupil, whiling away dead time for whatever reason, is a potential trouble-maker. On videotaped studies of mixed ability classes we found that the unocccupied child sometimes spread a trail of disruption by annoying occupied groups.

5. *Provision of special work* is one solution to the problems above. In a mixed ability class the teacher has to set special work for both ends of the ability range. This in turn means

6. *Increased preparation time* by the teacher. From our interview schedules it emerged quite forcibly that preparation time already looms very large for teachers faced with a mixed ability organization. Much of this time is spent on the devising of worksheets, and both slow learners and bright pupils need special attention regarding

7. *Linguistic and cognitive levels in worksheets.* The former need sheets with low reading ages, clear instructions and low cognitive levels relative to the rest of the class. Bright pupils need the precise opposite. In both cases it means extra work for the teacher, who not only has to cope with these professional hazards but also the

8. *Emotional and pastoral problems* of pupils who are 'different'. For the slow learner this may mean helping the socialization process, paying attention to the pupil's 'self-concept'; for the bright pupil the teacher may need to be aware of calculated under-achievement or help him to curb his impatience with slower classmates.

TEACHING STRATEGIES FOR BRIGHT PUPILS

The problems outlined above would be easier of solution if there were widespread access either to specialist help or to in-service training. While teachers of slow learners may often have these facilities, those who have to cater for bright pupils rarely experience them. In response to what was felt to be a growing need the Teacher Education Project produced a self-instructional handbook called Focus 3: Teaching Bright Pupils[4].

The handbook consists of 5 units. Units one and two are concerned with identification. The first unit seeks to improve the teacher's knowledge about the more obvious bright pupils in his class as well as to show gaps in his knowledge and to begin to point to patterns and characteristics for spotting bright pupils. Unit 2 sets out a suggested profile of the underachiever, and requests the teacher to search his class lists for such pupils.

Having completed these two exercises the teacher has a good idea about the scope and size of his problem, and unit three provides a short interlude for thinking about methods of grouping for teaching before the heart of the booklet is reached in units 4 and 5.

These last two units talk about teaching strategies and skills. Unit 4 sets out two dozen strategies, some quick and simple to carry out and others demanding a good deal of time and thought. In the present space only a few examples can be given.

It is suggested that a bright pupil may need just a moment or two extra of the teacher's attention in order to set him or her on a new thought train: the teacher might stop the pupil as he leaves the class and ask quite casually a question about work done by all pupils, but one formulated at a much higher cognitive level. Some bright pupils, as underachievers, may need help in social areas, and a key role in the production of a class magazine or play may provide opportunities both for co-operation and leadership. The value of competition is not played down, and various ways of setting creative competitive tasks are suggested. Teachers are asked, too, to review their own provision of learning resources such as workcards and to improve these with bright pupils in mind. It is also suggested that teachers could help to improve each other's performance by getting together and undertaking gentle critiques of one another's lessons.

The final unit of the workbook concentrates on a key skill for teaching bright pupils — questioning. Teachers are encouraged to tape-record their own lessons and to analyse their questioning technique using a specially prepared analysis system. By practising the kinds of questions which are more valuable in producing pupils' learning and improving pupils' thinking they can improve the work of their classes as well as their own skills.

THE RESPONSE

Keith Morgan, a teacher who participated in one of the Teachers' Centre courses during 1978 discussed the Focus 3 materials that were used with the author, Trevor Kerry.

Trevor Kerry: Perhaps you could begin, Keith, by saying a word or two about why you chose to come on a course concerned with bright pupils.

Keith Morgan: I think most teachers are aware of having bright pupils in their classes; and if one works in a mixed ability setting, as I do, one is conscious of the need to keep up both the pressure and the stimulus for these youngsters. I hoped the course would broaden my horizons about teaching strategies.

TK: The course began by looking at identification procedures for bright pupils and underachievers. How helpful were these?

KM: I'm not sure that they helped me to find any bright pupils of whom I was unaware, but I became much more conscious of the presence of these pupils in the class during lesson. Also, I followed the advice given, to probe more deeply into the background and attainments of these pupils; and in the process I found myself looking in detail at all the other pupils in the class too. (See Table 1: Pupil Proforma.)

TK: What about the underachievers, could you identify those using the guidelines supplied? (See Table 2.)

KM: Yes, but again I'm not sure if it was so much 'discovery' that was needed as 'awareness'. Certainly I altered some aspects of my teaching style to cater for these pupils.

TK: I'll take you up on that in a moment, Keith; but first can I ask you if you have suggestions about the identification procedures themselves. For example, would they be useful if more widely adopted in schools?

4. SUPPORT

KM: At present I'm not sure that the format of the identification procedures would be universally applicable. On the other hand I am convinced that informal screening for all children, not just testing on academic attainment which we carry out at our school on a formal basis, should be undertaken in all schools. I wish we had been taught to think about individual pupils in this analytical way during initial training. I've become extremely self-critical now of the ways in which I approach teaching Michael, Sharon, Dave and Carol, my underachievers.

KT: Perhaps that's a good cue to switch the conversation to teaching strategies. The Focus 3 booklets suggest 24 strategies, some short-term and others involving a considerable investment of time in, for example, Saturday morning clubs. You were asked to choose several strategies and try them out.

Which did you choose?

KM: I tried three. The 'quicky' was to set optional special homework in some groups which stretched the bright pupils. Longer-term, I decided to have a go at revising my whole resourcing of the curriculum of one 2nd year classs: and I established a drama group which attracted a lot of attention from some bright and lively fourth year girls.

TK: Let's take these in turn. Special homework — any comments on this?

KM: I got some bright youngsters from my fourth year to do additional homework on Shakespeare's *Julius Caesar*. This really was optional, but many bright pupils opted in. In a few weeks they had decorated the classroom walls with the results. Among the initiatives they took were making up crossword puzzles about the play, producing maps, drawing cartoons, translating key speeches into dialect paraphrases, devising quizzes and making visual aids that I could use with a parallel group. The level of interest escalated and their knowledge increased as well.

TK: I saw that display, Keith; it was very dynamic. How did you get on with your resource-based learning experiment for the 2nd year class?

KM: My classroom has a communicating door with the library so, as a teacher of English, I can always get instant resource materials. However, I also compiled a special project collection for some group-work with a class of second years who were exploring interest themes such as birds, aircraft, coal and oil, and transport. I got a lot of professional satisfaction from the way pupils took to using the collection, though oddly enough it was the underachievers who got most from the new approach.

TK: Well, there is some evidence to suggest that underachievers are more likely to respond well to curriculum change than the more obvious bright pupils are. After all, the bright achievers are riding high in the status quo so they are perhaps less motivated to change their ways. But I know you followed up your thematic work by asking the pupils to say what they thought of the time spent on it. How did you react to their comments?

KM: I was pleased that most of the pupils, not just the bright and the underachievers in the class, said they had enjoyed this and wanted to spend more time on it. At the same time they made it clear that it wasn't a soft option and that it had cost them a lot in effort and energy. Ferreting out resources on some of the more obscure themes had been difficult for them. One group became very self-analytical, saying exactly how each individual member felt about the project and why.

TK: Let's turn to the other teaching strategy. You set up a drama group. That had to be a firm commitment of time on your part.

KM: Yes. There are no half-measures with this kind of exercise and there is a limit to the added stimulus which an individual teacher can bring to a school by activities like this.

TK: But, of course, where each member of a large staff is committed to just one activity quite a range of educational and leisure pursuits can be on offer at a single school. In contrast to the Swedes, where there are no extra-curriculum activities and things like dramatic productions eat into the school day itself, we are very fortunate in this country in being almost able to take for granted that every teacher will give up some spare time to the pupils.

KM: Yes. I used lunchtime and after-school sessions. Our drama group decided to produce a half-hour comedy for presentation in School Gala day and to pupils at the end of term.

TK: How was this useful to the pupils?

KM: It gave me a chance to concentrate on things for which there is limited time in the classroom. I was less of an authority figure, so they confided more. It was possible to develop their personalities a bit, to give them poise and confidence. Also they had to work together as a production team. They felt, too, it helped them relax from pressure of classroom work.

TK: The last unit of the Focus 3 booklet looks at questioning as teaching skill. It suggests that questions can be either 'open' or 'closed', and there is a suggested category system (see Table 3) for analysing one's own questions during a lesson by tape recording the lesson and playing it back later. Did you try this out?

KM: Yes. I found that it was difficult sometimes to classify some of my questions into one of the ten suggested types. However, I quickly became conscious of whether a question was 'open' or 'closed' and I was aware of this as I taught, not just on tape. It was clear that open questions were more effective at helping bright pupils to reason and deduce.

TK: In the light of this, albeit brief, course about teaching bright pupils have you any summary comments about how it helped you, where it failed?

KM: It raised a lot of problems but didn't necessarily provide the answers. Maybe there are no answers yet. But it fired my enthusiasm. For example, I have a kind of remedial workcard kit which I devised prior to the course. If I mark a pupil's work and find he can't use a comma properly I send him off with the 'comma' workcard to practise on his own. Since coming on the course I've seen scope for developing this idea. So it's all pupils, not just the more able, who are likely to benefit from the teaching strategies I've put into practice.

But now let me turn the tables for a moment and ask if you, as tutor, got anything from the course to change your thinking.

TK: I thought that course threw up some very good ideas from individual teachers. Let me give you just one illustration. A primary teacher who was not satisfied with my identification procedures invented one of his own. It's very simple, but a good way of spotting verbal fluency and creativity. It's simply a 'fill in the missing phrases' game; so he might put down "John turned quickly and saw . . . . ." or ". . . . . and disappeared without trace". The pupil adds the rest. I think that's a promising idea.

I'm also getting quite excited about the idea of doing away with traditional Remedial Departments and training specialist teachers of pupils who have special learning needs, whatever the cause. The implications of this for teacher training leave plenty of food for thought.

Table 1: Pupil Proforma

PUPIL PROFORMA

List pupil's characteristics and abilities with reference to the following areas:

1. *Academic performance*
Strengths *and* weaknesses. eg 'outstanding at mathematics'; 'can cope with logarithms in her head', 'Grade VIII pianist at 11 yrs', 'motor co-ordination poor', 'written and drawn work messy', 'Reading age 3 years above chronological age'; 'exceptional vocabulary for age', 'much quicker than I am'.

2. *Personal interests*
Record all known hobbies and enthusiasms including comments on time spent on them and levels of knowledge gained eg 'plays chess at local adults' club', 'outstanding left half with boys' county team', 'two evenings per week at St. John's Ambulance, with advanced F.A. certificate' etc.

3. *Extra-curricular (school-based) activities*
'Form captain', 'junior eleven cricketer', 'goalkeeper-hockey team', 'school choir, drama group, film club, ornithology club'. 'Rushes straight home after school each night'.

4. *School relations and personality*
'Recluse', 'is bullied as being teacher's pet', 'extrovert'. 'Sociometric star'. 'Often organizes a group of classmates in the laboratory'. 'No-one will sit with her', 'friendly, relaxed pupil', 'popular without being assertive'.

5. *Physical description*
Healthy/unhealthy; alert, energetic. Nature of health problems if any. Neat/untidy. Physically advanced/retarded/normal for age. Level of co-ordination etc.

6. *Home background*
Parental occupations. Socio-economic background. Relations with parents, if known. Other children in family and relations with them. Information about the child's behaviour at home; etc.

(Ask a teacher friend who knows the child to record his/her impressions of the pupil using the same six items listed above. How do the two sets of impressions compare?)

Table 2

A suggested profile of the underachiever

he/she may be
   anti-school
   orally knowledgeable but poor in written work
   apparently bored
   restless or inattentive
   absorbed in a private world
   tactless and impatient of slower minds
   friendly with older pupils and/or adults
   excessively self-critical
   unable to make good social relations with peer group and/or teachers
   emotionally unstable
   outwardly self-sufficient

but also,
   creative in motivated directions
   quick to learn
   able to solve problems
   given to abstract thought
   able to ask provocative questions
   persevering when motivated
   inventive in response to open-ended questions/activities

4. SUPPORT

Table 3. Analysis of Questions

Question type	Explanation
1. a *data recall* question	Requires the pupil to remember facts, information without putting the information to use. Eg "What are the four rules of number?"
2. a *naming* question	Asks the pupil simply to name an event, process, phenomenon etc. without showing insight into how the event etc is linked to other factors. Eg "What do we call the set of bones which cover the lungs?"
3. an *observation* question	Asks pupils to describe what they see without attempting to explain it. Eg "What happened when we added litmus solution to hydrochloric acid?"
4. a *control* question	Involves the use of questions to modify pupils' behaviour rather than their learning. Eg "Will you sit down, John?"
5. a *pseudo-question*	Is constructed to appear that the teacher will accept more than one response, but in fact he/she has clearly made up his mind that this is not so. Eg "Do you feel beating slaves was a good thing then?"
6. a *speculative or hypothesis generating question*	Asks pupils to speculate about the outcome of an hypothetical situation. Eg "Imagine a world without trees, how would this affect our lives?"
7. a *reasoning* question	Asks pupils to give reasons why certain things do or do not happen. Eg "What motivates some young people to get involved in soccer violence?"
8. a *personal response* question	Allows pupils to say exactly how they themselves feel about something without pressure to conform to the teacher's or the group's viewpoint. Eg "How would you react if you were on a hijacked airliner?"

9.	a *discriminatory* question	Is one which makes a pupil weigh out the pro's and con's of a situation or argument. Eg "How much evidence is there for the existence of an after-life?"
10.	a *problem solving* question	Asks pupils to construct ways of finding out answers to questions. Eg "Suppose we wanted to discover what prompts birds to migrate, how could we go about it?"

NB Question types 1-5 clearly are more 'closed' than types 6-10. Type 1-5 demand shorter answers, less thought and little competence in language use by the pupils. Types 6-10 are clearly more demanding for brighter pupils.

REFERENCES

1. In our case 'effective' meant teachers specially selected by knowledgeable PGCE tutors as good teachers of mixed ability classes in their own curriculum areas.
2. These include:
P. DOOLEY et al (1977). *Teaching mixed ability classes: heads reports of problems and procedures in 40 schools.* Nottingham University School of Education publication.
T. KERRY (1978), *British Educational Research Journal vol 4 no 2.* Teaching bright pupils in mixed ability classes.
T. KERRY (1978) *Spectrum vol 11 no 1,* August 1978. Mixed ability RE: a case study.
T. KERRY (1978) *Remedial education vol 13 no 3.* Remedial education in the regular classroom.
E.C. WRAGG, (Summer 1978) *Forum for the discussion of new trends in education.* Teaching mixed ability classes: a ten point attack.
3. Her Majesty's Inspectorate (1978) *Gifted children in primary and middle schools,* Matters for discussion series, no 4, and *Mixed ability teaching in comprehensive school no 6.*
4. A list of Teacher Education Project publications can be obtained from the Project Coordinator, School of Education, Nottingham University.

LOOK Who's in the Counselor's Office

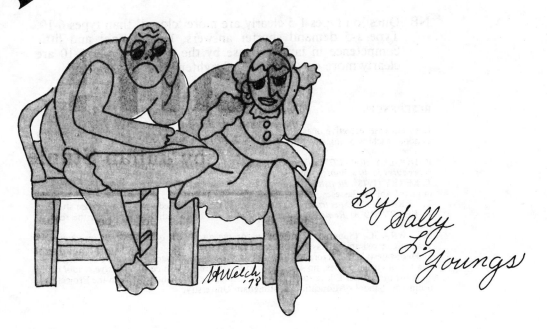

By Sally L. Youngs

Dear Mr. President:

Please change the Pledge of Allegiance by adding these words to the last sentence, ". . . who have reached the age of eighteen."

Thank you very much.

Sincerely,

Owen Grey

Owen met his parents in the school office. He and his parents had an appointment with the school counselor. He joined his parents in the blue chairs flanking the counselor's door.

A slight noise from the direction of the secretary's desk drew his attention. "What's that?" asked Owen pointing to the desk. His mother responded automatically to the pointing finger she had responded to even before Owen could talk. In the pattern she had developed over the past seven years she answered his question to the best of her ability. "It probably holds the names and addresses of every child in the school" she said.

The secretary dialed a number and spoke, "Mrs. Murphy, this is Bill's school calling. This is the second day he's been absent. Is he ill? . . . . I'm happy to hear it isn't another case of chicken pox. Thank you."

The cards in the box spun again. Owen was still watching. "How come the cards don't fall out?" he asked. His father also had learned an automatic response and answered this time. "There's a rib on the core and each card has a slot in it that fits around the rib, sort of like the tongue and grooves on the drawers. The cards can be taken out and put back in." As he spoke he used gestures with his fingers to demonstrate the card encircling the rib.

Just then the door opened and the counselor said, "Come in Owen. And you must be Mr. and Mrs. Grey? . . . " There was a warm feeling about the room as they entered and took seats. The counselor began by expressing how happy she was that they had come to help Owen with his problem.

Owen wanted to touch the cards on his way past the desk, but jammed his hands into his pockets instead. It crossed his mind that some day when he got big like the student aide working the copy machine that maybe he'd be allowed to replace the cards.

Being very good at guidance matters, the counselor knew her job was to help Owen understand himself and his world. The parents, too, must understand Owen and his world to be able to help him adjust to the world around him. She had reviewed his records and had discussed his recent work and behaviors with his teachers.

The counselor glanced at Mr. Grey and asked, "has Owen had any problems with his work this week?" The father said that he did not know of any. He believed that Owen was caught up in his math. However, he related that they had discussed it at home and felt that they would like Owen to be taken out of the gifted program. The mother indicated he still came home very unhappy and still seemed to be having problems. (Every time Owen heard the word 'problem' he sank a little lower in his chair).

The counselor turned to Owen and asked, "What do you think about being in the gifted class?" Owen explained how he liked both of his classes and both of his teachers. He told of how he was working with a group of other boys on a pretend town and had given the peninsula the name Penny, but hadn't named the island yet because he wanted to call it Quarter, but Tommy wanted it to be Gasbowl because it was marshy and smelly and Bob wanted it to be Aiwakii, just because it was a neat word he made up like a Hawaiian word.

"Did you write a story about your town?" asked the counse-lor. "No. We just drew the water reservoir, the peninsula with its island in the bay and the delta of the river beside the peninsula. You know the one that comes from the reservoir lake." (For a moment the counselor recalled how Mrs. Black had said all they do in enrichment is play. Maybe she was right after all.)

Owen admitted that he had not completed all of his work in Mrs. Black's room and had dropped from near perfect 'A' work to low 'C' work or in his own eyes almost failing. He knew his parents were disappointed in him and he knew Mrs. Black was, too. Even now he could hear her saying, "What has come over you? You did such fine work at the beginning of the year, but since you started going to enrichment in Mrs. White's room it seems you just don't care about your work." It was the same way when he got caught hitting his best friend. "What has come over you?" It seemed he couldn't do anything right in Mrs. Black's room any more. It had been fun, but now it seemed that when he told Mark about the island he was in trouble for talking, or if he needed to sharpen his pencil he was in trouble for being out of his seat at the 'wrong' time. He couldn't pick a right time anymore.

"Do you understand that in Mrs. White's room you can be out of your seat occasionally and there are discussions, but in Mrs. Black's room it is quiet work time?" asked the counselor. Owen replied that he did understand the difference, but that sometimes he forgot. "Do you understand that you need to do all the assignments you miss when you are at Mrs. White's?" "Yes, but when I ask the kids what they are doing, I get in trouble for talking," Owen replied. "Well, Owen it is your responsibility to ask Mrs. Black. Perhaps you could ask her at the beginning of class," helped

4. SUPPORT

Miss Counselor. (Owen didn't bother to explain he had tried that method and had only learned it seemed to upset Mrs. Black so she complained to him about how he did everything.) He couldn't do anything right in Mrs. Black's room anymore.

He and his parents had talked about his unhappiness and problems the night before and Owen now stated the conclusion they had come to that while he liked enrichment, his basic work did have to come first. He couldn't explain it, but he 'just knew' that he'd be happier if he stayed in Mrs. Black's room all of the time.

Miss Counselor and Owen's parents then discussed some of his test results showing he was definitely qualified for the gifted program. While they talked about his achievement scores Owen understood only that they were worried that he might drop by the end of the year if he continued to rush sloppily through his workbooks and not do some pages.

Then they discussed his behavior and outbursts of frustration both in school and at home. His parents were worried, but Miss Counselor consoled them that it was not unusual, that he like many second graders was bright, but not mature enough to handle having two teachers. Soon, they were in agreement that to be responsible for himself was beyond him at this point and it would be best for his happiness to be removed from the gifted program.

Miss Counselor said that she would make the necessary arrangements of rescheduling and wrote Owen a pass to return to Mrs. Black's class. Owen's parents thanked the counselor and left. As Miss Counselor glanced up to watch Owen leave for a moment she thought she saw Mrs. Black in one of the blue chairs flanking the door of her office. She pushed the mirage and thought from her head. She was there to counsel students, not teachers. Ridiculous that a teacher would be in that chair!

Owen entered Mrs. Black's class as they were beginning a writing assignment. Mrs. Black received him with a big grin. There was no need to explain where he had been as he took his seat.

She spoke pleasantly to him for the first time in months as she asked him to get out pencil and paper. He just knew he and his parents had made the right choice and his troubles would go away now.

Owen half listened while Mrs. Black explained that they were to write a letter to someone and went over all the commas, etc.. He daydreamed about all the people he'd like to write to while she was concerned with grammar. When they were told they could pick up their pencils he began assuredly.

December 1, 1977

Dear Mr. President,

Please change the Pledge of Allegiance by adding these words to the last sentence, ". . . who have reached the age of eighteen."
Thank you very much.

Sincerely,

Owen Grey

He knew he'd get an 'A' on this as all the grammar was correct and he had written neatly and finished it.

Bobby came in from enrichment class, sat behind Owen and whispered, "Where were you? We named the island Gasbowl." They both **giggled** a bit. Mrs. Black barked, "Bobby! When you come in you should be quiet and not disturb. Can't you see we are writing letters? Get your pencil out and get going. You only have ten minutes to finish your letter." Bobby got his pencil out and all was quiet.

Owen had come through his first counseling session well. The counselor had done a fine job of helping her client adjust to the world around him. He will probably not be sitting in the blue chair again. He has resigned himself to respecting the wishes of others. Perhaps when he reaches eighteen he will find a college with courses that are as much fun as enrichment was. Or, perhaps society will welcome him for the benefit of his talents and restore his self concept. Until that time his parents can be depended upon to help him find the answers to all of his questions.

THE END

No! It is not the end. Next week it may be Bobby or Tommy or your daughter. The client in the counselor's office should have been the regular classroom teacher, Mrs. Black. She needs to make a better adjustment to herself and the world around her.

There is a current trend to expand the role of counselor to include more consultation with teachers. Much of this arises out of Public Law 94-142 which requires mainstreaming of handicapped children.

Roger Aubrey in The Personnel and Guidance Journal *supports the trend with the conclusion that where elementary school counselors have used consultation with teachers there has been a successful adjustment by the teacher to the various learning styles of the students. Aubrey recommends that counselors avail themselves of course work to gain information on the nature and needs of the exceptionalities to successfully guide the teachers in their school.*

Charles W. Humes II in The School Counselor *views PL 94-142 as bringing more work to* the counselor such as meetings with teachers to establish Individual Education Plans. One aspect of these sessions would also be consulting with teachers in regards to appropriate educational services with instructional and curricular recommendations.

In the November, 1977 issue of The School Counselor *Douglas J. Mickelson and Jerry L. Davis* proposed a consultation model for the school counselor. They viewed consulting as a preventative guidance program, averting the need for so much remedial and crisis-oriented work in the profession. They saw it as an expansion of counseling services to reach greater numbers of students. Consulting with a teacher could in turn affect large numbers of students. They suggested a counselor begin by ". . . increasing the teacher's interpersonal competencies and understanding of human behavior in order to reduce the number of students who need individual attention at a later date."

I view consulting as a step in the right direction in relation to the situation in the gifted sector of our school population. If the regular classroom teacher better understands the gifted child's style of learning and his needs, I'm sure it will help.

However, I see the problem of the teacher such as Mrs. Black engaging in voice inflections, ridicule, and negative behaviors toward the child as well as the "Catch 22" tactics of not making assignments available to the student, but requiring them done to avoid failure, or expecting the child to ask for assignments, but disciplining him for talking as in need of much more than consulting from the counselor services before our gifted will truly get an appropriate education in the least restrictive environment.

These "Catch 22" tactics arise out of personal prejudice, jealousy, and fears of self-worth on the part of the classroom teacher. These are the same things that bring the student to the counselor's office. Until we label the actions of our teachers correctly and deal with such things as the teacher's fear that the child's loyalty will be shared with the teacher of the gifted, or the fear that the administrator will evaluate the regular classroom on the same objectives and basis as the gifted room putting the Mrs. Blacks at a gross disadvantage leading to job insecurity, and until we face prejudice and jealousy, the losers will continue to be our gifted children. Can we afford to give them anything but an appropriate education?

The literature in both the gifted area and the counseling area has politely ignored what is actually going on in the schools. At conferences and conventions the subject is widely discussed among teachers and parents as a problem, but no solutions are approached. It is not yet a topic open to analysis. After all who wants to accuse a professional such as a teacher of having such human weaknesses as prejudice, jealousy, or fears. To be human might jeopardize the teacher's authority. Or would it make him/her a better teacher? Isn't it about time for such action? How long are you willing to let the gifted children you know suffer the consequences through torpedoed gifted classes and through personal assault to their self concepts? Let's state the problem that exists so we can get on with the process of solving it. NOW!

What a University Can Do for the Gifted

Twelve-year-old university students getting the highest grades in the class isn't unusual in the PACE (Pre-Accelerated College Enrollment) program at California State University, Los Angeles, says Barbara Clark, Professor, Dept. of Special Education. These eighth, ninth, and tenth graders are participating in summer classes at the large, metropolitan Cal State U. which "enrolls students from a wide variety of ethnic and racial backgrounds," Clark continues. "These students in the programs described here are largely minority gifted students—often the first of their families to be involved in university work."

Clark says she hopes that other universities and colleges can see ways they too can participate in the education of gifted students. "We have all become aware of how valuable higher educational institutions can be in providing unique services to gifted learners through the radical acceleration project being conducted by Julian Stanley at Johns Hopkins University," she adds.

The programs offered at Cal State U., L.A. are the Mentally Gifted Minors (MGM) Friday afternoons for sixth, seventh and eighth graders; PACE, mentioned above; ACE (Accelerated College Enrollment) for 11th and 12th graders; General Education Honors Program for gifted college students; and a graduate program for teachers working with the gifted.

The MGM Friday afternoon sessions on the university campus are taught by professors who volunteer their time. Transportation and supervision is provided by participating school districts that also conduct asessment and follow-up monitoring. Because of the volunteer nature of staffing Clark says, the biggest probem is an inability to accommodate all the gifted students who want to participate.

The PACE program, described above, allows qualified students to participate as regularly enrolled members in a large variety of classes with all the attendant rights and responsibilities! Their parents take care of transportation to the campus. College credits accumulate on their university transcripts, to be used when they attend Cal State U. as fulltime students or to be transferred to any other school they attend.

Participants in ACE, for the gifted students in their last two years of high school, take university courses during all four quarters, with credit accumulating on their transcripts. Aside from special admission procedure, these students are treated the same as their older classmates. They provide their own transportation to the university.

When the gifted students enter the university fulltime, they may participate in the General Education Honors Program for more stimulating and challenging opportunities. This program also provides support and a sense of community for the freshman and sophomore high-potential student. The faculty for the General Education Honors Program classes are encouraged to include more student participation in these classes, additional interdisciplinary content, and innovations in their presentations.

For gifted juniors and seniors at the university some departments offer honors programs with continued flexibility and challenge. "The entire series of programs allows for acceleration," Clark says, "as the class designations—freshman, sophomore, etc.—are only dependent upon the number of units accumulated, not the time spent on campus."

In the graduate program for teachers preparing to work with the gifted, Cal State U., offers a credential specializing in the area of gifted; a Master of Arts in Special Education: Option Gifted; and a joint doctoral program with the University of California, Los Angeles for a Ph.D. in Special Education: Option Gifted.

The teacher education and higher degree programs specializing in the area of gifted at California State University, Los Angeles, are based on the following assumptions:

- Children who are gifted are atypical learners, requiring programs significantly differentiated from the more typical learner to develop their potential.
- To provide these differentiated programs, teachers must develop an understanding of the needs of the atypical learners and competencies needed to plan and implement such programs including the curricular and environmental modifications necessary.
- The most critical component in any program is the teacher, and that teacher's attitudes and abilities toward the facilitation of the thinking, feeling, sensing, and intuitive functioning of gifted students as well as the nurture of their creative growth and societal commitment.
- The instructional skills and attitudes of teachers are measureably improved by knowledge of and experience with the population they wish to serve.
- For teachers to facilitate high levels of development in others, it is necessary that they themselves pursue self-knowledge, and regard themselves with self-esteem.
- Learning occurs most efficiently when optimal conditions for human learning are available in the environment and in the instruction, and when the learner is highly involved in the learning and evaluation processes.

From the *Bulletin of the National/State Leadership Training Institute on the Gifted and the Talented,* November 1978. Barbara Johnson, Editor.

Mentorships, internships and apprentice-ships—all are forms of Youth Participation, yet there are subtle differences between the three types of programs. Generally, internship and apprenticeship are career-oriented. The young person may work with several adults in the course of an apprenticeship; one adult may supervise a number of young people in an internship. In contrast, a mentorship involves a one-to-one relationship between student and mentor. Student and mentor are matched on the basis of a mutual interest, usually in the mentor's career, but may pursue other common concerns as well.

MENTORSHIPS: WHAT ARE THEY? WHO NEEDS THEM?

When Odysseus left home to fight the Trojan War, he entrusted the education of his young son, Telemachus, to Mentor, his most respected friend. Mentor did a good job because Homer describes Telemachus as a "god-like young man, thoughtful and daring."

Contemporary parents may not go on such strenuous adventures, but young people—especially gifted and talented young people—still need wise and caring counselors like Mentor. "The only adults most kids know are parents, relatives and teachers," says Nat Hentoff, an observer of American education. "That's a narrow selection of the kinds of people they might grow up to be, so kids need other models."

Mentorship provides such models by deliberately matching young people in one-to-one relationships with adults. A mentor can be anyone—judge, novelist, corporation president, veterinarian, meteorologist, actor or orchestra conductor. The key requirements are that the adult care about the student and that their relationship be grounded in a strong mutual interest, usually related to the mentor's career or avocation.

Although young people at all levels of ability benefit from mentorships, NCRY has observed that the results are especially gratifying for gifted and talented young people. "At some point, gifted kids have special needs," says one coordinator, "needs that can be met by a mentorship."

For example, gifted youngsters need the freedom to explore subjects more deeply than is possible in most classrooms. A mentor who respects and appreciates a student's talents can provide individualized stimulation to stretch and test his or her abilities. Also, gifted young people are sometimes pressured to develop their talent at the expense of other aspects of their personalities.

In addition to students who are readily identified as gifted, mentorship is often an excellent way of revealing previously undetected talents. Although academic excellence and test scores are good measures of certain types of ability, they overlook many others. Some experts now admit the limitations of these vehicles and are trying to devise new ways of identifying undiscovered gifts. In the meantime, a mentorship in which a student explores his or her capabilities with adult encouragement often discloses unexpected talents.

Finally, some young people conceal their talents—perhaps intentionally, afraid of being "different" or perhaps because they are shy, unable to communicate, or disruptive. A mentor can reassure these young people about their value and give them the courage to develop their abilities fully. In every case, mentors support students, sharing knowledge and experience and guiding them into rewarding and challenging learning situations.

Perhaps the essence of mentorship is best expressed by a Boston teacher who said, "It's important to me to know I have arranged for an older person and a child to get together in a relationship where both are thinking, learning, exchanging. In short, they are living. I just get them together and allow that magic thing to happen."

"That magic thing" is what this newsletter is all about. Inside you'll find descriptions of mentorship programs, interviews with coordinators and strategies for starting or improving a mentorship program of your own.

From *Resources for Youth*, Vol. VII, No. 2, February 1978. Resources for Youth is the quarterly newsletter published by the National Commission on Resources for Youth, Inc.

4. SUPPORT

PROGRAMS THAT WORK

Mentorship programs can be organized in many ways, depending upon student needs, staff availability, school restrictions and community resources. The programs described below include mentorships oriented toward specific subjects such as science (PAT), creative arts (CAC), and law (Law Institute), as well as two additional programs.

The programs also illustrate diversified organizational structures, ranging from a nonprofit community agency to a regional council supported voluntarily by participating schools. In one program, mentorships were arranged by an individual teacher; in another, a district coordinator places students from an entire school system.

Yet, despite drastic differences in external structure, the heart of a mentorship program is always the one-to-one relationship between student and mentor.

Project LEARN
Westport, Connecticut

Project LEARN, an elective alternative for sixth through eighth graders, earns full academic credit in the Westport school system. Students spend an average of one day a week at the community Nature Center where they work with mentors on nature-related subjects like meteorology, animal care, taxidermy, ecology, etc. (For more information, write Project Director, Nature Center for Environmental Activities, P.O. Box 165, Westport, CT 06880.)

Apprenticeships in Career Exploration (ACE)
San Francisco, California

ACE is a volunteer organization which arranges after-school mentorships for talented high school juniors and seniors. The students can choose to work in business, the arts, science, the professions, communications or public affairs. The object of the program is to help students discover whether they have "the talent, discipline and interest to pursue the field as a career." (Project Director, ACE, 1948 Pacific Ave., San Francisco, CA 94109.)

The Switching Yard
San Anselmo, California

As the youth division of the county volunteer bureau, The Switching Yard coordinates credit-carrying work experiences, including mentorships for the gifted, for 14 county high schools. For more detailed information, see RFY, v. VI, no. 2. (Project Director, The Switching Yard, Volunteer Bureau of Marin County, Inc., 1022 Sir Francis Drake Blvd., San Anselmo, CA 94960.)

Joan of Arc Medical Program
New York, New York

William works in a microbiology lab, processing blood from diabetic mice. As a student in the Joan of Arc/New York University Medical Center program, he spends one day a week at the center, working with a mentor in the morning. In the afternoon, he attends a special seminar, a lab session and a feedback period where he writes a brief report about his work.

The Joan of Arc program started in 1966 with placements for only 30 students. Today over 140 students—mostly black and Puerto Rican—work with doctors, technicians, nurses, researchers, surgeons and other staff members. Their assignments are usually sophisticated and challenging—one student teaches mentally handicapped children under the supervision of his mentor; another performs skin grafts on rats; a third is learning x-ray techniques. "Our program introduces them to careers in health," says the director, "and provides them with reasons for persevering through the school system." (Project Director, Joan of Arc Medical Program, New York University Medical School, Dept. of Urban Health Affairs, 550 First Ave., New York, NY 10016.)

Learning Web
Ithaca, New York

Mentorship programs can also be operated successfully by nonprofit agencies, churches, youth bureaus or private contributors. The Learning Web, for example, was founded to provide a link between school and community, a setting in which young people have "hands on" experiences. So far, the Web's young clients have had their hands on everything from carpentry to weaving, veterinary science to dentistry, automechanics to dance.

Before student and mentor agree to work together, they undergo a two-week trial period. If all goes well, they sign a formal contract. In placing students, says one staff member, "We look for a combination which builds carefully on a student's interests and abilities, has clearly defined goals and is interpersonally satisfying." (Project Director, The Learning Web, 318 Anabel Taylor Hall, Ithaca, NY 14853.)

Del Mar Mentor Project
Tiburon, California

This program grew out of a series of mini-courses taught by community adults. Students responded so well that the teacher arranged informal mentorships after school and on weekends. The elementary school students who are intellectually gifted explore interests like architecture, journalism, aviation and conservation with their mentors. (Project Director, Del Mar School Mentor Project, 105 Avenida Miraflores, Tiburon, CA 93272.)

As these programs show, mentorships can be rewarding for many different students studying a broad range of subjects in a variety of settings. For more information about specific programs, write to the National Commission on Resources for Youth, 36 W. 44th St., New York, NY 10036.

Creative Arts Community (CAC)
Hartford, Connecticut

Mentorships can be unusually rewarding for students with exceptional talents in the arts because they offer an intensive involvement often unavailable in school. Creative Arts Community draws artistically gifted students from a large region and matches them with professional artists or people in charge of arts institutions.

All CAC students have been identified as gifted, but the director is careful not to stereotype their interests. "Brahms and Beethoven are not for everyone," he explains. "Drums and guitar may be the essential equipment for a given youngster. One student developed an ethnic music group which performs at street festivals; another is apprenticed to the conductor of a symphony orchestra."

In every instance, staff members closely monitor mentors and students. "We don't put a student with a mentor and say 'Go to it,'" says the director. "We try to develop individualized goals. It's extremely fulfilling to match an aspiring young artist who's hungry for experience with an artist who can provide that experience." (Project Director, Creative Arts Community, 45 Oak St., Hartford, CT 06106.)

Heritage of Art
Minneapolis, Minnesota

In this two-part program, gifted young artists spend one semester taking an advanced art history course taught by staff members from the Minneapolis Art Institute. In the second semester, students work with artists and museum curators to prepare a special exhibition. For an exhibit called "Imagination: Dreams, Fantasies, Nightmares," students planned the theme, assembled the art, wrote descriptive materials and arranged for publicity. (Project Director, Minneapolis Institute of Art, 2400 Third Ave. South, Minneapolis, MN 55803.)

Visions of the City
Minneapolis, Minnesota

Visions of the City is an intensive study of urban life in which students investigate the city by electing brief mentorships with leaders in human service, cultural or business organizations. (Project Director, Minneapolis Institute of Art, 2400 Third Ave. South, Minneapolis, MN 55803.)

Community Involvement Program
Minneapolis, Minnesota

All the Youth Participation programs for junior and senior high schools in Minneapolis are coordinated by a central office. Mentorship is one of many options.

"It's important to exercise judgment about the type of students who are likely to benefit from a mentorship," says the coordinator. "The best mentors are often super busy people who can't give constant attention to a student. The student needs to be self-directed enough to learn by observing and asking questions as well as by working."

The Minnesota program pools the resources of several schools, so staff members have developed placements to satisfy diverse needs. For example, in a consumer education course, mentorship complements a seminar and involvement in a consumer action service. Class discussions are enriched by insights which students get while working with mentors such as an FDA official, a state consumer fraud investigator, a housing inspector, an insurance adjustor or a quality control supervisor. (Project Director, Community Involvement Program, Southwest High School, 3414 W. 47 St., Minneapolis, MN 55410.)

Food Science Research Project
Minneapolis, Minnesota

For another mentorship, the coordinator tapped the resources of General Foods, a large local corporation where students do research on nutrition and food processing under the supervision of GF scientists. Though the placements are varied, the purpose is the same. "In each case," says the director, "we try to give

4. SUPPORT

the kids a larger slice of life than they would get in the classroom." (Project Director, Marshall University High School, 1313 S.E. Fifth St., Minneapolis, MN 55414.)

John Dewey Law Institute
Brooklyn, New York

Judges, lawyers, policemen, probation officers and other law-related professionals have been mentors for students at the Law Institute of John Dewey High School. The mentorship is the culmination of a five-course program in which students study law and government.

At the beginning of the mentorship, each student establishes learning objectives in cooperation with his or her mentor. Students keep logs evaluating each day's work and write a final paper related to one of the mentorship objectives. An in-school seminar allows students to compare their experiences to see how different aspects of the legal system interlock. "We learn a lot from each other," says one student, "because each placement has a different point of view." (Project Director, John Dewey Law Institute, 50 Ave. X, Brooklyn, NY 11223.)

Program for the Academically Talented (PAT)
Emeryville, California

Six years ago, a teacher in Emeryville became concerned that the aspirations of her gifted students were too narrow for their talents, so she developed PAT to give them a glimpse of advanced academic possibilities. One day a week, selected students work with university science majors in subjects like architecture, medical physics, microbiology, and linguistics. The students are third through eighth graders from blue-collar families, and PAT is often their first exposure to the challenges of higher education. (Project Director, PAT, Emery High School, 1100 47 St., Emeryville, CA 94608.)

Executive High School Internships
Boston, Massachusetts, and Stamford, Connecticut

In this nationwide program, exceptional students work with mentors who are executives in industry, communications, media, government, social agencies, medicine, etc. One day a week students attend a special seminar on management. For more detailed information, see RFY, v. VI, no. 3. (Project Director, Executive High School Internships, EDCO Metropolitan Education Center, 7 Marshall St., Boston MA 02108; Project Director, Executive High School Internships, Stamford Public Schools, Stamford, CT 06902.)

TROUBLE-SHOOTERS GUIDE

The directors of NCRY's model mentorship programs have identified a few problems that crop up over and over again. Anticipating these difficulties may make your program run more smoothly.

Credit. Whenever possible, students should receive credit for work with their mentors. Student performance can be evaluated through a report from the mentor, a day-to-day log kept by the student, a paper or seminar presentation on some aspect of their work.

In addition, a contract will help clarify the expectations of both parties at the beginning of the mentorship. The contract between student and coordinator should describe the mentorship placement, specify services or tasks which the student will perform, and list the student's objectives as specifically as possible.

Scheduling. A mentorship program can develop as one component of a traditional class, an elective alternative or even an extracurricular activity. NCRY has seen successful mentorships scheduled

all day, everyday for a semester,
one day a week,
one period per day,
half a day,
after school or on weekends.

In some of these arrangements, students may miss regularly scheduled classes, so be sure to secure the cooperation of effected teachers.

Transportation. Whenever possible, develop mentorship sites within walking distance of the school. For longer distances, you might consider hiring a district bus (this works best when students are grouped at one location such as a hospital), obtaining special passes from public transportation, or recruiting parents to drive on a rotating schedule. One program coordinator got a chauffeur's license and conducted a seminar on the bus while transporting students to their mentorship sites.

Supervision. Mentorships, like other off-campus programs, may be of concern to administrators. Some of these fears can be allayed if the coordinator involves administrators in the program from the beginning, asking them to recommend mentors, keeping them informed of progress, etc.

The coordinator must also monitor each placement, first to see that students arrive safely and, second, to be sure that the mentorship is satisfactory for both parties. Sometimes after starting well, a mentorship deteriorates and requires intervention to get it going again.

Legal Matters. Mentorships could involve legal liability for the school or mentors, so clear your project with the school attorney. The National Association of Secondary School Principals has two brochures which may prove helpful—*Responsibilities for Student Injuries Occuring Off School Property* and *Negligence*. Copies are available for a quarter from NASSP, 1904 Association Drive, Reston, VA 22001.

HOW TO FIND GOOD MENTORS

Match-making, always a delicate process, is especially challenging for a mentorship coordinator. S/he must take into account objective facts such as the student's interests and abilities, the mentor's skills and resources, transportation and scheduling as well as subjective considerations such as personalities and expectations.

As coordinator of the Columbia Teachers College Evaluation Center for Gifted Students, Lynn Kurtz has placed dozens of high school students in successful mentorships, so we asked her how she finds mentors. "I'm a kind of detective," she replied. "Naturally, I start with my own resources—I know a lot of people. Then I use the resources of the university and other local institutions. When you start looking, a lot of bright people are interested in working with kids."

Other program directors get suggestions about mentors from parents, teachers, administrators, local government officials, volunteer bureaus, associations for the retired, and social agencies. One program even advertised for mentors at the beginning. Often after the first few semesters, the program gains a word-of-mouth reputation and persons volunteer to be mentors.

The possibilities for placements are limitless. As the project descriptions in this newsletter prove, mentorships can flourish in any of the following settings:

> hospitals,
> law offices,
> corporations,
> ecology centers,
> arts programs,
> day care centers,
> consumer programs,
> crisis intervention centers,
> and many other places.

"I've placed kids in some situations, whatever seems to meet their needs best," explains Ms. Kurtz. "One student is working with a psychologist, learning about the enormous battery of tests used in that profession. Since psychology isn't even taught in most high schools, that's a tremendous opportunity. Another student is working on brain research with a mentor in a university science lab. She's learning her way around a lab, learning to use sophisticated experimental instruments."

Once a coordinator has a list of mentorship possibilities, s/he will want to contact the people involved and assess their potential as mentors. This is best accomplished in an interview where the coordinator can talk directly to the mentor about his or her special competencies, reasons for wanting an apprentice and expectations for the program.

What are the characteristics that distinguish a good mentor? "He or she is tremendously motivated to do this," says Ms. Kurtz. "You don't have to persuade him or her—this is something the person wants to do. There are other things, too, of course—knowledge of the subject, compatibility with young people, flexibility, sense of humor, an ability to listen. Those are all essential, but enthusiasm is very important. With a good placement, it's hard to tell who gets a bigger kick out of the thing, the student or the mentor."

NCRY Associates have also observed that successful mentors take a personal interest in their students and are able to provide guidance without smothering initiative. Often the mentor treats the student like a junior colleague, sharing information and providing creative situations in which the student can use what he or she has learned.

The motivations of mentors vary tremendously. They may simply enjoy the company of young people, find satisfaction in teaching or feel a moral obligation to future generations. Sometimes the motivation is partly practical. "One professor said, 'We can always use another pair of hands in the lab,'" says Ms. Kurtz. "Of course, I knew he would be a good mentor because he said he needed the insights the student might have into his research."

The other half of the mentorship placement is, of course, the student, and the coordinator must be equally insightful about the young person's interests and goals. "I use tests—IQ, aptitude, personality—and information I get by talking to parents, teachers and the student," say Ms. Kurtz. "Most of the time, the student gives the clues. By talking to him or her, you get a good picture of what they want."

The coordinator should also be alert to the possibility that some students may not be ready for mentorship. Occasionally, a student

4. SUPPORT

is enthusiastic about the idea of having a mentor but lacks the sustaining interest that will make a placement worthwhile. In such cases, the coordinator may encourage the student to postpone involvement in the program.

Of course, the coordinator's role does not end once a student is matched with a mentor. Because the quality of a mentorship is influenced by very subtle factors, the coordinator must maintain contact with both parties, says Ms. Kurtz, "so I stay in touch with mentors, parents, students. I just keep asking, 'How's it going?' Usually, when things aren't working out, you can tell. People are uncomfortable. For the most part, problems don't come up. Oh, we make mistakes, but usually it's a good marriage."

Throughout the mentorship experience, the coordinator is a pivotal person. "The work is demanding," concludes Ms. Kurtz. "It's a continual process of advocacy for the kids. But when you do make a good placement, you get a unique kind of interaction. Then people turn to each other and say, 'Oh, yeah! Why didn't we do this all along?' "

PERTINENT LITERATURE

An Introductory Manual on Youth Participation for Program Administrators. National Commission on Resources for Youth. Washington, DC: 1977. 48 pages. Free. Available as DHEW Publication No. OHD/OYD 76-27045, DHEW/Office of Youth Development, Division of Youth Activities, 200 Independence Ave., SW, Washington, DC 20201.

Prepared by NCRY for DHEW, Office of Youth Development, our practical manual advises personnel in a wide range of agencies "who want to start or who want to improve existing Youth Participation projects." This booklet shows how to overcome barriers to Youth Participation, provides a continuous management scheme, and describes the components of continuous evaluation.

"Coming of Age in the Space Age" by Dorothy Sisk. *Bulletin of the National/State Leadership Training Institute on the Gifted and the Talented.* November 1977, vol. 4, no. 11. 316 W. Second St., Ste. PH-C, Los Angeles, CA 90012. $11 per year.

USOE Director of the Office of the Education of Gifted and Talented Dorothy Sisk outlines "specific directives in gifted education." Her directives *stress the value of mentorship.* "Scholars need to be utilized in the classroom as mentors," she writes. "Internships with experts, especially in science and mathematics, need to be conducted throughout high school." The *N/S-LTI-G/T Bulletin* includes conference notices, book order forms, project listings and information of interest to parents, teachers and others interested in the development from infancy to adulthood of gifted and talented youngsters.

Students in Decision-Making: A Guide Book and *Massachusetts Students in Decision-Making.* Student Service Center-Student Advisory Council Project, Bureau of Student Services/Massachusetts Department of Education. 56 and 72 pages, respectively. Free.

Here are two important reports of nationwide relevance. They describe the creative and responsible participation of students in the design and legislation of their own schooling, as well as the definition and solution of their own school and community problems.

Student Essays, published by the San Francisco Public Schools Commission. Reprinted by The National Commission on Resources for Youth, Inc., 1977. 30 pages. Free.

Over 700 San Francisco students (K-12) responded to an essay contest on the subject of their schools — changes they want, what they like and do not like. The youthful concerns expressed in this collection of excerpts are serious, involving their education and the quality of life. Samples: "At passing times, my life is imperiled." "I wish there weren't any prejudices." "I would like to see green grass in our school yard." "Anti-littering laws should be drawn up." "Some school books are out of date." "If we were able to go to a hospital, and a doctor would show us around, I think we would learn something." "I like the teachers in my school who enjoy their work." "We should be treated like people."

REVIEWS

Experience-Based Learning: How to Make the Community Your Classroom. Northwest Regional Education Laboratory. Portland, OR: 1977. 246 pages. $9.45.

This well-developed textbook describes 25 successful Youth Participation programs. The textbook is supplemented by four pamphlets: *Student Competencies Guide: Survival Skills for a Changing World* (44 pages, $1.95), *Student Record of Community Exploration* (16 pages, plus an 8-page site information record, $1.50), *Student Guide to Writing a Journal* (16 pages, $1.50) and *The Community Resource Person's Guide for Experience-Based Learning* (24 pages, $.95).

THE IDENTIFICATION OF GIFTED CHILDREN: A COMMUNITY BASED DECISION-MAKING PROCESS

Theodore R. Storlie

Patrimpas G. Prapuolenis

October, 1979

The development of a valid process for identifying gifted and talented children in a local school district is a crucial first step in the implementation of an educational program designed for gifted children. It is virtually impossible to make meaningful statements about the effectiveness of such a program unless one has confidence that those children for whom the program has been designed are indeed being correctly identified. The development of a comprehensive system for identifying gifted children may be viewed essentially as a decision-making process. Specifically, several kinds of decisions are required:. Who should be involved in the decision-making process? How is "giftedness" to be defined? What criteria shall be established for judging giftedness? What single or composite cut -off score shall be applied in selecting children for the program?

As a joint venture, the Flint Community Schools (Flint, MI) and Educational Testing Service developed a two-stage model for the early identification and selection of gifted children in kindergarten through grade 3 for a full time gifted program in Flint. The project evolved out of an increasing concern that traditional methods of identifying gifted children often resulted in the under-representation of children from disadvantaged backgrounds. Consequently, a model was developed to increase the pool of eligible children and to minimize the impace of biases of opportunity, language, and cultural saturation which mitigate against the selection of gifted children from less advantaged environments.

The problem was addressed by extensive applications of an interactive group decision-making process, which involved Flint school administrators, school psychologists, teachers, parents, and other community members. Where differences of opinion occurred with respect to any specific problem, the process provided equal participation by all group members in generating ideas, discussion, information sharing, and problem resolution by use of a ranking procedure. Project activities also included a series of seminars on relevant topics such as creativity, early childhood, instrumentation, language arts, and mathematics, all focusing on the gifted child. The seminars provided project participants with a sound basis for decision-making.

By means of this interactive group process, project participants formulated a ranked list of six criteria for judging giftedness. These were, in order of importance: creativity, intellectual potential, learning ability, motivation, leadership and social/self awareness, and academic achievement. These criteria formed the basis for implementing Stage 1 of the model: the *identification* of potentially gifted children. Three identification procedures were established: 1) parent nominations by means of an eleven-item questionnaire, 2) school faculty nominations based on a list of behavioral indicators of each criterion, and 3) achievement data. Children were to be placed in the identification pool if nominated by any one or any combination of these three procedures. To provide an additional source of information, teachers of nominated children were to complete a "teacher check-list of their nominated pupils.

Stage 2 of the model, *selection* of pupils for participation in the gifted program, was to be implemented by a specially formed selection committee comprised of community representatives, balanced by sex and race. On the basis of individual pupil information derived from the identification process, the committee was to generate a ranked list of eligible candidates for the gifted program.

"The Identification of Gifted Children: A Community Based Decision Making Process," T.R. Storlie, P.G. Parpuolenis, Educational Testing Service, Midwestern Regional Office, October 1979.

4. SUPPORT

The children's cultural background, sex, or social class were not factors in the committee's decisions because such information was deleted from information provided to the committee. Given the ranked list of eligible candidates prepared by the committee, Flint Community Schools' administrators were to make final admission decisions, given consideration to those variables (social class, ethnic origin, race, or sex) which would best further the goals and philosophy of their gifted program.

This two-stage identification and selection model was implemented, first on a pilot basis involving five schools, and then, during the first part of the 1978-79 school year, on a district-wide basis. Results of the pilot implementation were encouraging. Of the 316 children identified as potentially gifted, 56 were selected as eligible for the gifted program. This represented a major accomplishment for schools that in the past had not identified any pupils as even potentially gifted.

Analysis of data generated by the district-wide implementation of the model also supported the effectiveness of the identification and selection process. The new process was found to be successful in selecting a group of gifted children which was significantly more representative of the Flint community with respect to ethnic composition than was attained by means of the traditional process which relied solely on recommendations made on the basis of IQ testing. Furthermore, those children who were found by the selection committee to be most eligible for the gifted program did rank higher with respect to the selection criteria than children only identified as potentially gifted as a result of stage 1 of the process. Finally, those children selected by the new process did not differ significantly from children selected by the old process with respect to the selection criteria, indicating that implimentation of the new process did not result in a lowering of standards with respect to the kind of students selected.

As more and more public interest is directed toward special programs for gifted and talented children, and as federal and state funding for such programs increases, the programs and the process by which a particilar child is deemed eligible for them, will likewise undergo increasing scrutiny. It is not unlikely that recipients of various funds intended for gifted and talented children will be required to document and demonstrate their eligibility for such funding, much the same as is required in the administration of compensatory education programs. This will require the application of defensible procedures for identifying and selecting gifted children that would be culturally fair, valid, and capable of being implemented within the ordinary kinds of constraints in which a typical school district must operate. In this regard, our project was a success.

Much work remains to be done in this area. Much could be learned from a closer look at existing programs for the gifted. It is becoming clear that the identification of gifted children cannot be considered as a separate issue from the specific program one has in mind for the education of these children.

Models need to be developed which link the two processes of identification and education with clearly defined constructs, objectives, and goals. Designs need to be developed for investigating the interrelationships among the variables linking the two processes. Finally, much greater emphasis must be placed on application of sound measurement practice to the identification of gifted children and the evaluation of gifted programs.

REFERENCES

1. The specific process used is known as the Nominal Group Technique, fully described in *Group Techniques for Program Planning,* by Delbecq, A.L., Van de Ven, A.H., and Gustafson, D.H.: Scott, Foresman and Co., Glenview, IL, 1975.

2. For a full report on the development of the model and the pilot study see *The Development of a Culturally-Fair Process for the Early Identification and Selection of Gifted Children.* Storlie, T.R., et. al., Evanston, Illinois: Educational Testing Service, 1978. (Available through ERIC ED#159-229.-

3. For a full report on the district-wide implementation of the model and subsequent follow-up analyses see *The Implementation of a Culturally Fair Process for the Identification of Gifted Children In Flint, Michigan; A Follow-up Study,* Prapuolenis, P.G. and Storlie, T.R. Evanston, Illinois: Educational Testing Service, 1979. (To be available from ERIC.)

PARENT INVOLVEMENT A KEY TO THE EDUCATION OF GIFTED CHILDREN

Kathleen Kenney O'Neill

How can the needs of gifted children be met in a situation lacking in special teachers or funds? Parent involvement is one solution. Last September I was faced with the difficult task of meeting the needs of children whose abilities ranged from gifted to well below average. Judging from scores on The Metropolitan Readiness Test and from my own observations, I felt that most of the nine children in my top reading group would qualify as gifted. I would have this gifted group for homeroom and reading activities; they would go to another classroom for math. I was determined that these children not be overlooked, and that they be challenged during their first year in school. At this point, our school has no special program for gifted children at the first grade level. It was apparent, however, that the needs of these children could be met only by extending beyond the program provided by the general first grade curriculum.

I decided that the most effective way to deal with this problem would be to enlist the aid of the parents of these children to supplement the school program with their assistance in teacher-planning homework activities. In this way, I could develop a variety of enrichment activities, and, although I would not be able to spend time during the day on this work, the parents would be able to give their time in the evenings.

During school, each of the three reading groups met for thirty minutes, and all groups worked with the Ginn 360 Reading Series. Although the children in the top group came to school reading fluently, they could benefit from the variety of grammar and language skills of a formal reading program. The Teacher's Manual proved to be a useful resource for enrichment ideas. Listed in the manual are ideas for creativity and language development, which can be extended so that they require the children to use higher levels of thought in cognitive and affective domains. Some of the homework activities were related to the stories in the book, although many were unrelated or related only indirectly.

When parent conferences were held early in the year, I discussed with the parents of these children my desire for them to participate actively in their children's education, and indicated that I would send home assignments periodically for the children to complete with the aid of their parents. All of the parents welcomed this opportunity for involvement, especially since they were aware of their children's ability and knew that there was not as yet a special program designed to meet their needs. The parents were concerned that their children view school as a positive experience and one that would be a constant and exciting challenge.

I began home assignments in November. Each assignment was sent home with instructions for the parents, indicating how I hoped they would be able to assist their children. On the day that an assignment was sent home, we discussed it in class and the children knew what was expected of them. Work was to be completed and returned to school within three or four days. This allowed busy parents to be able to have time to spend with their children without feeling burdened. As assignments were returned to school, the children had the opportunity to read their works to the group.

Types of Homework Activities

Homework activities have included three types of projects: 1) Group Projects, 2) Theme Projects, 3) Independent Projects. Projects that we worked on early in the year were Group Projects. One example of this type of project involved the study and comparison of Fairy Tales, Folk Tales, and Tall Tales. The children learned characteristics of each, chose a tale to read, identified its genre, and defended their choices. In addition, all children were asked to answer several questions, such as, "Did you like the main character in the story? Why, or why not?" and "If you could meet the main character, what three questions would you ask him or her?" Another group activity was exploring our school's library and learning to use the card catalogue. This was fascinating to the children, and they have since become able to do more independent work as a result of this study.

The second type of activity, Theme Projects, would include our study of Autobiographies and Biographies. The children wrote their own autobiographies, then read a biography. After reading, and with the help of parents, the children wrote reports and presented them to the rest of the group. We graphed the lifespan of each historical figure, discussed his or her importance, and discussed how we thought our present world might be different if not for these people and their contributions.

The third type of activity, Independent Projects, are projects decided upon by the children and can involve anything that is of interest to them. The children use resources from the school library, and with help from parents, write short reports and make a display of some sort, for example a collage, a diorama, or a model.

Parent participation in these homework assignments is essential to the success of this program. Parents are invited to give as much assistance as is needed. They often are asked to write answers dictated by their children. In this way, the children can express themselves freely and not be discouraged by the time it would take for them to write. In addition to writing, parents are asked to help out with general language skills, such as making sure that sentences convey a complete thought, and composition skills when they assist in writing reports.

At conferences held later in the year, I have received helpful feedback. One idea that a parent had was to have his child use a tape recorder to dictate his answers, and at a later time the parent would write down what the child had recorded. This allowed the child to speak naturally and not be slowed by the pace of the writer. This method proved effective: the child's reports were always quite long and fluent.

Other parents gave feedback on some difficulties that they were having, particularly involving the writing of reports (as opposed to answering questions). In some cases the children were inclined to copy directly from the book they were reporting on, and in other cases the children would state facts but in no particular sequence, and perhaps only stating phrases. Two of the parents came up with the idea of going back and re-reading the book, this time having their children stop them at important points of interest, and the parent would make a note. By the end of the reading, the notes could be easily assembled into a report. This seemed like an effective and valuable way of learning to report, and would certainly facilitate research and writing that the children would do in the future.

This feedback has helped me in planning for other projects and has given me some insight into how to better prepare the children for their homework assignments.

Homework has been an integral aspect of these children's development this year. The children enjoy doing it, and have produced excellent work. Involving the parents has proven to be a successful alternative in a situation where no special classes or financial resources exist. It has also provided an opportunity for the children and parents to work together on a given task, and has created an environment in which the child can see the interest that his parents take in his education.

Examples of Homework Activities
Below are some examples of the assignments, including letters to the parents, that the children have completed this year. In some cases, excerpts from the children's work are included following the assignment.

Dear Parents,
We have completed the first unit in our reading book, *May I Come In?* We have read and talked about several animals, in particular elephants, raccoons, and snowshoe rabbits. We have discussed the environments in which various animals live, and some ways that animals deal with danger.

As a wrap up of this unit, I would like to ask you to work with your child on the following questions, by writing down the answer as dictated. Some questions require simple recall of facts in the stories, while others require higher levels of thought.

1. Where do elephants live? What kinds of work can they do?
2. Why are elephants better able to work in teak forests than big machines?
3. Tell about the climate and types of animals in each of these environments: desert, Arctic region, jungle, woodland.

4. Which environment would you like best? Why?

5. What are some dangers that all animals face?

6. Suppose that the jungle became overpopulated with lions. What would happen to the lions? What would happen to the other animals?

7. What does "nocturnal" mean? Name a few nonturnal animals.

8. Baby animals depend on their mothers. How do the mothers help the babies?

9. In the story "A Surprise for Pat" how did Pat help animals? What do you think of Pat? Would you like him for a friend?

In response to question number four, all children thought that the woodland would be the most desirable, but for a variety of reasons: ". . . it's shady, and you can take a nap without turning off the lights. . ." "You can make tree houses in the trees," ". . . the climate is just right."

Dear Parents,

We are now working on a unit entitled "All for Fun." The first story in the unit is "Mr. Big." Ask your child to retell the story for you, and identify these three parts of the story: The problem; The course of action; The solution. Now, using the program given in the story, ask your child to decide on a different course of action, and a solution. You may want to discuss the feasibility of the suggestions, and discuss a variety of alternatives before beginning to write the final decision. Please write what your child dictates, but help him or her to use complete sentences.

Response varied: "I would tell the animals to be quiet, put earplugs on, and feed the animals so they might not make so much noise;" ". . . put his animals out in the fields as far away from his farmhouse as possible. Then he could put cotton in his ears, and pull his pillow over his head so he couldn't hear the noise the animals made;" ". . . sell all of his animals."

Dear Parents,

We have recently read the story "Carlo." Carlo is a monkey who runs away from his owner, Mr. Babbit. He meets several people along his way who attempt to make him stop. Finally, Mr. Babbit finds him, and by this time Carlo has decided that running away wasn't as much fun as he'd expected it would be, and he was glad to see his owner.

In connection with this story, we have read several versions of *The Gingerbread Boy*. Please help your child fill in the chart below, and discuss how the patterns of the stories are similar and different. To fill in the last column, your child will need to make up a new set of characters and a new ending.

"Carlo" *The Gingerbread Boy* or Your own title *The Pancake*

Who
ran
away?

Who
did it
run away
from?

Who
did it
meet?

How did
the story
end?

Dear Parents,

We have just completed a unit entitled "Boys and Girls" which depicted real-life situations to which children can easily relate. Along with our reading, the children have written short autobiographies.

At this time we will take a few days off from our formal reading program while the children read and report of biographies. Your child has chosen a book to read. Hopefully the content and vocabulary will not be difficult to the point of causing frustration; at the same time I hope the book will contain a few new words which the children can add to their rapidly growing vocabularies.

I have asked the children to write a report which they will present to the group. Please help in any way that you can -- spelling, sentence structure, form, suggestions for oral presentation.

Please encourage your child to include the following points, if applicable:

1) the period in which the person lived; 2) major contributions or accomplishments; 3) persons or situations that were inspirations; 4) obstacles overcome; 5) personal opinion of person 6) list of new vocabulary.

It is my hope that through this experience, the children will:

1) complete an independent assignment; 2) write an interesting report; 3) give an oral presentation; 4) enjoy the satisfaction of dissemenating new and interesting matter to their classmates; 5) enjoy the opportunity of learning from their classmates.

Reporting went extremely well. All of the children were proud of their first attempt at writing, which had been a valuable learning experience for everyone.

There are many genre of literature. *Genre* means kinds, or types. This year we have read Fables, and Folk Tales. Other genre we will read include Fairy Tales and Tall Tales. Each type of story is different from the others in certain ways. When you hear or read a story, you can sometimes determine its genre if you know the characteristics of each. Study the guidelines below.

Fable - 1. Characters are usually animals
 - 2. Very short
 - 3. Teaches a moral

Folk Tale - 1. Told over and over, by word of mouth
 - 2. Animals and people as characters
 - 3. Repetition
 - 4. Many versions of the same story

Tall Tale - 1. People and animals do impossible things
- 2. Everything is exaggereated
- 3. Very funny

Fairy Tale - 1. Tales of kings, queens, princes, fairies
- 2. Magic things happen
- 3. Good conquers evil

Dear Parents,

We are completing Level Five, and in conjuction ith the last unit in that book we are taking some time to study several forms of literature. We have discussed the four genre outlined above.

I have asked each child to chose a story to read, and practice at home, so that they will be able to read it to the group with fluency and expression. Please help your child to determine the genre of literature to which the story belongs.

Please assist your child in answering the following questions. This assignment should be hand written by the children, with your help in spelling and sentence structure as needed.

1. Who is the main character in the story? How do you feel about him or her?

2. If you could meet that character, what would you ask him? Write three questions.

3. Find as many words in the book that you can that describe the main character.

4. List as many words as you can think of to describe the character.

5. Write three questions that can be answered only by reading or hearing the story. We will answer them in class.

REFERENCES

Beckman, Lucille "The Use of the Block Design Sub Test of the WISC as an Identifying Instrument for Spatial Children" GIFTED CHILD QUARTERLY, Spring 1977

Gallagher, James J. *Teaching the Gifted Child*, Allyn and Bacon, 1975.

Gazzaniga, Michael S. "The Split Brain in Man", *Scientific American*, August 1967

Guilford, J. P. *The Nature of Human Intelligence*, New York McGraw-Hill, 1067

Hamilton, W. J. ed. *Textbook of Human Anatomy*, MacMillan & Co Ltd, 1956

Kohlberg, Lawrence and Gilligan, Carol "The Adolescent as a Philosopher: The Discovery of the Self in a Post-conventional World" *12 to 16: Early Adolescence* ed. by Jerome Kagan & Robert Coles, American Academy of Arts and Sciences, 1972

Netter, Frank *The CIBA Collection of Medical Illustrations: Nervous System*, Colorpress, New York 1958

Piaget, Jean "How Children Form Mathematical Concepts" *Scientific American* November 1953

Sperry, R. W. "The Great Cerebral Commissure", *Scientific American* January 1964

Turner, Johanna *Cognitive Development* Methuen & Co Ltd London, 1975

Williams, Frank E. *Ideas For Encouraging Thinking and Feeling* D.O.K. Publishers, Inc. 1970

SUGGESTIONS FOR ORGANIZING A PARENT ASSOCIATION

"My child has been identified as gifted and I'd like to help in planning for what he needs now and later."

"My child is gifted, but our local school has no program for the gifted."

"Our school program for gifted needs improvement and we would like to know what kinds of programs exist in other places."

"My child has problems with boredom. . .work load. . .other children. . . teachers. . .is not interested in achieving what he could. Where can we find help?"

"I'd like to work with other adults to improve opportunities and programs for the gifted."

Immediate personal needs and interests motivate formation of organizations for parents of gifted children. A group has a stronger voice than an individual, in asking for what it wants and explaining why it is needed to a legislator, a board of education, an educator, or the community. Alert educators realize that parents, as voters, can become a supportive part of the political process, not limited by the constraints affecting professionals in education.

Some one must start the action. This can be any parent who is willing and able to devote time to these initial steps. Items one and two can be covered concurrently, of course.

1.   Write to established organizations for copies of materials and suggestions (see page 78 for parent associations to contact). These organizations have developed bylaws, procedures, programs, publicity brochures, and educational materials for parents which are invaluable to a new group. Because such groups are supported by volunteers, we urge that requests be accompanied by money for postage and printing costs.

2.   Form a committee composed of several concerned, articulate parents, influential school personnel, prominent community members, students.

Select a temporary chairman.

Discuss problems, need for organization, benefits to be derived, possible activities.

Plan an initial organizing meeting. Choose a topic and speaker of certain appeal to parents of the gifted.

3.   Contact key school administrators about the proposed meeting. Enlist their support and involvement, and ask them to facilitate publicity to parents of the gifted via

"Suggestions for Organizing a Parent Association, J.L. Delp and R.A. Martinson, *A Handbook for Parents of Gifted and Talented,* sponsored by the National/State Leadership Training Institute on the Gifted and Talented, and a Grant from the U.S. Office of Education, Department of Health, Education and Welfare.

4. SUPPORT

notices to be mailed to known parents of gifted children by the school. Or make contacts independently through a telephone committee.

4.   Use part of the first meeting to get sign-up list of parents interested in forming an organization; ask those present to list others who should be contacted.

5.   Check mailing list initially with school system consultant for the gifted, if there is one, or with an administrator. Add names.

6.   At the first meeting, survey parents regarding their special needs and suggestions for activities. Through the organizing committee, appoint a nominating committee, and establish an initial list of needed committees: *Constitution*, *Finance*, *Community Resources*, *Liaison with School Board and School Personnel*, *Legislative*, *Special Interest Groups for Children* and *Program* are a representative list. You may wish to start with some of these, and add others later.

7.   Meeting two can be a combined business and informational meeting: nominations, announcement of committees, communicating results of survey, and speaker with topic of vital interest to the parents. After elections, conducted either at the meeting or by mail, the organization is on its way.

ASSOCIATIONS HAVE MULTIPLIED

Associations of parents promoting the interests of the gifted have multiplied since the emergence of large, effective organizations during the '60s. Their growth has resulted from the potential they hold. This power is realized by forming the parent component of the modern educational system into an efficient instrument for informing the community, planning with educators, sharing in decision making, and providing support and services for gifted programs. The organizations provide a forum for parents, teachers, administrators, counselors, and consultants to air the problems, goals, limitations, methods and philosophies germane to gifted education. Their existence provides a line of communication often otherwise unavailable within local school districts. Groups have been successful at local and state levels in securing the support of legislators and school boards for initiating and maintaining specialized programs for the gifted.

Parent organizations typically take several of the following forms, often with overlapping membership:

1.   *Advisory councils operating at local schools in cooperation with school personnel.* These are a source of initial information about gifted children and the program available within the school for parents. Parents often function as support and resource people when needed, and participate in planning and dialogue.

2.   *Area advisory councils with representatives from local schools sharing experience and information with similar groups from adjacent geographic areas.* These groups become a valuable two-way information pipeline, bringing back to the local level ideas, information, and solutions to shared problems from other groups. Consultants from larger educational administrative areas often attend these meetings and find them invaluable in an effective communication network.

3.   *City-wide advisory councils.* These groups offer the opportunity for parents to meet with representative professionals in formulating coherent plans, setting priorities and goals, and discovering and solving problems within the gifted program in a city. The Los Angeles Central Advisory Committee for the Gifted is such a group and includes representatives from the school board, Mayor's office, counselors, teachers, principals, area coordinators, parent advisory councils, and other parent and community groups.

4.   *Independent parent associations.* These organizations usually serve parents and

children from larger geographic areas and are not directly connected with any single school. Their independence allows them the freedom to work directly with every level of the community and to undertake projects of extended depth and duration. Their supportive efforts, marked by enthusiasm and energy, have mobilized the initiation of programs for gifted in areas where there were none and have helped to change the climate of opinion regarding gifted children through promoting understanding of their problems, nature, and needs.

5. *State-wide organizations.* These may be loose associations of parent groups for the purpose of the exchange of information or may be a component of groups of professionals in gifted educations such as California Association for the Gifted. Information is shared through an annual conference and circulation of periodic publications.

Local and area advisory councils require the simplest organizational structure. Their efforts offer the satisfaction of seeing change and improvement within the school that parents are working to help. Their projects reflect local needs and have ranged from coffee/information sessions at members' homes to publication of newsletters, parent-information brochures, and to the planning of area conferences for parents, educators, and children.

Independent associations reach farther into the community and because they are often legally incorporated, non-profit corporations, they require somewhat more formal structures and record keeping to satisfy federal and local requirements. A lawyer among the membership is often in a position to advise the membership concerning such matters. Formal incorporation affords them tax-exempt status, limited personal liability, and eligibility for non-profit mailing rates through the post office. Establishing an independent association requires a major effort which may be unnecessary if there is an existing group in the area willing to accept an affiliate. Projects which such associations undertake may include parent education meetings with experts speaking on various areas of concern to parents of gifted children, newsletter publication, establishment of reference and resource libraries for members, compilation of bibliographies and review of current literature in the field, field trips of a unique nature for families and children, publicity for community resources and events of interest to students in various fields, information for members and schools of legislation affecting the status of gifted programs, guidance for parents and a place for them to share their problems, workshops and conferences, campaigns for program support, extended enrichment classes and opportunities, representation for parents at local and statewide meetings and conferences.

Budgets for parent councils are negligible and are often absorbed as part of school administration costs. Membership dues provide the funds for independent associations. Dues in most groups range between $10-$25 annually and cover organizational operating costs such as postage, printing, office equipment, clerical help, conference fees, purchase of library materials, professional staff, office rent, and telephones.

Groups of all kinds would do well to establish a permanent mailing address or post office box as they take their place in the communication chain to share their printed information and newsletters with others concerned with gifted. Such idea sharing maximizes the results of everyone's efforts and provides the inspiration needed to keep working for improved gifted programs.

TYPICAL QUESTIONS AND BRIEF ANSWERS

FRAME OF REFERENCE

Parents of gifted children, like any other parents, constantly face questions regarding school and home practices. Many of their questions come from trying to decide whether a given school offering will benefit or harm their child. Often they have remained uneasy with decisions they made. Questions on whether they should encourage or discourage certain activities, how they handle uneven abilities within the family, and others plague them. Often, action cannot be postponed.

The questions which follow have been gleaned from contacts with many parents, both individually and in groups. They represent many of those most commonly asked. The brief responses are given as suggestions rather than as complete answers, since responses to cover all of the possible ramifications would be voluminous, if not impossible. The questions are regarded as a *framework* for discussion and further amplification, perhaps in parent study groups.

1.   How can I tell if a program is good?

A good program should cause the child to go to school eagerly. He should carry his interests into the home through discussions, through *voluntary* search for added information, through voiced enthusiasm. The content he is using should be appropriately challenging. Homework should be based on key ideas or issues, not on isolated facts. The amount of homework he is assigned means nothing; a large assignment is not more valuable than a small one. The program should extend the child's talents, skills, and interests into new or expanded areas.

2.   How can I train him to get his homework done and not leave it until the last minute? Should parents enforce regular periods of study?

First, determine casually if the homework is legitimate. If it is repetitive, lengthy, and deals with isolated facts, the child's resistance is warranted. You may need a conference with the teacher. If the assignments seem interesting and worthwhile, a regular time and quiet place are important. But, it is also important that parents, by their own example, provide respect for intellectual and aesthetic pursuits. The parent who wants his child to do homework so that he can watch television undisturbed is unfair and is a poor model as well. The parent who demands homework for his child also should consider the parallel in his being required to spend an added two or three hours on his own work at home, day after day.

3.   How do you handle the older children when this one seems to know more than the rest?

Avoid comparison. Comparison invites competition. Evenly and amply distributed love and affection and recognition for various accomplishments of different kinds will let each child know that he is valued for himself. If questions arise, discuss them in the context of each person's being especially good at something; one child likes books, another one art, another is especially good at sports—or music, cooking, helping others, or whatever particular contribution the individuals can make. Some learn earlier, other take a little longer; the *use* made of any learning for worthwhile contributions is the important thing.

"Typical Questions and Brief Answers," J.L. Delp and R.A. Martinson, *A Handbook for Parents of Gifted and Talented,* sponsored by the National/State Leadership Training Institute on the Gifted and Talented, and a Grant from the U.S. Office of Education, Department of Health, Education and Welfare.

4. *How can we keep them from getting "smart"?*

Avoid centering on a child's "giftedness." The child who is singled out and set apart for any attributes can easily develop erroneous attitudes toward himself and others. This applies to the handicapped as well as the gifted. In the case of the gifted, the child may develop an unrealistic sense of his own importance and become quite obnoxious. Then it often helps to sit with the child, ask him to assess the impact on others of his specific behavior, and ask him how he might change the relationships for the better. The discussion should be on a private, person-to-person basis, analytical in nature, with the *child* providing the analysis.

Trouble also may arise when adults become impatient with youth's views and forbid their expression. It is important that children have full opportunity to discuss peace movements, politics, ethics, religion, values, fears, discrimination, or strong feelings on any subject with adults who respect and understand them. The home should provide a secure base within which the child can express his feelings and examine them honestly with others. Any question at any age deserves a thoughtful response.

5. *Would you encourage these children to take service-type courses?*

Service-type courses are commonly understood to be such courses as shop, homemaking, and typing. The answer is yes. One reason is that some of the techniques are useful tools in learning. Speed typing assists the student in many ways, and metal shop may be of use in the production of necessary equipment for physics experiments, for example. Another reason is that, *given the right teacher,* the study of such topics as foods and clothing may be handled in such a way that students deal with many important economic, historical, political, and aesthetic issues and problems.

6. *What can be done about the problem caused by the enthusiasm of teachers in a departmental situation, and the resultant overload for students?*

This is a question which can be handled best in a group meeting of parents and department heads at the secondary level. Students at this age do not want parents to contact individual teachers regarding their particular problems. Often teachers are completely unaware of the accumulated overload, and calling the problem to their attention probably will suffice. It is helpful if parents prepare for such discussions by documenting the homework load of their children for a specific period of time, such as two weeks.

7. *Is it good to let the faster learners help the slower children?*

Not if it is done on a regular basis. Then it cuts down the time that the fast learners have for their own learning, and the child is working as a teacher substitute at the expense of his own education. An added danger in consistent help to the slower children is that other children in the class may react to "teacher's pet." If the help is occasional and for a specific need, yes. The experience is more valuable if the bright child plans the teaching experience, carries it out, and evaluates it with the teacher afterwards.

8. *What can you do with a child who is a perfectionist and becomes discouraged?*

Often gifted children will tackle topics which are so general that they are unable to handle them. They then become fustrated as they attempt to complete their studies. Parents can help by discussing with them their projected plans and by assisting them to choose realistically. For example, when a child announces that he or she is going to study the Civil War and make a report on it, the parent may ask what particular aspect of the Civil War? Or the parent may suggest scanning a book on the Civil War to choose among a number of topics and issues. The child should make the choice, however. Encouragement, support, and parent expectation that the child will do a worthy piece of work are helpful, but the expectations must be realistic.

9. *Should a program be for gifted children generally, or just for those with scientific interests?*

A good program should be flexible enough to meet the needs of all gifted and talented children. Any group of gifted children is extremely diverse in interests, abilities, and talents.

4. SUPPORT

This population is the most complex of any. Educational planning should be highly individualized to meet the diverse abilities of the gifted, whether in science, the arts, social sciences, or elsewhere.

Many gifted children are in fact interested in science and mathematics because of their fondness for system and logic, and if their real interests lie here, they should not be discouraged. But neither should children with primary interests and talents elsewhere be forced to concentrate heavily in the sciences.

10. Will this kind of program adversely affect the chances of a student getting a college scholarship?

It should enhance his chances, unless grades are used punitively. In such a case, parent contacts (preferably in groups) should be made with school department heads. *Parents should never accept punitive grades for their children.* We have heard too many expressions of bewilderment from parents about their children receiving "C's" and "D's" in subjects in which the parents had been informed that the child was functioning at a level four years or more beyond his age group. Parents rightly want to know how this can be. The answers lie in excessive and boring requirements, in punitive grading practices, in negative teacher-pupil relationships, or in student problems of long duration. But if the complaint is common within a class group, it should be discussed thoroughly in a meeting, and resolution should be attained. Many gifted children must earn scholarships in order to afford college attendance, and the program should not penalize them. We have known too many gifted students who have avoided certain courses and teachers in subjects they would have liked to take because they knew that high grades were given grudgingly, even though the students deserved them.

11. What can you do about underachievers?

The question is complicated and has been subjected to intense research. The problem may be educational, psychological, or physical in origin. Certainly a thorough physical examination should be made. If physical problems are ruled out, knowledge of some of the other factors involved help parents prevent this problem. Children who are underachievers are identifiable by the end of the primary grades; the early years, therefore, have a profound effect.

Teachers at this level have an important impact on children. Their attitude toward a child whose achievement is out of step with that of others tells him or her what this often-idolized person approves. With older children, peer approval increases in importance and their reactions are increasingly significant, especially to girls.

Children whose parents or other elders hold unreasonably high expectations may feel unable to cope and simply give up. This may occur where parents who are otherwise well educated lack information on child development.

Children who are subject to *reasonably* high expectations and are given early independence, especially by parents of the opposite sex, seem to become achievers. Those who are overindulged, pampered, or treated inconsistently, do not. Parent models are important. When children are exposed to new experiences in the company of their parents, such as concerts, visits to zoos, national parks, historical landmarks, and when they learn to seek information and answers to questions in reference materials, they become achievers. Growing up in an atmosphere in which learning occurs habitually is a great asset. Interesting people as visitors in the home can generate curiosity about far-off countries, about politics, the arts—unlimited subjects.

Support of curiosity and learning, and the latitude for early self-reliance help. One mother watched her five-year-old through binoculars as he crossed three busy intersections and a playing field on his half-mile trip to school for days after he had decided that he could go on his own. Her hillside vantage point enabled her to overcome her anxiety about whether he in fact could. Another child took a two-hundred-mile bicycle trip with two friends at the age of ten. Both of these children grew up in an intensely active learning atmosphere and became outstanding achievers. The parents were in close touch with them at all times, psychologically, but they allowed them to mature and make choices as they were ready.

Support of one's inclination and right to learn is important to the gifted at any age. Parents should never assume that the need for a friendly, communicative ally is past.

12. Should gifted children be given grades?

Grades are a folk custom of long standing, even though it has been shown repeatedly since 1922 that they are not especially useful and tell little about a child's actual achievement. However, if grades are used in a school system, all children expect to receive them. Gifted children in a regular class can receive high grades with little effort and actually can be underachieving "A" students. It is much more informative to a parent to confer with a teacher and discuss the specific accomplishments and needs of the child.

If grades are used in a special group of gifted students, they should be given as if the children were being compared to the *total* school population since the whole concept of grading is based on relative standing. If gifted students are measured on the basis of their real achievement, it is likely that they would receive "A's." If a program is good and the students are interested, they should be producing, and their grades should be high. In no case is grading the gifted on a curve justified within a special group.

13. Should I let my child attend a special class?

This question usually is based on fear that the children will develop feelings of superiority, or on fear that they will be punished by others who are not in a special group. Membership in a good special class can be beneficial in several ways: (1) the content is likely to be more relevant to the child's interests and abilities than in a regular class; (2) the child may learn that there are other children whose abilities are as high or higher than his or hers and thus may develop a wholesome aspect for others and a sense of humility regarding self; (3) the child is able to work with others who understand and respect him or her; (4) the child is likely to relate to others with similar interests and to develop new interests; and (5) the child is more likely to have a teacher who has some special interest in and preparation for teaching the gifted.

14. Will a special class create competition and bad feeling?

Not if it is properly planned and taught. Special classes should not be given publicity beyond that given other groups; nor should the children be singled out to display their "giftedness" for the public. If children develop special materials and presentations for parents and other groups, this should be done by other groups of children as well. The class should not be designated the "gifted class," or the teacher the "gifted" teacher, but should be known as "Mr. Jones'" or "Mrs. Smith's" class, as are others. Competition within the class will not be a problem if the program is adequately individualized; indeed, the children will assist one another with resources and solutions to mutually challenging problems.

Punishment for the gifted by other children or other teachers occurs when resentment and jealousy result from improper publicity and exploitation.

15. How can we find out about our child's ability level?

Ask. Teachers are more willing to discuss comparative achievement levels than IQ, especially when the IQ is derived from group tests. School psychologists may discuss a child in terms of his or her ability, which places him or her in the upper three percent of the general population; this indicates that the child can succeed at the college graduate level, given proper home and school conditions. If the child is in the one-in-a-hundred, or the one-in-a-thousand, his or her abilities are, of course, higher. The fallacy in pinpointing a *specific* IQ lies in the allowable margin of error in tests, even when given individually under ideal conditions; in the relatively few items suitable for the gifted; and in the fact that within this population, other factors such as self-concept, motivation, health, and persistence also count heavily for ultimate success.

It is helpful to parents to know that an eight-year-old child is reading at a sixth-grade level and is particularly interested in certain topics. It also is helpful to discuss a child's home reading and other interests with the teacher.

4. SUPPORT

16. *Is there danger in putting too much pressure on young gifted children too soon?*

The answer to a loaded question like this must be yes. However, fear on this subject has been founded on the practice of assigning large quanities of material rather than on the use of topics of real interest to children, and on the imposition of adult requirements rather than on the use of child interests. When pressure is **self-imposed** in the sense that children are intrigued with a problem and want to find out all they can, pressure is enjoyable. In an unpublished study we conducted on this question, more than two hundred gifted children at various grade levels reported that they enjoyed the experiences in special programs of being able to delve into topics in-depth, without restriction, and they enjoyed using their minds fully. Self-imposed pressure can produce great satisfaction in a task well done. Harmful pressure may also operate when the gifted child is pressured to conform to the middle-ground and to be average.

17. *My child has more homework than ever before and doesn't seem to have much time for relaxation. Should this be so?*

No. All children should have time for play and relaxation and for doodling, dreaming, and idling. Adults do. A problem of this sort should be discussed with the teacher.

18. *How can we prevent negative feelings in others toward our child's being identified as "gifted"?*

Avoid discussion of the fact with others. The knowledge is important to you and the teacher in understanding the child and in working with him appropriately. No useful purpose is served by overt pride in the "chip off the old block." Children should be valued as children, and not as labels, nor should they be used for the satisfaction of adult needs. Parents who boast about their child over the back fence guarantee resentment and hostility.

If remarks are made by adults, it is good to counter with something like this: "We know that he is bright. We don't talk about it, because we don't want him to feel that his IQ is our source of pride. We want to bring him up so that he can use his ability constructively as an adult. . .

When classmates or other children make remarks, a parent has an indication that the matter should be discussed with the teacher. No child wants to live under a label, including the gifted.

19. *Is it good for children to know they are gifted?*

Most gifted children know that they achieve better than others, although occasional children may feel vaguely different and even suffer from inferiority complexes. Gifted children generally can be expected to meet reasonable demands and can be asked to work out real-life problems with adults with the comment that they are bright and can do so competently. The child who feels inferior may require special counseling. In most cases, gifted children do not need any special interpretation or discussion of their abilities. Any such discussion may be most useful when a plan for a special remedial program with a tutor is outlined (as with a child who requires temporary special help in mathematics), or when a student is discussing college and carrer alternatives.

20. *Our daughter does so well in reading. Shouldn't she do better in math?*

Although social and cultural mores are changing, and girls are able to work in broader fields than formerly, they are still subject to pressures. Girls especially are subjected to comments by peers and adults which cause them to feel that failure in mathematics or science is frequent in girls, that being a "brain" is bad, or that girls shouldn't like math. Reading is less subject to direct teaching than mathematics since gifted children especially do a great deal of independent reading. While we cannot expect identical accomplishments in all areas, it is possible that some time spent in private tutorial contacts and weekly conferences by the teacher with the pupil on her progress might improve her performance markedly. The problem should be discussed with the teacher, in any event.

21. *I heard that IQ tests are inaccurate. What do they actually measure?*

The individual IQ test is the best measure of potential that we have *at present.* Group IQ tests are much less accurate and are the most commonly used in schools because they are less expensive. The individual examination gives a fairly reliable picture of how well a child will perform academically in relation to others of his age. It does not measure personal factors which are also important in achievement. It also may be unfair to a child from a markedly different background.

22. *How do I know if my child is working up to capacity?*

If the child's expected achievement and actual achievement are fairly equivalent he or she is. These would be measured through population forms from standardized tests rather than through teacher-made tests. Another index, though informal, may be the type and extent of reading and interests. It is important to remember that "working up to capacity" is something that very few adults do and that a child needs time for childhood.

23. *I want my child to be happy and well-adjusted. Will this program cause one-sidedness?*

The meaning of happiness and good adjustment varies with individuals. The right of people to be themselves is paramount. A good program should be so designed that the children derive a great deal of satisfaction from their interests. If they specialize early, this is not necessarily a cause for concern. Harvey Lehman pointed out that many of the important contributions to mankind were made by persons still in their teens (5). Sidney Pressey wrote extensively on the same topic (11). For some persons, the work in which they are interested is so fascinating and satisfying that the work itself is recreational, and conflicting social or play activities are a nuisance (12). It is important, therefore, to look at children, their attitudes toward themselves, and their attitudes towards others. If the child is apparently one with a healthy self-regard and is able to relate to others satisfactorily, his or her desire to pursue interests intensively and/or to specialize early should not be denied. Gifted children often do this.

24. *What kind of vocational information should I give him?*

Gifted children have more complicated vocational choice problems than others simply because they face a bewildering array of thousands of potential occupations, most of which they could master successfully. Many gifted persons do have vocational problems, chiefly of under-placement in unchallenging jobs. Many schools and colleges have vocational counselors who also have specialized in scholarship possibilities. These persons should be consulted. It is possible, also, through arrangements by either school or parent groups, to give gifted young people opportunities for work experience with adults in their fields of interests. Parents can be of substantial help to their children in simply supporting their right to an occupational decision. For example, if a young person has marked talent in musical composition and wishes to work in that field, he or she should be allowed that right rather than be prodded to enter some "safe" and lucrative field. The influence of teachers who exploit the multiple talents of gifted young people by recruiting them into their own fields or who denigrate the interests of the gifted should be counterbalanced by discussions at home.

25. *Will she maintain her giftedness?*

Giftedness is maintained and enhanced if the enviroment is rich with opportunities. Giftedness can diminish, and outward evidence of giftedness can disappear in a sterile environment. We found a slight rise in measured ability among children who lived in a particularly desirable home-school environment. Some studies have shown that children of poverty who attend poor schools lose in measured ability as they grow older (8). Women, who in the past have encountered less opportunity for continuing learning than men, have shown some loss in ability from childhood to middle adulthood although this is less true at the present time. Parents who continue their own interest in learning are good examples for their children and probably are more interesting companions to them as well.

4. SUPPORT

26. What can I do about the school when they won't recognize that my child is gifted and do anything for him?

The best evidence (that most readily accepted by the school) comes from individual tests and study by a credentialled or licensed psychologist. Parents are more likely to encounter resistance or skepticism when they describe their own observations, however valid. Parents in most areas can find a person qualified to test, either through the school system, through private sources, or through a college or university. Parents shoud not expect the school to do the necessary studies automatically, even when resource personnel are available. Many times they are occupied with problems of the handicapped, and must be asked.

If the child has been identified and suitable provisions have not been made, the parent should make direct inquiry. This should start with the teacher, but may require contacts with a principal or supervisor who can give the teacher some help. Suggestions on working *with* the teacher, both in fact and psychologically, are given on page 59.

27. How can we persuade the school to start a gifted program?

In systems of small or medium size, we advocate discussion by a group of parents with the local Board of Education. In large school systems, this may need to take place with one or two members in an informal, exploratory session. Parents can prepare for such sessions by marshalling the arguments in favor of efforts from such sources as the Commissioner of Education's report on the gifted and talented (6), or from sources in the bibliography for parents.

It is wise to work closely with school personnel to minimize threat and promote cooperation. When school people are resistant, however, parents have every right to consult with any persons in decision-making positions, including school board members.

Somewhere there's a small foundation that would just love to give grant money to your schools

By Margery Thompson

NAME some foundations that give money to schools. Ford, Carnegie, Rockefeller—the giants, sure. But if you think of education grants exclusively in terms of the biggie foundations and their millions, you're overlooking an important source of scarce dollars: the numerous small foundations.* Pat Edwards, program officer at the Mott Foundation, says: "This group [of small foundations] is one of the least tapped resources for public education—maybe because their existence and activities are so little known."

What's more, chances are that one of these foundations is near your schools. Foundations of all sizes are in every state and territory from Alaska to Puerto Rico. Alabama, for example, has 139 foundations, which is more than the number of school districts (127) in the state. Pint-sized Connecticut has 544 foundations, and Illinois is home for no less than 1,443.

Compared with federal funding, the $2 billion that foundations disburse each year is small potatoes. Even if the impossible occurred and foundations ignored other claims and invested that money in public education, school systems would not become fat. So if you are looking to a small foundation for a windfall—don't. Still, when 80 percent or more of your budget is eaten up by salaries alone, you know how valuable "extra money" becomes.

To learn more about how foundations operate, where their interests lie,

and how schools can benefit from their largesse, the JOURNAL recently took a look at some foundations and interviewed a sample of foundation experts. What we found:

First, foundations can be divided into three groups according to the source of their money—and the source often dictates how and where the money is spent.

• Corporate foundations. Weyerhauser, General Foods, and General Electric are among the 462 corporations that have set up foundations; this group often prefers to make grants in towns where the corporate plants are located. Also, many corporations make grants directly, much as your local bank or hardware store will make a donation to community activities. These two corporate programs (direct grants and grants through foundations) operate independently and the foundation is the more likely source of funds for school systems.

• Family or independent foundations. As the name suggests, the money entrusted to these foundations comes from family fortunes—the Fords, Mellons and Ketterings, and many lesser-known families. "The small independent foundations are often better able to respond to local needs than are the big national foundations," says Mott's Edwards, "because many families restricted grants to a specific geographic area."

• Community foundations. Some 219 communities have established foundations; their money comes from many sources—from small donations to large gifts by wealthy donors—and it all goes back to support local community institutions and activities, including schools. Saul Richman, of the Council on Foundations, urges school systems to explore their common interests with their community foundations. These foundations are apt to be more accessible than private or corporate founda-

tions, he says, because they publish descriptive annual reports of their activities and because their boards are drawn from a more representative group of local citizens than are trustees of private foundations.

So how do you get the money? First, *you* have to go to the foundations, because they're unlikely to come to you. Few small foundations have paid professional staff, so few initiate and manage their own programs. Trustees of small foundations are, however, open to requests from outside organizations, including schools—in effect, they are waiting to be asked. A foundation officer describes the policy this way: "We believe that people in education, health care, or recreation know their business much better than we do. They know their own needs, and we are willing to sit down and listen while the professional outlines a problem. We can't offer money in every instance, but together we can always explore ways we might be able to help."

To keep in touch with their potential recipients, foundation trustees often are urged to take on more management tasks—to interview grantees more frequently and to make more site visits. School board members, particularly those in small school systems, can profit from this advice, too. In other words, visit your peers on foundation boards—not to request money but to exchange information. "If I were a school board member," a Michigan foundation representative advises, "I'd sure make myself familiar with the foundations in my state—find out what kinds of projects those people are funding and then let them know who I was and what I was interested in."

And if you do become involved in your system's funds-raising efforts, observe these important guidelines: Work closely with your superintendent, preferably in a small subcommittee. Be cer-

---

* "Small" is a relative term when you're dealing in millions. *The Foundation Directory,* the standard reference book on foundations, describes a "small" foundation as having assets below $25 million; but of the 26,000 foundations in the United States, 23,000 are smaller than "small." These 23,000 are not listed in the directory because their assets fall below $1 million and their annual grants average $100,000 or less.

Margery Thompson is an associate editor of the JOURNAL.

Here's what
other schools get:

Here are a few examples of the kinds of programs small foundations support:

The Bush Foundation in Minneapolis pumps $300,000 a year into a statewide management training fellowship program for public school system superintendents and assistant superintendents. The foundation chooses 25 fellows each year to attend classes based on the case-study method taught by a professor from the school of business administration at the University of Minnesota. "When you have 430 school districts in the state of Minnesota alone," says Stanley Shepherd, Bush program associate, "you have to try to be even-handed. We believe we can reach a good many school systems in this way, over time, and help upgrade school system management."

The Danforth Foundation in St. Louis thinks the flash point of education takes place at the individual school and with the help of the school principal. In the St. Louis schools, Danforth provides funding and support for teams of citizens, students, principals and community representatives to study education issues. Nationally, the foundation has initiated a program for urban school principals that seeks to improve their management skills and to help them deal with the problems peculiar to big city schools.

The Flint (Michigan) school system is unique in the degree to which it benefits from a local foundation. The Mott Foundation, in addition to its national programs, provides—each year—$5 million of the system's $89 million operating budget. Some typical grants for the Flint schools include $25,299 for an early childhood development program, $11,220 for an "artist in the schools" program, $83,246 for police-related programs—and $35 to a teacher who wanted some special materials for a math class.

Restricted to three areas in South Carolina, the Elliott White Springs Foundation puts much of its funding into local public elementary and second-ary education—unlike many others, this foundation *does* invest in bricks and mortar. One such grant helped build a vocational school in Lancaster County, which the Springs Foundation further supported by providing $20,000 for vocational students in carpentry, electrical work, plumbing, and other skilled trades to put classroom theory into practice by building a house. The house later was sold for a profit and the class has since built three additional houses and now has $30,000 (plus a pickup truck) for the next venture.

"Some of the best money we spend," says Springs Foundation President Charles A. Bundy, "is for our school assistance program—a special fund based on $3 per student enrolled in the school district. In the Lancaster area, it's worth about $25,000." Part of the money is used for tuition for any teacher who wants to study for a master's degree and who maintains passing grades. "We've doubled the number of teachers with graduate degrees—from 30 percent to 60 percent," says Bundy.

School assistance money also is used to send teachers and administrators to conventions, workshops or professional meetings, and for in-service education. "If the superintendent wants to bring in a specialist in reading to talk to 30 teachers," explains Bundy, "we'll reimburse the school system for the cost." While the superintendent has discretion as to how the money is spent, Bundy says: "We'd like to see school assistance funds used to strengthen weak departments by further education for teaching staff."

Travel money for conventions is given serious consideration by foundation people. "Walking around money," as the foundations call funds for meetings, conventions and such, is not scorned by the smaller foundations, either. Gene Schwelke of Danforth says that this kind of training is needed and probably is the one item school boards are reluctant to include in school system budgets, given the current mood of taxpayers.

tain that you are well-briefed on the activities of the foundation to be visited and on all contacts the superintendent has had or intends to set up. Never bypass your own staff. For that matter, never bypass a foundation staff—even if it consists of only one person. One recommended approach is to ask for an appointment with foundation personnel to discuss common interests—and to request advice about educational problems that the foundation is interested in. You are asking for nothing—and you may get nothing, but it is worth the effort. Also remember that foundations "broker" for one another and can provide you with an entree to another foundation.

Remember, too, that you're going to get money only when your needs match foundations' guidelines for giving. Trends in that area:

• *Grants are small—and likely to get smaller.* Foundation rationale for the shift to smaller grants is twofold. First, foundations (like everyone) have been hit by inflation and their assets have diminished as a result of recent stock market slumps. Second, although most foundations believe their role is to provide seed money for experimental ideas or new programs, most foundation trustees realize that the problem school systems now face is finding ways to sustain current programs, not to explore new ideas.

Charles A. Bundy, president of the Elliott White Springs Foundation in South Carolina, says: "We are trying to be sure that we don't offer schools money to start new programs they really don't need and then run away and leave the community or school with a program they can't afford to maintain."

An examination of the effectiveness of seed money in Michigan is the subject of a current study by the Mott Foundation. "Along with several other foundations," says Mott's Pat Edwards, "we've found that if we give schools $15,000 and then drop down to $5,000 in the third year of a grant, schools can't afford to keep the program going. But when we start out giving schools smaller grants of $5,000 and then drop down to $1,000, schools are more likely to be committed to their project from the beginning, know what their goals are, and continue the program or activity after our funding ends."

In the light of curtailed school budgets, another official suggests that rather than start new programs, foundations might help schools maintain programs that originally were begun with foundation money—the many music, fine arts, and performing arts programs that are being swept away, along with experienced staff, by budget cuts.

• *Joint programs are booming.* Foundations are interested in stretching their dollars and ensuring that the programs they fund will last. One popular theory among foundation executives: the more people involved in a program, the stronger local commitment will be.

A classic example of cooperation among many groups is the experience foundations have enjoyed with Reading is Fundamental, Inc. (RIF). Designed to motivate children to read by providing them with inexpensive paperback books of their own choosing, local RIF programs now number 2,400, of which 1,600 are sponsored by individual schools, school systems and parent-teacher organizations (the remainder are sponsored by community service clubs). RIF is especially attractive to foundation donors because it works—the track record is a proven one. Other pluses: The

program addresses a basic problem by supporting school reading programs; it is staffed primarily by volunteers (with the exception of the national headquarters); and funds raised locally are matched by the federal government. The Levi Strauss Foundation's recent $60,000 grant to RIF, for example, is being spent in 17 communities where there are company outlets and, when matched with federal funds, the total money available to these towns will be $120,000.

• *Foundations are extremely interested in strengthening the ties between citizens of a community and their schools.* Support generally will be provided for (1) grants to help schools reach out to the community by using school facilities and developing education programs for all ages and (2) subsidies to develop or staff programs that bring local people closer to schools through citizen advisory councils, parent/school projects, and community/school programs, such as the consulting service and job counseling that

many business people now provide school systems.

Also, recommendations from local sources are becoming increasingly important to foundations. Says Saul Richman: "Most corporate foundations like General Mills or the Gannett Newspaper Foundation make grants in two ways. A small amount of money will go to national programs selected by foundation staff. But a greater sum of money is going into local communities, and these days it is the local General Foods plant manager or publisher of one of the Gannett newspapers who is telling headquarters staff how to make out the checks." With all this in mind, school board members might look to their own backyards for help from local foundations. Because many foundations are relatively small, it may be up to board members to initiate the first contact. It's worth a try: After all, they've got the money, you've got programs you'd like to support, and you both want to help schools contribute to a better life in your local communities.

Want to find out more?
This outfit knows all about small foundations

Where can school systems find out about foundations in their area that may make grants to schools? We're glad you asked—and so is the Foundation Library Center in New York City, which has compiled, collated, microfilmed, and generally sorted out useful information on small foundations. In addition to material from Internal Revenue Service reports, the Center has extensive collections of reports published by foundations (including annual reports, directories of foundations by state and region) and has developed three computerized data banks to keep its research current.

Along with its New York City operation, the Center now has a national library in Washington, D.C., field offices in San Francisco and Cleveland, a national cooperating collection in Chicago, and 72 regional cooperating collections throughout the country, all of which contain the Center's major reference materials and publications. (Addresses of all but the regional collections are at the end of this article.)

One Center publication you might want to get is *The National Data Book*, which lists over 21,000 founda-

tions—twice. In the first volume, foundations are listed alphabetically along with information about each foundation's total assets, the level of grants paid, and the name of the foundation's principal officer. A second volume lists foundations by state (in descending order of their total grants) and gives mailing addresses. The two-volume paperbound set sells for $40—and you can use your VISA or Mastercharge card to order it.

An even bigger bargain for school systems willing to spend $200 a year to do their research at home is the Foundation Center Associates Program. The Center publication, *About Foundations,* describes this custom service. Here is a brief summary:

• For quick answers to brief questions, members can call the Washington, D.C., office from anywhere in the United States on a toll-free WATS line. Unlisted private lines are available for residents of Washington or New York.

• Members also can plug in on the WATS line to hear short bulletins (taped weekly) that cover the latest foundation news—changes in personnel, recent grants, reports, and publications.

• Responses by mail to specific requests for foundation information is available to members; nonmembers get only general information.

• Copying services—photocopy, aperture card (reproductions of foundations' I.R.S. reports), or data sheets showing the address of a foundation, names, titles and business addresses of officers, total assets, and a complete list of grants awarded during a given year.

Here are the addresses you'll need to get the ball rolling:

Foundation Library Center:
National Libraries:
The Foundation Center, 888 Seventh Avenue, New York 10019; The Foundation Center, 1001 Connecticut Avenue, N.W., Washington, D.C. 20036
Field Offices:
The Foundation Center, 312 Sutter Street, San Francisco, Calif. 94108; The Foundation Center, Kent H. Smith Library, 739 National City Bank Building, 629 Euclid Avenue, Cleveland, Ohio 44114

National Cooperating Collection:
Donors Forum of Chicago, 208 South LaSalle Street, Chicago 60604

About Present and Needed Resources for Identifying and Evaluating Learning Materials

The National Information Center for Educational Media advertises that the indexes which they publish provide access to a half million annotated audio-visual titles.[1] This claim suggests the huge quantity of learning materials available on the commercial market. As the profusion of catalogs from publishers is studied, displays of materials at conferences visited, and media and materials libraries explored, the overwhelming amount of learning materials begins to be evident. No teacher can complain about the lack of available materials any longer.

For almost any goals and objectives stated in curricular plans, materials are available on the commercial market which were carefully designed to help students achieve them. No longer does the classroom teacher have to develop from scratch the materials needed for most learning tasks. Now finding appropriate materials is the major activity, and this activity can be defined in terms of two tasks: first, to identify what currently exists in any specific area of the curriculum and, second, to evaluate the materials so that a judgment can be made as to how good they are for teacher and learner. A variety of resources exists which will help in these two tasks.

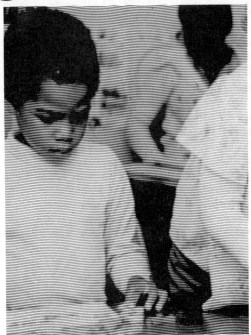

Resources for Identifying Materials

One readily available source for identifying what materials exist is the publishing companies themselves. Advertisements of the latest materials are very accessible and often appear in school mailboxes unsolicited. These advertisements and catalogs from publishers can become a very informative source regarding what learning materials are available.

The publisher's representative is eager to talk to prospective customers and is well-prepared to inform them about the company's products. He or she can highlight the strengths of the products and will sometimes demonstrate or conduct workshops on how to use the materials. Some publishing companies make available sampler kits of specific programs upon request, and these kits will provide a hands-on experience with the components included. The complete set of materials is sometimes made available for a limited time. This provides an even better opportunity for careful scrutiny of the product.

It should be recognized, of course, that advertisements and representatives are trying to sell you a product. While most publishing companies want to be honest about their products, remember that they do reflect a biased opinion.

Another resource for identifying learning materials is professional journals published by educational organizations: *The Arithmetic Teacher,*

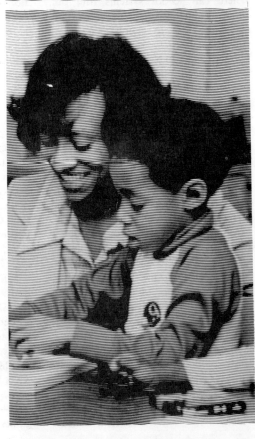

---

[1] National Information Center for Educational Media, University of Southern California, University Park, Los Angeles, California 90007.

Educational Leadership, and *English Journal,* for example, include advertisements about the latest materials from publishers. Some of these journals, such as *Social Education,* also include reviews of learning materials as a regular feature. These reviews provide more systematic and objective information about materials than do the advertisements.

Actual collections and displays of materials are another rich resource for finding out what is available. Local schools, school districts, and intermediate agencies such as county education associations have collections of selected materials. State agencies often make materials available for examination. Such collections may include only state-recommended materials or may contain all the materials which were submitted by publishers for consideration by state agencies. Workshops and conferences at the state and national levels also provide opportunities for viewing the newest materials.

One of the largest displays of materials is brought together at ASCD's Annual Conference held each year in March. Other conferences held by groups with specific subject matter interests, such as the National Council for the Social Studies and its state affiliates, usually sponsor displays of materials. Many colleges and universities which have teacher education programs maintain special libraries of learning materials. These collections are often available for examination by educators and lay people even if they are not enrolled as students at the institution.

A variety of publications, which might be considered directories, is a fourth resource for identifying learning materials. A number of these publications exist and each has somewhat different information included. Some include materials for only one subject field such as the *Social Science Consortium Data Books,* and others such as *Alert* select only major curriculum projects. (For bibliographical information on these and the following publications, see the annotated list immediately following this section.) The bimonthly publication, *Curriculum Review,* provides information about new textbooks and supplementary materials. *EPIEgram* provides subscribers with information about and reviews of equipment and learning materials by Educational Products Information Exchange (usually referred to as EPIE). EPIE also makes available more extensive evaluations of materials in selected subject areas such as reading, early childhood education, social studies, mathematics, and bilingual education.

Some of the major publications which have a primary focus on learning materials are:

- *ALERT, Sourcebook of Elementary Curricula: Programs and Projects.* Far West Regional Laboratory for Educational Research and Development. San Francisco, California, 1972. Order from Superintendent of Documents, U.S. Government Printing Office, Washington, D.C.

Compilation of a selected sample of innovative curricula, training programs, model projects, and resources for pre-kindergarten through grade six. Designed to provide information on type of student and grade level, outstanding characteristics, implementation requirements, and evaluation reports. Materials were selected for review on basis of: (a) produced by research and development agencies; (b) non-R and D programs with value established in the field; and (c) programs which were not rigorously evaluated, but show internal evidence of quality and innovativeness.

- *CEDaR—4th edition Volume I* and *Volume II.* Mary Kennedy Burton, editor. Compiled by the Council for Education Development and Research, Inc., Suite 206, 1518 K Street, N.W., Washington, D.C. (Published by Commercial Educational Distributing Service, P.O. Box 3711, Portland, Oregon 97208.)

Annual publication which includes programs and products selected from grants and contracts awarded from the Department of Health, Education, and Welfare and other agencies. Volume I provides abstracts of programs in process at research and development institutions and Volume II describes products which have not yet been published commercially. Volume II has information which includes product name, institution, principal investigator, programs, product links, target audience, product evaluation, and abstract of product.

4. SUPPORT

• *Curriculum Product Review.* A Bobbitt Publication, P.O. Box 1904, Clinton, Iowa 52732.

Publication issued nine times per year. Advertises new curriculum products from publishers. Very brief descriptions of materials given with feedback cards provided for obtaining further information.

• *Curriculum Review.* Published by Curriculum Advisory Service, 500 South Clinton Street, Chicago, Illinois 60607.

Bi-monthly magazine which publishes reviews and evaluations of texts, professional books, and supplementary materials for grades K-12 in all curriculum areas. Reviews and evaluations written by specialists in education may vary in information contained. May include information about description, rationale, objectives, organization, methodology, physical features, additional materials available, field testing, and recommendations.

• *EPIEgram, The Educational Consumers Newsletter.* Educational Products Information Exchange Institute, 475 Riverside Drive, New York, New York 10027.

Eighteen newsletters a year highlighting news, problems, and strengths about materials and audiovisual equipment and their use in schools.

Also available are the Educational Products Information Exchange Reports. Published six times a year as a membership service, including reports on materials for individualizing math instruction, secondary school social studies (31 textbook programs), elementary and junior high science programs, basic and supplementary reading materials, how to select and evaluate beginning reading materials, and early learning kits (25 evaluations). Analyses vary somewhat from report to report. May include information on physical description, target audience, content, objectives, methodology, conditions of use, instructional design, rationale, research and development, means of evaluation, and comments by reviewers.

• *Games and Simulations for School Use.* Board of Cooperative Educational Services, June 1974.

Index to games in the following major categories: ecology, economics, career education; physical health; alcohol, drugs, and tobacco; mental health; first aid and survival; history and geography; language arts; learning disabled; mathematics; political science; science; sociology; and computer games.

• *Gaming: An Annotated Catalogue of Law-Related Games and Simulations.* Special Committee on Youth Education for Citizenship, American Bar Association, 1155 East 60th Street, Chicago, Illinois 60637.

Descriptions of games to help the reader determine if further examination is warranted. Games are described in six major subject areas: basic concepts of law, Constitution, Bill of Rights, current issues, political process, and teacher resources.

• *Guide to Simulation/Games for Education and Training.* Hicksville, New York: Research Media, 1973.

Index to current games and simulations designed specifically with an educative purpose. Complete information on 613 entries is given which meet specifications of game/simulation format. Lists 473 additional items which are out of print, in development, or for which more information was needed.

• *Guide to Teaching Materials for English, Grades 7-12.* National Council of Teachers of English: Urbana, Illinois, 1975.

(Also a 1975-76 Supplement and a 1974-75 Guide.) Designed to provide comprehensive index of available instructional materials at secondary level. Provides basic description of materials in 16 subject areas for basal series (materials for 2 or more years) and single volumes and packages.

• Hawkins, John. *Teacher's Resource Handbook for Asian Studies,* 1976; *Teacher's Resource Handbook for Latin American Studies,* 1975; *Teacher's Resource Handbook for Russian and East European Studies* (with Jon Maksik), 1976; and *Teacher's Resource Handbook for African Studies* (with Jon Maksik), 1976. Regents of the University of California, University of California at Los Angeles.

Series of annotated bibliographies of curriculum materials designed for students in preschool through grade 12. Includes materials intended to instruct American students about the various regions of the world listed in the titles.

● Hendershot, Carl H. *Programmed Learning and Individually Paced Instruction* (Fifth edition), 1973. 4114 Ridgewood, Bay City, Michigan 48706.

Index to instructional materials in programmed or self-pacing format. Updated by supplements issued periodically. Ordering information and brief description given.

● *Indexes,* available from the National Information Center for Educational Media. University of Southern California: Los Angeles.

These indexes provide access to audiovisual educational products by media format and by selected subject areas.

● *Learning With Games.* Cheryl L. Charles and Ronald Stadsklev, editors. Published jointly by the Social Science Education Consortium and the ERIC Clearinghouse for Social Studies/Social Science Education, Boulder, Colorado, 1973.

Contains the 70 analyses of games included in the *Social Studies Curriculum Materials Data Book.* Also provides resources on development and use of educational games and simulations. Information provided on overview of the materials, available materials, cost, required or suggested time, intended user characteristics, rationale and general objectives, content, procedures, evaluative comments, and suggestions.

● Lewis, Darrel R., and Donald Wentworth. *Games and Simulations for Teaching Economics.* New York: Joint Council on Economic Education, 1971.

Annotated bibliography of materials which: (a) met definition of educational game or simulation, (b) involved use of economic behavior, goals, or concepts, (c) had general educational application, and (d) was commercially or publicly available. Part III annotates games and simulation. Part IV contains list of other bibliographies.

● *Materials and Human Resources for Teaching Ethnic Studies: An Annotated Bibliography.* Social Science Education Consortium: Boulder, Colorado, 1975.

Materials about ethnic groups in the United States, selected on bases of publication date, cost, and recommendations from scholars in ethnic studies. Annotations contain a rating on format, realism and accuracy, intercultural understanding, educational quality, and overall recommendation about quality and usefulness. Bibliography also contains sections on ethnic organizations and human resources and publishers.

● *Media and Methods Educator's Purchasing Guide.* Frank McLaughlin, editor. North American Publishing Co., 134 North 13th Street, Philadelphia, Pennsylvania 19107.

Annual guide designed to assist in the pre-adoptive search and selection process. Contains information from every known supplier of educational materials and equipment. Part I is an index to basic publishing and advertising information about educational materials. Part II focuses on educational equipment and supplies.

● *A Mexican-American Bibliography: A Collection of Print and Non-print Materials.* The Mexican American Curriculum Office, Toledo Public Schools, Manhattan and Elm Streets, Toledo, Ohio 43608. Produced by Xerox, University Microfilms: Ann Arbor, Michigan 48106.

Bibliographical information on materials which are addressed to the history, heritage, pride, and contributions of Mexican Americans.

● *Tenth Report of the International Clearinghouse on Science and Mathematics Curricular Developments.* Joint Project of the American Association for the Advancement of Science and the Science Teaching Center, University of Maryland, 1977.

Comprehensive annual report of new science and mathematics curricula from many countries. Provides brief description of project, personnel, history, headquarters, support, objectives, methods of instruction, age/grade level, materials available and being produced, language of materials, teacher preparation, facts on project implementation, evaluation, publicity, and plans for future.

● *Social Studies Curriculum Materials Data Book.* Social Science Education Consortium, Inc.: Boulder, Colorado, 1977.

Three volumes containing analyses of curriculum materials in the social studies. Designed to assist educators to select materials appropriate to their students, school, and community. Answers questions concerning what is available, physical description, cost, time required for use, students the materials are designed for, special training of teachers, authors' intent, content, teaching methodology, effectiveness, and evaluation. Selections based on: (1) availability, (2) accessibility of complete set of materials to Consortium Staff, (3) expertise of Consortium Staff, and (4) advice and help from Consortium Membership. Data book updated twice a year and data sheets on projects revised as necessary.

• Stadsklev, Ron. *Handbook of Simulation Gaming in Social Education.* Part I: *Textbook,* and Part II: *Directory,* 1974. Institute of Higher Education Research and Services, University of Alabama, P.O. Box 6293, University, Alabama 35486.

Volume I contains information on the what, why, and how of the theoretical aspects of gaming. Section on Evaluating Materials includes chapters by Judith A. Gillespee, "Evaluating Materials" (pp. 66-87) and Little Mac (Measuring Analytical Components) by Ron Stadsklev. Stadsklev presents GAS (Games Analysis System). Raises questions in areas of observable factors and judgmental factors. Part II, the *Directory,* gives answers to question of where the materials may be found. Updated by bimonthly magazine, *Simulation/Gaming/News.* Describes and evaluates current social studies materials in game format. Information provided on source, date of publication, grade level, cost, time required, participants, description, comments, and suggestions.

• Superka, Douglas P., Christine Ahrens, and Judith E. Hedstorm with Luther J. Ford and Patricia L. Johnson. *Values Education Sourcebook.* Social Science Education Consortium: Boulder, Colorado, 1976.

Provides information about materials available for teaching about values and characteristics of specific materials. Analyzes 84 sets of materials and contains extensive annotated bibliography of resources. Describes each project and provides analytical information on rationale, objectives, content, and procedures. Materials selected as a result of a survey of what was generally available. Bibliography contains materials discovered after project was completed.

• Troyen, Donald L., Maurice H. Kellog, and Hans O. Anderson. *Sourcebook for Biological Sciences.* Macmillan: New York, 1972.

Annotated bibliography of resources for teachers of biological science. Includes learning materials, curriculum projects, evaluation instruments, facilities and equipment, and professional associations.

Resources for Determining Quality

After identifying the learning materials available, the next major task becomes determining how good they might be for use in a specific school district or by a specific teacher and student. Several resources are available to help in evaluating and selecting learning materials.

Many of the publications on the preceding list would be a useful resource. The *Social Science Consortium Data Books, ALERT,* issues of *Social Education, Curriculum Review,* and publications of EPIE are examples. These publications do more than simply help identify materials; they include carefully prepared assessments to which educators can turn as one judgment of quality.

There are some limitations, however, to the usefulness of these published reviews. Each of these publications will differ in the extent to which the information provided is of a descriptive nature or is an evaluation of the materials. The bases used for evaluation also vary among the publications, which makes it difficult to compare learning materials reviewed in several publications. A different set of standards may have been used in each review. With these limitations clearly in mind, however, the above publications can be a resource for helping to determine the quality of materials.

It is very possible that the published evaluations or reviews do not contain enough detail to be useful for making a decision about a specific situation, or they may not contain any information on the specific program that is being considered. It then becomes a task for someone at the local district or school level to evaluate those learning materials. In order to engage in this task, some standards or criteria are needed. A number of authors have carefully formulated criteria to use in evaluating learning materials.

The sets of criteria can be divided into two major types—procedural and substantive. The procedural criteria help the user to answer questions about designing the processes to use as materials undergo evaluation. These include criteria by which the processes of setting up committees, procedures, and responsibilities for evaluating materials can be studied and improved. Substantive criteria provide the user with some criteria which can be applied to the materials themselves.

Some of these substantive criteria have been developed for special kinds of materials. For example, Henderson focuses upon educational games and simulations; Rinne upon materials designed to teach human relations; Rosenberg upon the degree of bias or stereotyping present in the materials; and Morrissett and Stevens upon materials in social science education. (See following section for bibliographical information on these publications.) Although these criteria have been developed with a very specific focus, some of them have a considerable amount of generalizability to other types of materials. Other sets of criteria have a broader focus and presumably can be used with a more general format and any subject matter.

The following annotated list contains some of the major publications and audiovisual programs available now for determining the quality of learning materials. Sources cited here are largely available through national circulation. Others can usually be obtained at state and district levels through appropriate agencies.

• Banks, James A. "Evaluating and Selecting Ethnic Studies Materials." *Educational Leadership* 31:593-96; April 1974.
Identifies criteria and examples of materials to help evaluate and select ethnic studies resources. Criteria include: 1. Accurate portrayal of perspectives, attitudes, and feelings of minority groups; 2. settings and experiences with which all students can identify and which accurately reflect ethnic cultures and life styles; 3. illustrations which are accurate, ethnically sensitive, and technically well done; 4. free of racist concepts, clichés, phrases, and words; 5. historically accurate; 6. comprehensive in terms of groups included and events discussed; and 7. discuss major events and documents related to minority history. In addition, the teacher should determine age level, interest and reading level, type of classroom situation, and how each resource will be used.

• "Criteria for Selection of Single Items of Equipment and Materials" (p. 28) and "Criteria for Selection of Packaged Instructional Materials" (p. 29). *Selecting Educational Equipment and Materials for Home and School*. Washington, D.C.: Association for Childhood Education International, 1976.
First set of criteria contains five broad categories of considerations: safety, durability, adaptability, accountability, and facilitation of growth in intellectual, physical, and social/emotional domains. Second set of criteria lists 14 questions to be answered regarding components, cost, characteristics of students, time, instruction, areas of growth, motivational factors, individualization, integration of experiences for use in future learning, discrepancies between advertising claims and staff evaluation and reactions. Part III of the publication is an annotated list of distributors and manufacturers of equipment and materials who responded to the survey of the organization.

• *Criteria for Teaching Materials in Reading and Literature*. Task Force on Racism and Bias in the Teaching of English. National Council of Teachers of English; 1111 Kenyon Road, Urbana, Illinois 61901, November 26, 1970.
Seven criteria are named which focus upon the style, subject matter, illus-

trations, photographs, and dialects in anthologies. Designed to help select materials which will portray non-white minorities in an accurate and in a balanced way.

• Davison, Dorothy, Chairman. "Evaluating Curriculum Guides." Reprint from *English Journal,* September 1968, pp. 1-8.

Report of a committee appointed to review curriculum guides. Identifies strengths of guides analyzed (clarity of objectives) and weaknesses (do not integrate English instruction, give little guidance in assessment and evaluation, little help provided to teacher in decision making, and lack of differentiation of instruction, for example). Presents the guidelines used for analysis. Includes criteria on philosophy and objectives, content, instructional methods, assessment and evaluation, and design of the guide.

• Eash, Maurice J. "Developing an Instrument for Assessing Instructional Materials." *Curriculum Theory Network,* Monograph Supplement, 1972, pp. 193-220. Also in: Herbert J. Walberg, editor. *Evaluating Educational Performance: A Sourcebook of Methods, Instruments, and Examples.* Berkeley, California: McCutchan Publishing Corporation, 1974.

Instrument contains criteria in four major categories: Objectives, organization of materials (scope and sequence), methodology, and evaluation. Also provides a comment section allowing reviewer to identify strengths and weaknesses of materials. Each category asks for a global rating of materials. Also reports a research study conducted on agreement of reviewers using the instrument.

• Henderson, Bob H., and W. G. Gaines. *Simulation Evaluation Form.* Department of Social Science Education, 218 Aderhold Hall, University of Georgia, Athens, Georgia 30601, April 1971.

Provides information about physical description and open-ended comments about simulations. Specific analysis criteria include comments on adequacy and clarity of directions, objectives, debriefing, evaluation, physical make-up, cost, math and reading requirements, usage requirements or recommendations about time and space, alternative versions, appropriateness for students and adequacy of simulation to the true-life model.

• *Instructional Product Selection Kit.* Southwest Regional Laboratory (SWRL) Educational Research and Development, 4665 Lampson Avenue, Los Alamitos, California 90720, 1975.

A multimedia kit designed for workshop use. Participants are trained to deal with criteria about outcomes, assessment materials and procedures, reports of previous use, instructional materials and procedures, orientation and training for installation of product, reporting, and time and cost.

• Klein, M. Frances, and George D. Thayer. *Selecting Curriculum and Instructional Materials.* Regents of the University of California: Los Angeles, 1973.

An audiovisual program with self-instructional guide. Eleven questions are identified which need answers for systematic selection of materials. Criteria include categories dealing with objectives, appropriateness, role of teacher, effective use, content, activities, evaluation, price, and special conditions.

• Kurfman, Dana G. "Choosing and Evaluating New Social Studies Materials." *Social Education* 36 (7): 775-82; November 1972.

Presents two teacher evaluation forms, one for preliminary teacher evaluation and another for teacher evaluation after classroom tryout. The preliminary form includes sections on the relevance of materials to teacher objectives, effectiveness in accomplishing the objectives, probable interest of students, level of difficulty, and cost. The evaluation form for after try-out includes descriptions of situations in which materials were used, students who used materials, time consumed, effectiveness, amount of student participation, and willingness to use materials again next year. Student evaluation form also included. It asks student to rate materials on interest, value, how much learning occurred, difficulty, recommendation of whether materials should be used again next year, and a description of what student thinks he or she learned from the material.

• Miller, Richard I. *Selecting New Aids to Teaching.* Association for Supervision and Curriculum Development: Washington, D.C., 1971.

Maps out a procedure by which evaluation and selection processes can be planned and studied. Identifies five major steps: initial probing of materials or unit of instruction, developing a plan of action, accomplishing the plan, making the decision, and revising and recycling. Raises questions about who will make decisions, community and personnel factors, curricular and instructional factors, evaluation procedures, cost and implementation factors.

For complete text of this document, see Appendix A of this booklet.

• Morrissett, Irving, W. W. Stevens, Jr., and Celeste P. Woodley. "A Model for Analyzing Curriculum Materials and Classroom Transactions." Chapter Eight in: Dorothy McClure Fraser, editor. *Social Studies Curriculum Development: Prospects and Problems.* Thirty-ninth yearbook of the National Council for the Social Studies. Washington, D.C.: NCSS, 1969. pp. 229-76.

System contains criteria in six major categories: descriptive characteristics, rationale and objectives, antecedent conditions, content, instructional theory and teaching strategies, and overall judgments. Chapter also reports how the system was developed and the variety of situations in which it has been used.

• Payne, Arlene. *The Study of Curriculum Plans.* Washington, D.C.: National Education Association, Center for the Study of Instruction, 1969.

Presents guidelines for evaluation in the first section and an analysis of a guide using the criteria in the second section. Plan of analysis includes a differentiation as to whether the curriculum plan is descriptive or evaluative in nature. Criteria for descriptive guides are at two levels of planning, general and specific. At the general level of planning, questions are raised concerning curriculum organization, goals, beliefs about learning, and evaluation. Each of these is examined regarding the justification for decisions about them and the form in which the decisions are presented. At the specific level of planning, nine questions are raised with emphasis on the local situation. Questions center upon organization and sequence, subject matter, activities for students, activities or methods for teacher, learning objectives, and evaluation. Clarity and internal consistency are named as two evaluative criteria which must be used in any descriptive analysis. Criteria for evaluative analysis include questions regarding the view of curriculum planning as an organizational process, learning and instruction, and models or rationales which identify types of curricular decisions and their relationships and bases.

• Rinne, Carl H. "Criteria for Evaluating Curriculum Materials in Human Relations." *Educational Leadership* 32:37-40; October 1974.

Suggests six criteria for judging potential effectiveness of instructional materials in human relations. Materials should provide for: performance of a task by learner, opportunity for the learner to experience consequences from his or her performance or consequences which can be viewed in context of a larger concept or model of interaction, repetition of experience when appropriate, protection from undue threat and emotional pain, and encouragement for students to relate exercise behavior to real world constraints.

• Rosenberg, Max. *Criteria for Evaluating the Treatment of Minority Groups in Textbooks and Other Curriculum Materials.* Michigan Association for Supervision and Curriculum Development Position Paper, no date. Western Michigan University, 105 North Division, Grand Rapids, Michigan 49502. Also reprinted as "Evaluate Your Textbooks for Racism, Sexism!", *Educational Leadership* 31(2):107-109; November 1973; and as chapter five in *Eliminating Ethnic Bias in Instructional Materials: Comment and Bibliography.* Washington, D.C.: Association for Supervision and Curriculum Development, 1974.

Identifies 20 questions which focus upon the content and illustrations of textbooks and other curriculum materials. Criteria try to assess degree to which materials portray minority groups in fair, accurate, positive, objective, and valued presentations in past and present society.

• *Instructional Materials: Selection and Purchase.* National Education Association and Association of American Publishers. Washington, D.C.: National Education Association, 1976.

Identifies 14 recommendations for developing selection procedures. Recommendations are in areas of the legal and administrative setting for selection, organizing for selection, selection processes, and guidelines for expenditures. Charts procedures for selection and purchase of instructional materials.

• *Sharper Tools for Better Learning.* National Association of Secondary School Principals, 1904 Association Drive, Reston, Virginia 22091, 1973.

Describes importance of training selection committee and identifies areas

4. SUPPORT

by which a school system might organize criteria to be used. Suggests criteria in areas of administrative requirements, curricular requirements, pedagogical requirements, and evaluation requirements. Also discusses how to refine and systematize examination and review procedures, pilot use and testing procedures, and expectations about improving materials through learner verification and revision.

• Tom, Alan. *An Approach to Selecting Among Social Studies Curricula.* Central Midwestern Regional Educational Laboratory, 10646 St. Charles Rock Road, St. Ann, Missouri, 63074, 1970.

Discusses a model for curricular decision making focusing primarily upon curricula for citizenship education. Although the intent of the model has a broader purpose of focusing upon the school situation in which materials are to be used, some questions deal directly with selection of materials. Analytical questions in the model are categorized into clarification of intent, logical analysis of intents, strategies and materials, curricular intent, making value judgments, curriculum evaluation, validity of content, and implementation issues.

• Tyler, Louise L., M. Frances Klein, and associates. *Evaluating and Choosing Curriculum and Instructional Materials.* Educational Resource Associates, P.O. Box 415, Glennville, California 93226, 1976.

Discusses 28 recommendations to be considered in evaluating and choosing learning materials. Recommendations are grouped broadly into seven categories: rationale, specifications, appropriateness, effectiveness, conditions, practicality, and dissemination. Includes chapters on the use of recommendations in research, organizing a curriculum, and reactions of a publisher.

• Tyler, Louise L., M. Frances Klein, and Ruby Takanishi. *Inner Teaching: Mastery in Selecting Classroom Materials.* Educational Resource Associates, P.O. Box 415, Glennville, California 93226, 1977.

Selects 15 tips from 1976 publication by Tyler, Klein, and associates. Presentation directed primarily to the classroom teacher. Criteria include statements about objectives, cost, evaluation, field-testing, special facilities, and care of materials, revision, learning opportunities, teacher skills, and content. Also demonstrates the process of using the criteria, and discusses how to open up the instructional and selection processes.

There are some general areas of agreement among many of the authors about what criteria are important. Several mention, for example, the importance of clearly stated objectives, various aspects of appropriateness such as age or grade level, the need to evaluate how well the students learn from the materials while they are still in developmental stages, and the role of the teacher in using the materials. There are criteria, however, that are unique to each of the authors. This seems to suggest that there is no agreement as to how certain criteria contribute to quality materials. While this may represent real disagreement to some degree, given the recent appearance of many of the publications, it may be due more to the newness or the developmental nature of the criteria by the various authors than to real disagreement among them.

The sets of criteria have varying degrees of research and validation behind them. A few authors have reported results of their research. For example, Eash conducted research on his criteria to determine the consistency of raters in using them to evaluate material. Tyler and Klein, in their 1976 volume, report research regarding the application of their criteria to a set of materials and how the perceptions of materials are affected, if at all, by the interactions of teachers, students, and materials in classrooms. They also report on several uses to which their criteria have been put: in the development of materials by a producer, in the formative evaluation of materials by a researcher, and in the organization of a curriculum materials library. Some other sets of criteria appear to be largely the opinions of the authors (all of whom are respected educators, however) with little or no research available to validate how well they contribute to selecting quality learning materials. This lack of research is cited as a major problem area of the field in the next chapter.

While these publications are a valuable resource in determining how good learning materials are, it should be made clear that in no case will simply applying any of these sets make a decision for anyone. What they will do is provide information upon which to base a judgment. Using a set of criteria increases the likelihood that the decision will be a rational, well-informed one rather than mainly a spur-of-the-moment or intuitive decision. Human judgment still plays a major part in the decision, however, even after applying the criteria.

Needed Resources for the Future

Information on the preceding pages suggests some of the major resources which are now available to help educators or any other interested persons identify what learning materials exist and determine their quality. These tasks would be made much easier, however, if other resources are developed in the future.

One resource which needs to be developed is a validation and synthesis of the various sets of criteria cited in the preceding section. Research is needed to determine whether each criterion is related to the learning process. This will require creative and systematic research as learning materials which are rated highly on the various criteria are actually used in a variety of classroom settings and with different types of students and teachers. A synthesis of those criteria which are identified through research as being significant in contributing to learning can then become the basis of several comprehensive systems from which interested people can choose as they prepare to evaluate learning materials. This would be an invaluable asset for all those who must engage in evaluating and selecting learning materials. It is possible, for example, that some of the criteria developed by Morrissett and Stevens for evaluating social studies materials could be combined with some by Banks for ethnic studies, Rinne on human relations, and Rosenberg for evaluating the treatment of minority groups into a comprehensive set of standards for evaluating social studies materials. (See preceding section for bibliographical information on these publications.) The criteria to be included in this comprehensive set of standards would need to be identified through research as being significant contributors to learning.

A second much-needed resource is a Learning Materials Yearbook. This resource could index the major learning materials produced during that year. The materials would be evaluated by reviewers, perhaps similar to the way tests and other assessment instruments are in the *Mental Measurements Yearbooks*[2] or as the Center for the Study of Evaluation rates tests available for use in early childhood education, elementary schools, and secondary schools.[3] It would be difficult, if not impossible, to include every set of learning materials currently available. What might be feasible, however, would be to establish a central clearinghouse where producers and publishers would send a set of any newly developed materials which were ready for distribution. These materials could then be inventoried, cited, and evaluated in an annual Learning Materials Yearbook. Such a publication would be a resource of great value to many people.

[2] Oscar K. Buros, editor. *Mental Measurements Yearbooks.* Highland Park, New Jersey: Gryphon Press.

[3] Ralph Hoepfner et al. *CSE-ECRC Preschool-Kindergarten Test Evaluation.* Los Angeles: UCLA Graduate School of Education, Center for the Study of Evaluation, 1971; Ralph Hoepfner, editor. *CSE Elementary School Test Evaluations.* Los Angeles, UCLA Graduate School of Education, Center for the Study of Evaluation, 1970; and Ralph Hoepfner, editor. *CSE-RBS Test Evaluations.* Los Angeles: UCLA Graduate School of Education, Center for the Study of Evaluation, 1972.

U.S. Office of Education
Regional Offices

REGION I
CT Harvey Liebergott
ME Office of Edu., Region I
MA John F. Kennedy Federal Bldg.
NH Government Center
RI Boston, MA 02203
VT (617) 223-5453 (202) 245-9661

REGION II
NJ Barbara Brandon, Commissioner
NY U.S. Office of Edu., Region II
PR Federal Building
VI 26 Federal Plaza
New York, NY 10007
(212) 264-4370

REGION III
DE Albert Crambert
DC U.S. Office of Edu., Region III
MD 3535 Market Street
PA P.O. Box 13716
VA Philadelphia, PA 19101
WV (215) 597-1011

REGION IV
AL N. Ellen Lyles
FL Prog. Officer, Gifted/Talented
GA U.S. Office of Edu. Region IV
KY 50 Seventh St., N.E., Room 545
MS Atlanta, GA 30323
NC (404) 526-5311
SC
TN

REGION V
IL Richard H. Naber
IN U.S. Office of Edu. Region V
MI HEW-OE 32nd Floor
MN 300 South Wacker Drive
OH Chicago, IL 60606
WI (312) 353-1743

REGION VI
AR Harold Haswell
LA U.S. Office of Edu., Region VI
NM 1114 Commerce Street
OK Dallas, TX 75202
TX (214) 749-2634

REGION VII
IA Pat Carruthers
KS Asst. Regional Commissioner
MO U.S. Office of Edu., Region VII
NE Federal Office Building
601 East 12th Street
Kansas City, MO 64106
(816) 374-2528

REGION VIII
CO H. John Runkel
MT Director, School Systems
ND (Also Edward B. Larsh)
SD U.S. Office of Edu., Region VIII
UT Federal Office Bldg., Rm. 9017
WY 1961 Stout Street
Denver, CO 80202
(303) 837-3676

REGION IX
AS Mary Ann Clark Faris
AZ Infomation Officer
CA U.S. Office of Ed., Region IX
GU Federal Office Building
HI 50 Fulton Street, Room 359
NV San Francisco, CA 94102
TT (415) 556-4921

REGION X
AK John Bean
ID Director, Urban & Community
OR Education Programs
WA U.S. Office of Edu., Region X
Mail Stop 628
1321 Second Avenue
Seattle, WA 98101
(206) 442-0493

State Educational Agencies

ALABAMA – Region IV
Sue Akers, Consultant
Program for Except. Children & Youth
416 State Office Building
Montgomery, AL 36130
(205) 832-3230

ALASKA – Region X
Judi Hayden, Consultant
Section for Exceptional Children
State Department of Education
Pouch F
Juneau, AK 99811
(907) 465-2904

AMERICAN SAMOA – Region IX
Dennis McCray, Program Director
Gifted and Talented
Department of Special Education
Pago Pago, AS 96799
Overseas Operator 2435

ARIZONA – Region IX
Diane Erbert, Consultant
Division of Special Education
Department of Education
1535 West Jefferson
Phoenix, AZ 85007
(602) 271-4361

ARKANSAS – Region VI
Natalie Pruett
Programs for Gifted/Talented
Department of Special Education
Arch Ford Education Building
Little Rock, AR 72201
(501) 371-2161

CALIFORNIA – Region IX
Siegfried Efken, Management Team
Gifted and Talented Education
State Department of Education
721 Capitol Mall
Sacramento, CA 95814
(916) 445-9420

Paul D. Plowman, Consultant
Education of the Mentally Gifted
(Northern California)
Department of Education
721 Capitol Mall, Room 641
Sacramento, CA 95814
(916) 322-3776

Jack Mosier, Consultant
Education of the Mentally Gifted
(Southern California)
Department of Education
601 West 5th Street, Room 1014
Los Angeles, CA 90017
(213) 620-2679

COLORADO – Region VIII
Jerry Villars, Consultant
State Coord., G/T Student Programs
State Department of Education
201 East Colfax
Denver, CO 80203
(303) 892-2111

CONNECTICUT – Region I
William G. Vassar, Consultant G/T
State Department of Education
P.O. Box 2219
Hartford, CT 06115
(203) 566-3444

DELAWARE – Region III
Connie Allen, Supervisor
Programs for Exceptional Children
Department of Public Instruction
The Townsend Building
Dover, DE 19901
(302) 678-4667

DIST. OF COLUMBIA – Region III
James Guines, Mary Harbeck,
Irene Rich
Presidential Building, Room 611
415 – 12th Street, N.W.
Washington, DC 20005
(202) 628-6385

FLORIDA – Region IV
Joyce Runyon, Consultant
Gifted and Talented
Bureau of Edu. for Except. Students
State Department of Education
204 Knott Building
Tallahassee, FL 32304
(904) 488-3103

GEORGIA – Region IV
Margaret O. Bynum, Consultant
Programs for the Gifted
State Department of Education
State Office Building
Atlanta, GA 30334
(404) 656-2414

GUAM – Region IX
Victoria T. Harper, Assoc. Supt.
Special Education
Department of Education
P.O. Box DE
Agana, GU 96910
(Dial 9-0) 772-8300 or 8418

D. B. Smith
Programs for Gifted/Talented
Division of Special Education
Box DE
Agana, GU 96910
772-8418

HAWAII – Region IX
Thomas Hale
Program Specialist, Gifted/Talented
State Department of Education
1270 Queen Emma St., Room 1206
Honolulu, HI 96813
(808) 548-2474 or 548-2211

IDAHO – Region X
Genelle Christensen, Coordinator
Gifted and Talented
State Department of Education
Len B. Jordan Building
Boise, ID 83720
(208) 384-2203

ILLINOIS – Region V
Joyce Van Tassel, Coordinator
Programs for the Gifted
State Department of Education
1020 South Spring
Springfield, IL 62706
(217) 782-7830

INDIANA – Region V
Walter Bartz
Gifted and Talented Education
Division of Public Instruction
Indiana State Dept. of Education
120 West Market, 10th Floor
Indianapolis, IN 46204
(317) 633-4507

IOWA – Region VII
Edith Munro, Consultant
Department of Public Instruction
Grimes State Office Building
East 14th and Grand Avenue
Des Moines, IA 50319
(515) 281-3264

KANSAS – Region VII
Clifford Curl, Consultant for Gifted
State Department of Education
120 East Tenth Street
Topeka, KS 66612
(913) 296-3866

KENTUCKY – Region IV
Joseph T. Clark, Coordinator G/T
1827 Capitol Plaza Tower
Frankfort, KY 40601
(502) 564-5587

LOUISIANA – Region VI
Ruth Buck, Coordinator G/T
State Department of Education
P.O. Box 44064, Capitol Station
Baton Rouge, LA 70804
(504) 389-6427

MAINE – Region I
Patricia O'Connell
Gifted and Talented
Dept. of Edu. & Cultural Services
Augusta, ME 04333
(207) 289-2181

MARYLAND – Region III
James L. Fisher, Consultant G/T Prg.
Department of Education
P.O. Box 8717
B.W.I. Airport
Baltimore, MD 21240
(301) 796-8300, Ext. 318

MASSACHUSETTS – Region I
Roselyn Frank
Div. of Curriculum and Instruction
Department of Education
182 Tremont Street
Boston, MA 02185
(617) 727-5750

MICHIGAN – Region V
Robert Trezise
General Educational Services
Michigan Dept. of Education
P.O. Box 420
Lansing, MI 48902
(517) 373-2484

MINNESOTA – Region V
Lorraine Hertz, Gifted Edu. Coord.
State Department of Education
Capitol Square
500 Cedar Avenue
St. Paul, MN 55101
(612) 296-4072

MISSISSIPPI – Region IV
Maryanne Baird
Division of Instruction
State Department of Education
P.O. Box 771
Jackson, MS 39205
(601) 354-6876

MISSOURI – Region VII
John D. Patterson, Consultant
Gifted/Talented, Special Education
Department of Education
P.O. Box 480
Jefferson City, MO 65101
(314) 751-3502

MONTANA – Region VIII
William S. Elliott, Consultant, Sp. Edu.
Capitol Building
Helena, MT 59601
(406) 449-3651

NEBRASKA – Region VII
Diane Dudley, Spvsr., Prog. for Gifted
State Department of Education
301 Centennial Mall South
Lincoln, NE 68509
(402) 471-2446

NEVADA – Region IX
Jane Early LoCicero, Consultant
Learning Disabilities & Gifted
Department of Education
400 W. King Street
Carson City, NV 89710
(702) 885-5700, Ext. 214

NEW HAMPSHIRE – Region I
James Carr, Consultant, Special Edu.
State Department of Education
64 North Main Street
Concord, NH 03301
(603) 271-3741

NEW JERSEY – Region II
Ted Gourley, Consultant G/T
Robert Swissler, Consultant G/T
State Department of Education
225 W. State Street
Trenton, NJ 08625
(609) 292-7604

NEW MEXICO – Region VI
Elic Guiterrez, Dir. of Sp. Edu.
State Department of Education
Education Building
Santa Fe, NM 87503
(505) 827-2793

NEW YORK – Region II
Roger Ming, Spvsr. Edu. for Gifted
Department of Education
Albany, NY 12234
(518) 474-4873

NORTH CAROLINA – Region IV
Cornelia Tongue, Section Coordinator
Exceptional Children
Department of Public Instruction
Raleigh, NC 27611
(919) 733-7931

NORTH DAKOTA – Region VIII
Janet M. Smaltz, Asst. Dir. Sp. Edu.
State Dept. of Public Instruction
Bismark, ND 58501
(701) 224-2277

OHIO – Region V
George R. Fichter, Cons., Prog. G/T
Department of Education
933 High Street
Worthington, OH 43085
(614) 466-8854

OKLAHOMA – Region VI
Larry Huff
State Department of Education
4545 North Lincoln
Oklahoma City, OK 73105
(405) 521-3353

OREGON – Region X
Mason McQuiston
Asst. Supt. for Special Education
State Department of Education
942 Lancaster Drive, N.E.
Salem, OR 97310
(503) 378-3598

PENNSYLVANIA – Region III
Noretta Bingaman, Spvsr., G/T
Department of Education
P.O. Box 911
Harrisburg, PA 17126
(717) 787-9880

PUERTO RICO – Region II
Maria L. de Jesus, Director
Office of External Resources
Department of Education
Hato Rey, PU 00924
(809) 765-1475

RHODE ISLAND – Region I
Carolyn Hazard, Consultant
Roger Williams Building
Providence, RI 02908
(401) 227-2821

SOUTH CAROLINA – Region IV
James Turner, Cons., Prog. for G/T
Rutledge Building, Room 803
Department of Education
1429 Senate Street
Columbia, SC 29201
(803) 758-2652

SOUTH DAKOTA – Region VIII
Robert Huckins, Consultant
Student Services, G/T
Div. of Elem. and Sec. Education
State Office Building No. 3
Pierre, SD 57501
(605) 224-3371

TENNESSEE – Region IV
Dixon Corum
Division of Special Education
State Department of Education
1837 N. Parkway
Jackson, TN 38301
(901) 423-2251

TEXAS – Region VI
Ann Shaw, Prog. Dir., G/T
Texas Educational Agency
201 East 11th Street
Austin, TX 78701
(512) 475-6582

TRUST TERRITORY – Region IX
David Ramarui, Dir. of Education
Trust Territory of the Pacific Islands
Saipan, Marianna Islands 96950

UTAH – Region VIII
Jewel Bindrup, Consultant, G/T
250 East 5th South
Salt Lake City, UT 84111
(801) 328-5061

VERMONT – Region I
Jean Garvin, Director, Special Edu.
State Department of Education
Montpelier, VT 05602
(802) 828-3141

VIRGINIA – Region III
Isabel P. Rucker, Director
Special Programs for the Gifted
State Department of Education
Richmond, VA 23216
(804) 770-3317

VIRGIN ISLANDS -- Region II
Robert Rogers, St. Dir. of Spec. Edu.
Department of Education
Box 630, Charlotte Amalie
St. Thomas, VI 00801
(809) 774-0100, Ext. 217

WASHINGTON – Region X
Mary Henri Fisher, Director of G/T
Department of Public Instruction
Old Capitol Building
Olympia, WA 98504
(206) 753-1140

WEST VIRGINIA – Region III
Division of Special Education
Building B, Unit 6, Room 315
Charleston, WV 25305
(304) 348-2707

WISCONSIN – Region V
Tom Diener, Supervisor G/T
Department of Public Instruction
126 Langdon Street
Madison, WI 53720
(608) 266-2658

WYOMING – Region VIII
Kathy Erickson, Coordinator, G/T
Department of Education
Hathaway Building
Cheyenne, WY 82001
(307) 777-7411

N/S-LTI-G/T

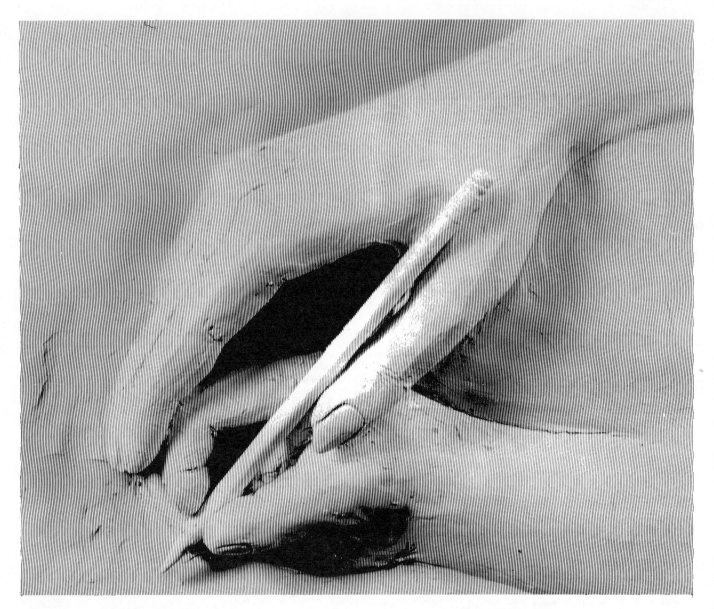

STAFF

0-89568-188-9

Publisher	John Quirk
Editor	Roberta Garland
Director of Production	Richard Pawlikowski
Director of Design	Donald Burns
Typesetting	Carol Carr
Production Ass't	Mary Kirkiles
Cover Design	Donald Burns

ORDER FORM

_____ Administration of Special Education (8.75)	_____ Hyperactivity (8.75)
_____ Autism (8.75)	_____ Individualized Education Program (8.75)
_____ Behavior Modification (8.75)	_____ Instructional Media & Special Education (8.75)
_____ Career & Vocational Education for the Handicapped (8.75)	_____ Law & Special Education: Due Process (8.75)
	_____ Learning Disabilities (8.75)
_____ Child Abuse (8.75)	_____ Mainstreaming (8.75)
_____ Child Psychology (8.75)	_____ Mental Retardation (8.75)
_____ Classroom Teacher & Special Education (8.75)	_____ Physically Handicapped (8.75)
_____ Counseling Parents of Exceptional Children (8.75)	_____ Pre-school Education for the Handicapped (8.75)
_____ Curriculum Development for the Gifted (8.75)	_____ Psychology of Exceptional Children (small) (8.75)
_____ Deaf Education (8.75)	_____ Psychology of Exceptional Children (large) (19.95)
_____ Diagnosis & Placement (8.75)	_____ Severely & Profoundly Handicapped (8.75)
_____ Down's Syndrome (8.75)	_____ Special Education (8.75)
_____ Dyslexia (8.75)	_____ Special Olympics (8.75)
_____ Early Childhood Education (8.75)	_____ Speech & Hearing (8.75)
_____ Educable Mentally Handicapped (8.75)	_____ Trainable Mentally Handicapped (8.75)
_____ Emotional & Behavior Disorders (8.75)	_____ Visually Handicapped Education (8.75)
_____ Foundations of Gifted Educations (8.75)	_____ Vocational Training for the Mentally Retarded (8.75)
_____ Gifted & Talented Education (8.75)	

_____ Abnormal Psychology: Problems of Disordered Emotional & Behavioral Development (8.75)

_____ Development Psychology: The Problems of Disordered Mental Development (8.75)

_____ Human Growth & Development of Exceptional Individual (8.75)

1. Orders will not be processed without _complete_ mailing address, including _zip code._
2. Orders not accompanied by a purchase order number must be prepaid.
3. Orders under $15. must be accompanied by check. Add 10% shipping & handling.
4. Orders less that $100., add 10% shipping & handling.
5. Orders over $100., add 2% handling, shipping will be charged via specific rate.
6. Orders of 5 or more of one title receive 20% discount, less than five will be billed at catalog price.

Checks payable to: SPECIAL LEARNING CORPORATION
Allow 3-6 weeks for 4th Class (book rate) delivery

NO POSTAGE
NECESSARY
IF MAILED
IN THE U.S.

BUSINESS REPLY MAIL

First Class Permit No. 142- Guilford

Postage will be paid by addressee

SPECIAL LEARNING CORP.
P.O. Box 306
Guilford, CT. 06437

SPECIAL LEARNING CORPORATION

COMMENTS PLEASE ! ! !

1. Where did you use this book?

2. In what course or workshop did you use this reader?

3. What articles did you find most interesting and useful?

4. Have you read any articles that we should consider including in this reader?

5. What other features would you like to see added?

6. Should the format be changed, what would you like to see changed?

7. In what other area would you like us to publish using this format?

8. Did you use this as a
( ) basic text?   ( ) in-service?
( ) supplement?   ( ) general information?

————————————— Fold Here —————————————

Are you a ( ) student ( ) instructor ( ) teacher ( ) parent

Your Name _____

School _____

School address _____

_____

Home Address _____

City _____ St. _____ Zip _____

Telephone Number _____

☐   **ORDER PLACED ON REVERSE SIDE**

CUT HERE ● SEAL AND MAIL